T0277756

Fast and Fabulous Knits

Fast and Fabulous Knits

18
Speedy Sweater and Top Patterns for Busy Knitters

Jaime Dorfman
Founder of the Knitwear Brand Jaime Creates

PAGE STREET
PUBLISHING CO.

PAGE STREET
PUBLISHING CO.

Copyright © 2024 Jaime Dorfman

First published in 2024 by
Page Street Publishing Co.
27 Congress Street, Suite 1511
Salem, MA 01970
www.pagestreetpublishing.com

All rights reserved. No part of this book may be reproduced or used, in any
form or by any means, electronic or mechanical, without prior permission in
writing from the publisher.

Distributed by Macmillan, sales in Canada by The Canadian Manda Group.

28   27   26   25   24   1   2   3   4   5

ISBN-13: 979-8-89003-984-2

Library of Congress Control Number: 2023936758

Cover and book design by Laura Benton for Page Street Publishing Co.
Photography by Alexandrena Parker and Jaime Dorfman

Printed and bound in the United States of America

Page Street Publishing protects our planet by donating to nonprof-
its like The Trustees, which focuses on local land conservation.

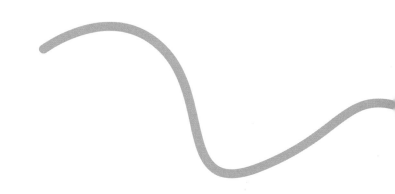

DEDICATION

In loving memory of my granny Dinky, who sadly passed not long before I started writing this book. She was always my biggest fan and I know she would have been so proud to see me become a published author.

Table of Contents

LACE IS MORE   165

INTRODUCTION

Welcome to the whimsical world of *Fast and Fabulous Knits*—a collection of 18 modern and stylish knitting patterns that will work up in a flash.

When most knitters think of quick projects, the first things that come to mind are typically projects such as scarves, beanies and gloves, whereas garment knitting is more commonly thought of as a marathon, not a sprint. What you may not realize is that by simply utilizing thicker yarns and larger needles, you can actually create an entire garment that you'll love to wear in a fraction of the time it would typically take.

Having been an avid crocheter for over a year when I first picked up the knitting needles, I was initially a little skeptical of how much I would enjoy knitting. Crochet had been great in helping me deal with what I now know is ADHD, but the main reason I wanted to start knitting was because I thought I'd get more wear out of knitted garments than crocheted ones. However, I was also aware that knitting is a notoriously slower craft than crochet, and I wasn't sure how my patience would fare. Luckily, I decided that my first knitting project would be a chunky garter stitch jumper, and I was

truly amazed by how quickly the project took shape, despite me being an absolute beginner. I immediately fell in love with knitting and then began experimenting with a multitude of patterns that utilized a wide range of yarn weights and techniques, but if it wasn't for that first chunky jumper project, I'm not sure I would have had the motivation to continue.

Don't get me wrong, one of the many joys of knitting is that it allows one to truly appreciate and savor the process of creating a garment by hand, but I think a common misconception is that this ethos is only pertinent when the garment takes what can feel like endless hours to complete. My experience with knitting has led me to wholeheartedly disagree with this idea, and I strongly believe that quick projects should not be seen as antithetical to the essence of knitting. Although I now very much enjoy knitting and designing with lighter weight yarns from time to time, my appetite for quick knit projects has persisted well beyond my days as a beginner, and I have come to understand the many benefits they can provide for knitters of all skill and experience levels.

First and foremost, not everyone has the time or patience to spend months knitting a single project. In today's fast-paced world, attention spans are only becoming shorter and our desire for instant gratification is increasing; therefore, the motivation of seeing your knitting project come to life quickly can be the difference between completing the project and a lingering pile of WIPs (works in progress) that will haunt you for months. As I mentioned earlier, I personally obtain a great deal of satisfaction not just from making my own clothes, but also from wearing my handmade knits. If you're anything like me, I'm sure you will agree that there is nothing more disheartening than finally completing a meticulously crafted jumper just in time for warm weather to roll around. The great thing about quick knit projects in this respect is that you can enjoy the comfort of knitting during the cooler months whilst also being able to reap the benefits of your handiwork when the timing is just right.

When the prospect of writing a pattern book first came about, I was, of course, incredibly excited, but was also initially quite overwhelmed. Despite my imposter syndrome, this feeling didn't stem entirely from my lack of self-confidence. In fact, what I experienced wasn't too dissimilar from the feeling of purchasing a knitting pattern book, when you just don't know where to start or how you'll ever have the time to get through all the patterns you want to make. My brain was inundated with ideas, and it soon occurred to me that writing a pattern book dedicated to quick knit garments would not only allow me as the designer to sustain my creative momentum without burning out, but it would also reassure knitters who purchased the book that they could achieve their knitting goals within a reasonable timeframe.

As a knitter and designer who revels in exploration and experimentation, writing this book was also the perfect opportunity to share my passion for diverse techniques, fibers, colors and stitches. Within this book you will find a delightful mix of size-inclusive jumper, cardigan and vest patterns that cater towards a range of skill levels, with each chapter shining a spotlight on a different technique: cables, texture, colorwork and lace. I have used yarns ranging from Aran to super bulky weight and numerous different fibers including wool, cotton, mohair and alpaca, as well as a wide range of needle sizes within these patterns to ensure there is something to satisfy every taste.

Writing this book was one of the most challenging, rewarding and, above all else, fun experiences I've ever had, and I am so incredibly proud of what I've created. I hope this book brings as much joy to your life as it has brought to mine. Happy knitting!

BEFORE YOU BEGIN

This section will cover all the things you will need to know before you begin knitting any of the patterns in this book. I have provided thorough explanations of all the pattern skill levels you will find in the book, as well as a detailed guide on how to find your perfect fit, which covers everything from taking your measurements to gauge swatching. I highly recommend you read through this section in its entirety to ensure you are set up for success!

Pattern Skill Levels Explained

Before you start knitting a pattern, it is important that you consider your level of experience and skill to determine if the pattern will be suitable for you, especially if you are relatively new to knitting. There are three skill level classifications that appear in this book: Confident Beginner, Advanced Beginner and Intermediate. Each skill level is explained below.

Confident Beginner

Patterns that fall into this category are suitable for beginner knitters who have mastered the basic stitches and are confident in their ability to apply these skills to a full garment. Preferably, you will have knitted one or two basic garments and are comfortable with reading and following a pattern.

Techniques you should know: casting on, binding off, knit stitch, purl stitch, knit decreases (k2tog, ssk), purl decreases (p2tog, ssp), picking up stitches, knitting in the round, placing stitches on hold and weaving in loose ends. Any other stitches or techniques included in patterns at this level will be explained within the pattern or in the Techniques section (page 207).

Advanced Beginner

These patterns include slightly more complex techniques that require a little more knitting experience and understanding of the craft to execute.

Techniques you should know: all techniques listed under Confident Beginner, yarn over, basic cable knitting, slip stitches and knit increases (M1R, M1L). Any other stitches or techniques included in patterns at this level will be explained within the pattern or in the Techniques section (page 207).

Intermediate

The patterns that fall into this category are suitable for experienced knitters who are not only very comfortable with the skills listed under Confident Beginner and Advanced Beginner but are also working with picking up and combining more advanced stitch patterns and techniques. For example, the Bambi Jumper (page 195) is classified as Intermediate as it combines a top-down raglan construction with lacework.

Choosing Your Size and Ensuring It Will Actually Fit

The patterns in this book include instructions for nine sizes, which range from sizes XS–5XL. Instructions for each size are distinguished by parentheses in the following format: XS (S, M, L, XL) (XXL, 3XL, 4XL, 5XL). If a set of instructions only pertains to some sizes, you will see a "-" used as a placeholder for the sizes that are not included in those instructions.

Choosing the correct size for your body and your desired fit is very important, as there is nothing worse than finishing a project that you are so excited to wear only to find that it does not fit as you had hoped. Here are some helpful tips to guide you through the process of finding your perfect fit.

Measure Your Bust

The first step you should take when determining your size is to measure your bust. This measurement will indicate where you sit within the size range and will be a useful tool in making the right sizing choice for your body.

Measuring your bust is super easy! Simply grab a measuring tape and wrap it around the fullest part of your chest. You'll need to make sure you aren't wearing any bulky clothing when you do so—ideally you will just be wearing an undergarment or a thin shirt. Make sure the measuring tape is parallel to the floor, and that you aren't pulling too tight.

Sizing Chart and Schematic

You'll notice that there is a sizing chart and schematic in each pattern. In each sizing chart, you will find a To Fit Bust section that will contain a range of measurements within which each size is intended to fit. This is where your bust measurement comes into play. If you have a 32.7-inch (83-cm) bust, you would be looking at a size S, which ranges from 32–34 inches (81–86 cm).

You will also find other measurements in the chart and schematic that refer to the finished measurements of different elements of the garment, such as width, length and sleeve length. These measurements will be a good point of reference for you to get an idea of how the garment will fit on your body and if there are any modifications* you would like to make, such as adding length, to ensure you are happy with the fit.

* If you choose to modify a pattern, keep in mind that the yardage (meterage) requirements will change, so it is best to decide on the changes you wish to make before acquiring yarn to help prevent running out of yarn mid-project.

Finished Bust and Ease

In addition to the sizing chart and schematic, you will also notice a section in the patterns that will provide you with the Finished Bust measurements for each size. It is important that you do not get these measurements confused with the To Fit Bust measurements. The Finished Bust measurement refers to the full circumference of the completed garment at its widest point.

There will also be a note on the intended ease of the garment. All patterns in this book are designed with positive ease, which means they will measure larger than the measurements of the body. Some are designed to have a lot of positive ease, which gives them an oversized fit, whereas others are designed to have a smaller amount of positive ease, which means they will fit closer to the body.

The intended ease of a pattern is very important to consider when choosing your size, especially if your bust measurement falls on the cusp or between sizes. If a garment is designed to be oversized (as is the case with most jumpers and cardigans in this book) you may want to consider sizing down if your bust measurement falls on the lower end of a size or in between sizes. The same logic applies to garments designed with a smaller amount of positive ease (as is the case with most vests in this book), so if your bust measurement falls on the higher end of a size or between sizes, you may wish to size up to ensure the garment won't be too tight.

Ultimately, these decisions are entirely up to you and will be determined by your desired fit of the garment. There are no strict rules, as personal preferences vary from person to person. The intended fit and ease are there for you as a guide, but the beauty of knitting your own clothes is that ultimately, you get to decide how you want a garment to fit your body.

Choosing Your Yarn

The patterns in this book use a range of different yarns, fibers and weights, ranging from Aran weight to super bulky weight. I understand that the recommended yarn may not always be accessible to you, which is why it is listed as a recommendation and not a requirement. There are also two alternative yarn options listed in each pattern, which I would consider to be almost exact dupes of the recommended yarn. It is important to note that if you are going to substitute yarn, you should do so thoughtfully and carefully. I always recommend using a yarn with similar fiber content to the recommended yarn where possible, as using a fiber that behaves very differently to the recommended yarn (for example, using cotton instead of wool) can impact the overall fit and drape of the garment. This isn't to say that it's not possible to use yarn with different fiber content to the recommended yarn, rather that it's something to keep in mind when making your selection. There are great resources available for substituting yarn, such as www.yarnsub.com, which will give you a list of alternatives to choose from and provides useful information on aspects to consider such as fiber content, yardage, price, etc.

Gauge Swatching (and Why You Need to Do It)

The most important yet probably the most frequently neglected step to ensuring a perfect fit is . . . you guessed it: knitting a gauge swatch.

If you're unfamiliar with gauge swatching, it essentially involves knitting up a small square using the recommended yarn and needles. You will then measure the number of stitches and rows you have for 4 inches (10 cm) and compare this with the gauge listed in the pattern. This process is used to determine if your gauge is correct, and by correct, I mean that it matches the gauge listed in the pattern, which is crucial to ensuring your garment ends up with the correct finished measurements. If the pattern specifies that the gauge should be achieved once blocked, this means you should block your swatch. See Blocking 101 (page 216) for more information.

When knitting your gauge swatch, make sure that you cast on at least four more stitches than the listed gauge states and that you knit at least four extra rows. This will ensure that you can easily measure your gauge swatch without including the edge stitches, as these stitches tend to curl and are not considered full stitches. Some patterns that use special stitch patterns will include instructions on how to knit your gauge swatch.

If you do not match gauge using the recommended needle size and yarn weight, there are several adjustments that can be made to resolve this. For example, if according to the pattern you should have 10 sts x 16 rows for 4" (10 cm), but your swatch tells you that you have 11 sts x 17 rows for 4" (10 cm), this means your gauge is too tight. In this case, the first step you should take is to size up your needles. The same logic applies if you have fewer stitches and/or rows for 4" (10 cm) than the pattern recommends, in which case you should try sizing down your needles.

Every knitter is different, so just because you use the suggested yarn and needle combination, it does not mean you will match gauge. For example, I am primarily a continental style knitter, which means I hold my working yarn in my left hand, rather than in the right hand. Whilst English style knitting, where the yarn is held in the right hand, is congruous with a tight, even tension, it is generally a slower method of knitting, whereas continental style makes for quicker knitting, but can result in a looser fabric.

In the spirit of *Fast and Fabulous Knits*, I knit all the samples using continental style, which is thus reflected in the gauge of each pattern. I am by no means saying you must knit these patterns continental style but rather flagging this as something you should consider, especially if you know you are a tight knitter, as you will more than likely need to make some adjustments to match gauge.

I also recommend that you measure your gauge throughout your project, as your tension can change over time, and you want to make sure your gauge remains consistent. If your pattern requires blocking, be sure to measure your gauge swatch before blocking as well as after, so you can use the unblocked measurement as a point of reference as you check your gauge whilst knitting your project. Additionally, some knitters will find that their tension differs when working flat versus in the round. This is important to keep in mind as many patterns in this book include both methods. If you find that your tension is tighter or looser when working flat or in the round, it may be helpful to switch needle sizes for either section to ensure your gauge remains consistent throughout the garment.

Choosing the right size for your measurements and desired fit is all well and good, but really is totally pointless if you decide to skip the swatch. Gauge swatching has become a semi-controversial topic amongst the knitting community. When you're so excited and eager to cast on a new project, knitting a swatch beforehand can feel like a major buzzkill, especially if you find out your gauge is wrong, and you have to repeat the process all over again—maybe even several times— before you can actually start your project.

However, the alternative, in my opinion, is much worse. Spending hours upon hours knitting a garment, only to find out it is far too big or too small, knowing that this could have been prevented if you only took a little extra time before starting to ensure your gauge was correct, is quite literally my worst nightmare. I completely understand that swatching may not be the most fun part of knitting, but I see it as a small pain for a world of gain. So, I beg of you, please do not skip the swatch. Even if you're only one stitch or row off and you think "that's close enough," remember that one stitch or row in a swatch is then multiplied across the entire garment, which makes a bigger difference than you realize (trust me, I've learned this the hard way). Especially in this book, where the patterns call for thicker-than-average yarn, this is not the time for taking chances.

All Aboard the Cable Train

I'll be the first to admit that I was incredibly intimidated by cables when I first started knitting—they just seemed so complicated! However, after years of avoiding them at all costs, I finally hopped onto the cable train, and I think it's fair to say I've never looked back. I was truly astounded when I realized how easy cables actually were. To be honest, I felt quite silly for judging a book by its cover when I had never even given cable knitting a go. It's safe to say I've learned my lesson.

I'm truly amazed by the endless possibilities of what one can create using essentially one simple, versatile technique. This chapter showcases the timeless beauty of cable knitting in four unique quick-knit patterns. Whether you're after a classic wardrobe staple like the dreamy Orla Cardigan (page 47) or a striking statement piece like the deliciously chunky Magnolia Jumper (page 37), this chapter has something for every occasion.

Sweet as Pie Jumper

The Sweet as Pie Jumper features the scrumptious Basket Cable stitch, which cleverly mimics the intricate lattice of a freshly baked pie crust. Don't be intimidated by the cable work; this stitch is easier than it looks, making it an ideal choice for advanced beginners looking to expand their skills. While the overall construction of this jumper remains basic, the thoughtful design elements set it apart. The Sweet as Pie Jumper boasts a luxurious roll neck, providing an extra layer of warmth for those cold winter days, whilst the inclusion of side slits adds a touch of comfort and flair, allowing for ease of movement and a fashionable silhouette. The creation of this pattern marked a personal challenge for me to step outside my comfort zone and explore new design territories. The result? One of my absolute favorite pieces from this book and a knitting experience that promises to be as sweet as a warm slice of pie.

Construction Notes

This jumper is worked mostly flat in stockinette stitch and charted cables from the bottom up. You will first work the back panel flat, followed by the front panel. You will join the shoulder seams to create the neck hole using the Three Needle Bind Off method (page 207). To create the armholes, you will use the Mattress stitch (page 209) to seam the sides together. The neck trim and sleeves are worked in the round by picking up stitches along the neck hole/armhole edges.

Skill Level

Advanced Beginner

Sizing

XS (S, M, L, XL) (XXL, 3XL, 4XL, 5XL)

Finished bust: 34.6 (38.6, 42.6, 46.4, 50.4) (54.4, 58.2, 62.2, 67)" / 88 (98, 108, 118, 128) (138, 148, 158, 170) cm, blocked

Recommended ease: This jumper is designed with approximately 4.7–6.7" / 12–17 cm of positive ease

Sample shown is knit in Size S.

MATERIALS

Yarn

Bulky weight, Wool and Works, Merino Chunky (100% Superwash Merino), 110 yds (100 m) per 100-g skein, shown in Glacier colorway

Any bulky weight yarn can be used for this pattern as long as it matches gauge. A good substitute would be Wool and the Gang, Alpachino Merino or Drops, Andes.

Yardage/Meterage

880 (998, 1113, 1203, 1325) (1460, 1553, 1717, 1871) yds / 805 (913, 1018, 1100, 1212) (1335, 1420, 1570, 1711) m

Needles

For body: US 11 (8 mm) straight needles or 24- to 32-inch (60- to 80-cm) circular needle

For sleeves: US 11 (8 mm) 24- to 32-inch (60- to 80-cm) circular needle

For bottom ribbing: US 8 (5 mm) straight needles or 24- to 32-inch (60- to 80-cm) circular needle

For neckline and sleeve cuffs: US 8 (5 mm) 24-inch (60-cm) circular needle

Notions

Cable needle

Stitch markers

Tapestry needle

Scissors

Stitch holders

Measuring tape

GAUGE

18 sts x 18 rows = 4 inches (10 cm) in Basket Cable stitch (explained in following section) using larger needle (blocked)

To Knit Gauge Swatch

CO 30 sts.

Rows 1–5: Work in stockinette stitch, starting with a purl (WS) row.

Row 6 (RS): K3, *C8B*, rep ** until last 3 sts, k3.

Rows 7–11: Repeat rows 1–5.

Row 12: K7, *C8F*, rep ** until last 7 sts, k7.

Work at least 18 rows.

ABBREVIATIONS

BO - Bind off

BOR - Beginning of round

C8B - Cable 8 back (place 4 sts on cable needle and hold to back of work. K4, k4 from cable needle)

C8F - Cable 8 front (place 4 sts on cable needle and hold to front of work. K4, k4 from cable needle)

CO - Cast on

K - Knit

K2tog - Knit 2 stitches together

K3tog - Knit 3 stitches together

P - Purl

P2tog - Purl 2 stitches together

PM - Place marker

Rep - Repeat

RS - Right side

Sl - Slip

Ssk - Slip, slip, knit 2 stitches together through the back loops

Ssp - Slip, slip, purl 2 stitches together through the back loops

St(s) - Stitch(es)

WS - Wrong side

SIZING CHART

Size	XS	S	M	L	XL	XXL	3XL	4XL	5XL
To fit bust	28–30"/ 71–76 cm	32–34"/ 81–86 cm	36–38"/ 91.5– 96.5 cm	40–42"/ 101.5– 106.5 cm	44–46"/ 111.5– 117 cm	48–50"/ 122–127 cm	52–54"/ 132–137 cm	56–58"/ 142–147 cm	60–62"/ 152–158 cm
(A) Width	17.3"/ 44 cm	19.3"/ 49 cm	21.3"/ 54 cm	23.2"/ 59 cm	25.2"/ 64 cm	27.2"/ 69 cm	29.1"/ 74 cm	31.1"/ 79 cm	33.5"/ 85 cm
(B) Length	18.1"/ 46 cm	18.9"/ 48 cm	19.7"/ 50 cm	20.5"/ 52 cm	21.3"/ 54 cm	22"/ 56 cm	22.8"/ 58 cm	23.6"/ 60 cm	24.4"/ 62 cm
(C) Sleeve Width	7.1"/ 18 cm	7.1"/ 18 cm	7.1"/ 18 cm	8.7"/ 22 cm	8.7"/ 22 cm	8.7"/ 22 cm	10.2"/ 26 cm	10.2"/ 26 cm	10.2"/ 26 cm
(D) Sleeve Length	16.9"/ 43 cm	17.7"/ 45 cm	17.7"/ 45 cm	17.7"/ 45 cm	18.5"/ 47 cm	18.5"/ 47 cm	18.5"/ 47 cm	19.3"/ 49 cm	19.3"/ 49 cm

SPECIAL TECHNIQUES

Three Needle Bind Off (page 207)

Tubular Bind Off (page 209)

Magic Loop method (page 207)

Mattress stitch (page 209)

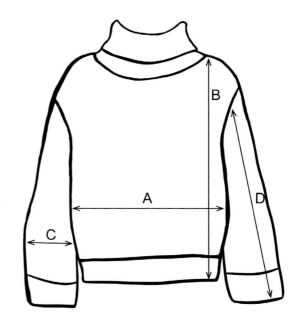

BACK PANEL

Using US 8 (5 mm) straight needles or 24- to 32-inch (60- to 80-cm) circular needles and the Long Tail Cast On, CO 80 (88, 96, 104, 112) (122, 130, 140, 150) sts.

Sizes XS (S, M, L, XL) (-, -, 4XL, -) only

Rows 1–9: *K2, p2*, rep ** until end of the row.

Sizes - (-, -, -, -) (XXL, 3XL, -, 5XL) only

Row 1 (RS): *K2, p2*, rep ** until last 2 sts, k2.

Row 2 (WS): *P2, k2*, rep ** until last 2 sts, p2.

Rows 3–9: Repeat rows 1–2. *You should end after a RS row.*

All sizes continue

Switch to US 11 (8 mm) straight needles or 24- to 32-inch (60- to 80-cm) circular needles. Restart your row count here.

You will now begin working in the Basket Cable stitch.

Repeat the following 12 rows until you have worked 71 (75, 79, 83, 87) (91, 95, 99, 103) rows **total (not including ribbing)**. *You should end after row 11 (3, 7, 11, 3) (7, 11, 3, 7) of the Basket Cable stitch.*

Rows 1–5: Work in stockinette stitch, starting with a purl (WS) row.

Row 6: K4 (4, 4, 4, 4) (5, 5, 2, 3), *C8B*, rep ** until last 4 (4, 4, 4, 4) (5, 5, 2, 3) sts, k to the end of the row.

Rows 7–11: Repeat rows 1–5.

Row 12: K8 (8, 8, 8, 8) (9, 9, 6, 7), *C8F*, rep ** until last 8 (8, 8, 8, 8) (9, 9, 6, 7) sts, k to end of the row.

> **Note:** If you would like to add or subtract length to/from your jumper, do so here, but make note of how many total rows you work and which row of the Basket Cable stitch you end after so that you can work your Front Panel to match. You should still end after a WS row.

BACK SHOULDERS

You will now make decreases to shape the back neckline, whilst continuing to work in pattern. *You should now be on row 12 (4, 8, 12, 4) (8, 12, 4, 8) of the Basket Cable stitch.*

> **A note on working in pattern:** As you decrease during this section, you may no longer always be able to complete a full repeat of the Basket Cable stitch pattern at the inner edges of the neckline. This will only come into effect if/when you reach a cable row. This means you will not necessarily begin with the stitch you would normally begin the row with when it says "work in pattern"; instead, you would start with the stitch that vertically matches the stitch column below it. If/when you reach a cable stitch and no longer have enough sts to work that cable, simply knit those sts instead.

Row 1 (RS): Work in pattern across the first 21 (24, 28, 32, 36) (41, 44, 49, 54) sts, turn.

Row 2 (WS): P1, p2tog, p to the end of the row.

Row 3: K across.

Cut yarn and place these 20 (23, 27, 31, 35) (40, 43, 48, 53) right shoulder sts on a stitch holder. *You will come back to them later for the Shoulder Seams.*

Place the middle 38 (40, 40, 40, 40) (40, 42, 42, 42) sts on another stitch holder. *You will come back to them later for the Neck Trim.*

Reattach yarn on the RS to the remaining 21 (24, 28, 32, 36) (41, 44, 49, 54) left shoulder stitches.

Row 1 (RS): Work in pattern to the end of the row.

Row 2 (WS): P to last 3 sts, ssp, p1.

Row 3: K across.

Cut yarn and place these 20 (23, 27, 31, 35) (40, 43, 48, 53) left shoulder sts on a stitch holder. *You will come back to them later for the Shoulder Seams.*

FRONT PANEL

Follow Back Panel instructions until you have worked 66 (70, 74, 78, 82) (86, 90, 94, 98) rows **total** of Basket Cable stitch (not including ribbing). *You should end after row 6 (10, 2, 6, 10) (2, 6, 10, 2) of the Basket Cable stitch.*

> **Note:** If you are adding or subtracting length to/from your jumper, work 5 rows less than you did for the Back Panel. You should still end after a RS row.

FRONT SHOULDERS

You will now make decreases to shape the front neckline, whilst continuing to work in pattern. *You should now be on row 7 (11, 3, 7, 11) (3, 7, 11, 3) of the Basket Cable stitch.*

If/when you reach a cable stitch and no longer have enough stitches to work that cable, simply knit those stitches instead.

Row 1 (WS): P across the first 26 (29, 33, 37, 41) (46, 49, 54, 59) sts, turn.

Row 2 (RS): K1, ssk, work in pattern to the end of the row.

Row 3: P to last 3 sts, ssp, p1.

Rows 4–7: Repeat rows 2–3.

Row 8: K across.

Cut yarn and place these 20 (23, 27, 31, 35) (40, 43, 48, 53) right (as worn) shoulder sts on a stitch holder. *You will come back to them later for the Shoulder Seams.*

Place the middle 28 (30, 30, 30, 30) (30, 32, 32, 32) sts on another stitch holder. *You will come back to them later for the Neck Trim.*

Reattach yarn on the WS to the remaining 26 (29, 33, 37, 41) (46, 49, 54, 59) left (as worn) shoulder sts.

Row 1 (WS): P across.

Row 2 (RS): Work in pattern to last 3 sts, k2tog, k1.

Row 3: P1, p2tog, p to end of the row.

Rows 4–7: Repeat rows 2–3.

Row 8: K across.

Leave these 20 (23, 27, 31, 35) (40, 43, 48, 53) sts on your needle and do not cut the yarn. *Proceed to "Shoulder Seams."*

SHOULDER SEAMS

You will now be using the Three Needle Bind Off method (page 207) to join the shoulder seams.

1. Turn your work inside out and place the RS of your front and back panels together.

2. Your front left (as worn) shoulder stitches should still be on your needle. Place the corresponding 20 (23, 27, 31, 35) (40, 43, 48, 53) sts left on hold for the back left shoulder onto the other needle. Make sure both needles are facing the same direction.

3. Insert a third needle (US 11 [8 mm] or smaller) knitwise into the first st of the panel that is facing you, then insert that same needle knitwise into the corresponding st of the other panel.

4. Continue, following the instructions for the Three Needle Bind Off method (page 207).

5. Repeat all steps for the right shoulder, using the corresponding front and back right shoulder stitches left on hold.

SIDE SEAMS

Flip your work so that the RS are now facing out (your shoulder seams should be invisible).

1. Take a measuring tape and measure from the shoulder seam down. Place an interlocking stitch marker on the outside edge of your work at the 7.9 (7.9, 7.9, 9.4, 9.4) (9.4, 11, 11, 11)-inch / 20 (20, 20, 24, 24) (24, 28, 28, 28)-cm mark. Repeat this on both sides.

2. Measure from the cast-on edge up. Place another stitch marker on the outside edge of your work at the 4.7 (4.7, 5.1, 5.1, 5.5) (5.5, 5.9, 5.9, 6.3)-inch / 12 (12, 13, 13, 14) (14, 15, 15, 16)-cm mark, or one-quarter of your total length. Repeat this on both sides.

3. Use the Mattress stitch (page 209) to seam the sides together between the two markers. *This will create the armhole as well as a slit along the bottom quarter of the body.*

4. Seam until you reach the second stitch marker (you may now remove the markers).

NECK TRIM

Using US 8 (5 mm) 24-inch (60-cm) circular needles, pick up stitches in the following fashion:

1. Pick up 4 sts along the side of the back right shoulder.

2. Pick up and knit the 38 (40, 40, 40, 40) (40, 42, 42, 42) live sts from the stitch holder at the back neck.

3. Pick up 4 sts along the side of the back left shoulder.

4. Pick up 7 sts along the side of the front left (as worn) shoulder.

5. Pick up and knit the 28 (30, 30, 30, 30) (30, 32, 32, 32) live sts from the stitch holder at the front neck.

6. Pick up 7 sts along the side of the front right (as worn) shoulder.

You should now have 88 (92, 92, 92, 92) (92, 96, 96, 96) sts. PM to mark the BOR.

Rounds 1–29: *K2, p2*, rep ** until end of the round.

You will now work a setup round before working the Tubular Bind Off.

1. K1.

2. Insert the right needle purlwise into the back loop of the 2nd st on the left needle.

3. Sl this st off the left needle, which then forces the 1st st off the left needle as well and will result in a live st.

4. Catch the live st with the left needle at the front of your work.

5. Sl the st on your right needle back onto the left needle (you should have reversed the order of the two sts now at the tip of your left needle, with the new 2nd st crossed in front of the new 1st st).

6. P1, k1, p1.

Repeat steps 1–6 to the end of the round.

BO all sts following instructions for the Tubular Bind Off (page 209).

SLEEVES

Using US 11 (8 mm) 24- to 32-inch (60- to 80-cm) circular needles, starting at the underarm point, pick up 64 (64, 64, 72, 72) (72, 80, 80, 80) sts, evenly spaced, around the armhole. PM to mark the BOR.

You will now begin working the Basket Cable stitch in the round.

Repeat the following 12 rounds until you have worked 53 (56, 56, 56, 59) (59, 59, 62, 62) rounds total. *You should end after round 5 (8, 8, 8, 11) (11, 11, 2, 2) of the Basket Cable stitch.*

Rounds 1–5: K across.

Round 6: *C8B*, rep ** until end of the round.

Rounds 7–11: K across.

Round 12: K4, *C8F*, rep ** until last 4 sts, k4.

Note: If you would like to add or subtract length to/from your sleeves, do so here, but be sure not to end after a cable row, and keep in mind the sleeve cuff will add approximately 3.1 inches (8 cm). Make note of how many total rows you work and which row of the Basket Cable stitch you end after so that you can work your second sleeve to match.

You will now make decreases before working the sleeve cuffs.

Sizes XS (S, M, L, XL) (XXL, -, -, -) only

Next round: K3 (3, 3, 1, 1) (1, -, -, -), *k2tog, k3*, rep ** until last st, k1.

Sizes - (-, -, -, -) (-, 3XL, 4XL, 5XL) only

Next round: *K2tog, k3*, rep ** until end of the round.

All sizes continue

You should now have 52 (52, 52, 58, 58) (58, 64, 64, 64) sts.

Switch to US 8 (5 mm) 24-inch (60-cm) circular needles. *You will need to use the Magic Loop method (page 207).*

Sizes - (-, -, L, XL) (XXL, -, -, -) only

Round 1: K3tog, k1, p2, *k2, p2*, rep ** until end of the round.

You should now have 56 sts.

All sizes continue

Next 13 (13, 13, 12, 12) (12, 13, 13, 13) rounds: *K2, p2*, rep ** until end of the round.

Follow instructions for the setup round for Tubular Bind Off in the *Neck Trim* section (page 25).

BO all sts following instructions for the Tubular Bind Off (page 209).

FINISHING

Weave in any remaining loose ends.

Wash and block (see Blocking 101 [page 216] or use your preferred blocking method).

Heartstrings Vest

Fall in love with the Heartstrings Vest, a gorgeous piece that effortlessly combines warmth, style and a touch of romance. Crafted with super bulky yarn and designed for those seeking a quick and satisfying knitting project, this pattern is sure to get your heart racing with excitement. At the center of this pattern lies the Celtic Heart Cable stitch, which weaves its magic to create a stunning heart-shaped motif, adding an extra touch of beauty and elegance. The Heartstrings Vest is designed to have a cropped fit with a little positive ease, allowing it to be worn with versatility, so you can layer it effortlessly over your favorite outfits or showcase it as a standalone piece. You will become totally infatuated as you watch the dreamy heart motif emerge row by row, creating a garment that captures both the warmth of your hands and the beauty of your heart.

Construction Notes

This vest is worked mostly flat in reverse stockinette and charted cables from the bottom up. You will first work the back panel flat, followed by the front panel. You will join the shoulder seams to create the neck hole using the Grafting method (page 214). To create the armholes, you will use the Mattress stitch (page 209) to seam the sides together. The neck and sleeve trims are worked in the round by picking up stitches along the neck hole/armhole edges. Instructions on how to adjust the body length of your vest are included.

Skill Level

Intermediate

Sizing

XS (S, M, L, XL) (XXL, 3XL, 4XL, 5XL)

Finished bust: 32.2 (36.2, 40.2, 44, 48) (52, 56, 59.8, 64.6)"/ 82 (92, 102, 112, 122) (132, 142, 152, 164) cm

Recommended ease: This vest is designed with approximately 2.4–4.3 inches / 6–11 cm of positive ease

Sample shown is knit in Size S.

MATERIALS

Yarn

Super bulky weight, Cardigang, Chunky Merino Wool (100% merino wool), 87 yds (80 m) per 200-g skein, shown in Flossy Pink colorway

Any super bulky weight yarn can be used for this pattern as long as it matches gauge. A good substitute would be Wool and the Gang, Crazy Sexy Wool or Malabrigo, Rasta.

Yardage/Meterage

164 (190, 209, 241, 273) (306, 350, 416, 448) yds / 150 (174, 191, 220, 250) (280, 320, 380, 410) m

Needles

For body: US 19 (15 mm) straight needles or 32-inch (80-cm) circular needle

For bottom ribbing, neck and sleeve trims: US 17 (12 mm) 32-inch (80-cm) circular needle

Notions

Cable needle

Stitch markers

Tapestry needle

Scissors

Stitch holders

GAUGE

7 sts x 10 rows = 4 inches (10 cm) in stockinette stitch using larger needle

ABBREVIATIONS

1x1 rib(bing) - *Knit 1, purl 1*

BO - Bind off

BOR - Beginning of round

C4B - Cable 4 back (place 2 sts on cable needle and hold to **back** of work. K2, k2 from cable needle)

C4F - Cable 4 front (place 2 sts on cable needle and hold to **front** of work. K2, k2 from cable needle)

CO - Cast on

K - Knit

K2tog - Knit 2 stitches together

LPC - Left purl cross

P - Purl

P2tog - Purl 2 stitches together

PM - Place marker

Rep - Repeat

RPC - Right purl cross

RS - Right side

SM - Slip marker

Ssk - Slip, slip, knit 2 stitches together through the back loops

Ssp - Slip, slip, purl 2 stitches together through the back loops

St(s) - Stitch(es)

WS - Wrong side

SIZING CHART

Size	XS	S	M	L	XL	XXL	3XL	4XL	5XL
To fit bust	28–30"/ 71–76 cm	32–34"/ 81–86 cm	36–38"/ 91.5–96.5 cm	40–42"/ 101.5–106.5 cm	44–46"/ 111.5–117 cm	48–50"/ 122–127 cm	52–54"/ 132–137 cm	56–58"/ 142–147 cm	60–62"/ 152–158 cm
(A) Width	16.1"/ 41 cm	18.1"/ 46 cm	20.1"/ 51 cm	22"/ 56 cm	24"/ 61 cm	26"/ 66 cm	28"/ 71 cm	29.9"/ 76 cm	32.3"/ 82 cm
(B) Length	16.5"/ 42 cm	17.3"/ 44 cm	17.3"/ 44 cm	18.1"/ 46 cm	18.9"/ 48 cm	19.7"/ 50 cm	21.3"/ 54 cm	23.6"/ 60 cm	23.6"/ 60 cm
(C) Armhole Depth	8.3"/ 21 cm	8.3"/ 21 cm	8.3"/ 21 cm	9.8"/ 25 cm	9.8"/ 25 cm	10.6"/ 27 cm	10.6"/ 27 cm	11.8"/ 30 cm	11.8"/ 30 cm

SPECIAL TECHNIQUES

Alternating Cable Cast On (page 208)

Grafting (page 214)

Magic Loop method (page 207)

Mattress stitch (page 209)

2/2 Right Purl Cross

Place 2 sts on cable needle and hold to back of work. K2, p2 from cable needle.

2/1 Right Purl Cross

Place 2 sts on cable needle and hold to back of work. K1, p2 from cable needle.

2/2 Left Purl Cross

Place 2 sts on cable needle and hold to front of work. P2, k2 from cable needle.

2/1 Left Purl Cross

Place 2 sts on cable needle and hold to front of work. P1, k2 from cable needle.

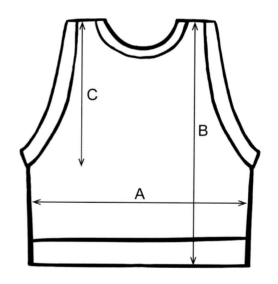

BACK PANEL

Using US 17 (12 mm) 32-inch (80-cm) circular needles and the Alternating Cable Cast On (page 208), CO 28 (32, 36, 40, 44) (48, 52, 56, 60) sts.

Rows 1–5: *K1, p1*, rep ** until end of the row.

Switch to US 19 (15 mm) straight needles or 32-inch (80-cm) circular needles. Restart your row count here.

Row 1 (WS): K across.

Row 2 (RS): P across.

Repeat rows 1–2 until you have worked them 8 (9, 9, 8, 9) (9, 11, 13, 13) times **total** (meaning 16 (18, 18, 16, 18) (18, 22, 26, 26) total rows). You should end after a RS row.

Place an interlocking stitch marker on the outermost stitch on both edges of the last row you just worked.

Note: If you would like to add or subtract length to/from your vest, do so here. Make note of how many rows you add or subtract so that you can work your Front Panel to match.

You will now begin making decreases for the armholes. The decrease sequence is as follows:

Row 1 (WS): K1, ssk, k until last 3 sts, k2tog, k1.

Row 2 (RS): P across.

Repeat rows 1–2 until you have worked them 5 (5, 5, 6, 6) (7, 7, 8, 8) times **total** (meaning 10 (10, 10, 12, 12) (14, 14, 16, 16) total rows). You should end after a RS row and have 18 (22, 26, 28, 32) (34, 38, 40, 44) sts.

Work 8 (8, 8, 10, 10) (10, 10, 10, 10) straight rows in reverse stockinette stitch with no decreases. *You should end after a RS row.*

BACK SHOULDERS

Setup row (WS): K4 (6, 8, 8, 10) (11, 12, 13, 15), BO 10 (10, 10, 12, 12) (12, 14, 14, 14), k to end of the row.

You will now be working across only the first 4 (6, 8, 8, 10) (11, 12, 13, 15) sts. Leave the remaining sts on the cord or place them on a stitch holder. *You will come back to them later for the left shoulder.*

Row 1 (RS): P to last 3 sts, ssp, p1.

Row 2 (WS): K across.

Cut yarn and place these 3 (5, 7, 7, 9) (10, 11, 12, 14) right shoulder sts on a stitch holder. *You will come back to them later for the Shoulder Seams.*

Reattach yarn on the RS to work the remaining 4 (6, 8, 8, 10) (11, 12, 13, 15) sts for the left shoulder.

Row 1 (RS): P1, p2tog, p to end of the row.

Row 2 (WS): K across.

Cut yarn and place these 3 (5, 7, 7, 9) (10, 11, 12, 14) left shoulder sts on a stitch holder. *You will come back to them later for the Shoulder Seams.*

FRONT PANEL

Using US 17 (12 mm) 32-inch (80-cm) circular needles and the Alternating Cable Cast On (page 208), CO 28 (32, 36, 40, 44) (48, 52, 56, 60) sts.

Rows 1–5: *K1, p1*, rep ** until end of the row.

Switch to US 19 (15 mm) straight needles or 32-inch (80-cm) circular needles. Restart your row count here.

You will now place markers to mark where you will work the Celtic Cable Heart stitch.

Setup row (WS): K2 (3, 4, 5, 6) (7, 8, 9, 10), p2, k2 (3, 4, 5, 6) (7, 8, 9, 10), PM, k2, p12, k2, PM, k2 (3, 4, 5, 6) (7, 8, 9, 10), p2, k to end of the row.

Row 1 (RS): P2 (3, 4, 5, 6) (7, 8, 9, 10), k2, p to marker, SM, p2, k2, C4B, C4F, k2, p2, SM, p2 (3, 4, 5, 6) (7, 8, 9, 10), k2, p to end of the row.

Row 2: K2 (3, 4, 5, 6) (7, 8, 9, 10), p2, k to marker, SM, k2, p12, k2, SM, k2 (3, 4, 5, 6) (7, 8, 9, 10), p2, k to end of the row.

You will now begin to follow the chart for the Celtic Cable Heart stitch (page 35). Restart your row count here.

> **Note:** Odd (RS) rows of the chart are read from right to left, and even (WS) rows are read from left to right. On WS rows, the knit symbols on the chart are worked as purl stitches and vice versa.

During Row 1 below, begin with Row 1 of the chart where it says "work next row of the chart."

Row 1 (RS): P2 (3, 4, 5, 6) (7, 8, 9, 10), k2, p to marker, SM, work next row of the chart, SM, p2 (3, 4, 5, 6) (7, 8, 9, 10), k2, p to end of the row.

Row 2 (WS): K2 (3, 4, 5, 6) (7, 8, 9, 10), p2, k to marker, SM, work next row of the chart, SM, k2 (3, 4, 5, 6) (7, 8, 9, 10), p2, k to end of the row.

Repeat rows 1–2 until you have worked them 6 (7, 7, 6, 7) (7, 9, 11, 11) times **total** (meaning 12 (14, 14, 12, 14) (14, 18, 22, 22) total rows). You should end after a WS row. *You should end after row 2 (4, 4, 2, 4) (4, 8, 2, 2).*

Repeat row 1. *You should end after row 3 (5, 5, 3, 5) (5, 9, 3, 3) of the chart.*

Note: If you would like to add or subtract length to/from your vest, do so here, but be sure to add or subtract the same number of rows as you did for the Back Panel. This will impact which row of the chart you end on. This is fine; just continue to work from whichever row you are up to.

Restart your row count here. You will now begin making decreases for the armholes, whilst continuing to follow the chart between your stitch markers, and work the non-charted edge stitches that have been established during the previous section where it says "work in pattern." You should be on row 4 (6, 6, 4, 6) (6, 10, 4, 4) of the chart.

A note on working in pattern: As you decrease during this section, some sizes will no longer be able to work the k2/p2 within the non-charted edge stitches. If/when this happens, when it says "work in pattern," you would start with the stitch that vertically matches the stitch below it.

The decrease sequence is as follows:

Row 1 (WS): K1, ssk, work in pattern until last 3 sts, k2tog, k1.

Row 2 (RS): Work in pattern.

Repeat rows 1–2 until you have worked them 5 (5, 5, 6, 6) (7, 7, 8, 8) times **total** (meaning 10 (10, 10, 12, 12) (14, 14, 16, 16) total rows). You should end after a RS row and have 18 (22, 26, 28, 32) (34, 38, 40, 44) sts. *You should end after row 3 (5, 5, 5, 7) (9, 3, 9, 9) of the chart.*

Work 5 (5, 5, 7, 7) (7, 7, 7, 7) straight rows in pattern with no decreases. *You should end after row 8 (10, 10, 2, 4) (6, 10, 6, 6) of the chart.*

FRONT SHOULDERS

You may now remove your stitch markers.

Setup row (RS): Work in pattern across the first 5 (7, 9, 9, 11) (12, 13, 14, 16) sts, BO 8 (8, 8, 10, 10) (10, 12, 12, 12), work in pattern until the end of the row.

You will now be working across only the first 5 (7, 9, 9, 11) (12, 13, 14, 16) sts. Leave the remaining stitches on the cord or place them on a stitch holder. *You will come back to them later for the right shoulder.*

Row 1 (WS): K to last 3 sts, k2tog, k1.

Row 2 (RS): P across.

Rows 3–4: Repeat last 2 rows.

Row 5: K across.

Cut yarn and place these 3 (5, 7, 7, 9) (10, 11, 12, 14) left (as worn) shoulder sts on a stitch holder. *You will come back to them later for the Shoulder Seams.*

Reattach yarn on the WS to work the remaining 5 (7, 9, 9, 11) (12, 13, 14, 16) right (as worn) shoulder sts.

Row 1 (WS): K1, ssk, k to end of the row.

Row 2 (RS): P across.

Rows 3–4: Repeat last 2 rows.

Row 5: K across.

Leave these 3 (5, 7, 7, 9) (10, 11, 12, 14) sts on your needle and do not cut the yarn. *Proceed to "Shoulder Seams."*

SHOULDER SEAMS

You will now be using the Grafting method to join the shoulder seams.

1. Place the WS of your front panel and back panel together.

2. Your front right (as worn) shoulder stitches should still be on your needle. Place the corresponding 3 (5, 7, 7, 9) (10, 11, 12, 14) sts left on hold for the back right shoulder onto the other needle. Make sure both needles are facing the same direction.

3. Cut working yarn leaving a tail that is 2–3 times longer than the width of the shoulder.

4. Continue, following the instructions for Grafting (page 214).

5. Repeat all steps for the other shoulder, using the corresponding front right (as worn) and back right shoulder stitches left on hold.

SIDE SEAMS

1. Use the Mattress stitch (page 209) for reverse stockinette to seam the sides, starting at the bottom.

2. Seam until you reach the stitch markers (you may now remove the markers).

NECK TRIM

Using US 17 (12 mm) 32-inch (80-cm) circular needles, pick up stitches in the following fashion:

1. Pick up 2 sts along the side of the back right shoulder.

2. Pick up 10 (10, 10, 12, 12) (12, 14, 14, 14) sts along the back neck.

3. Pick up 2 sts along the side of the back left shoulder.

4. Pick up 6 sts along the side of the front left shoulder.

5. Pick up 8 (8, 8, 10, 10) (10, 12, 12, 12) sts along the front neck.

6. Pick up 6 sts along the side of the front right shoulder.

You should now have 34 (34, 34, 38, 38) (38, 42, 42, 42) sts. PM to mark the BOR.

Rounds 1–2: *K1, p1*, rep ** until end of the round. *You will need to use the Magic Loop method (page 207).*

BO all sts loosely in 1x1 rib pattern.

SLEEVE TRIMS

Using US 17 (12 mm) 32-inch (80-cm) circular needles, starting at the underarm point, pick up stitches in the following fashion: *Pick up 4 sts, skip 1 st.* Make sure you have an even number of stitches. PM to mark the BOR.

Round 1: *K1, p1*, rep ** until end of the round. *You will need to use the Magic Loop method (page 207).*

BO all sts loosely in 1x1 rib pattern.

FINISHING

Weave in all your loose ends.

Blocking super bulky yarn is not necessary. However, if you do wish to block your vest, it is suggested that you use the spray blocking method (do *not* wet or steam block).

CHART

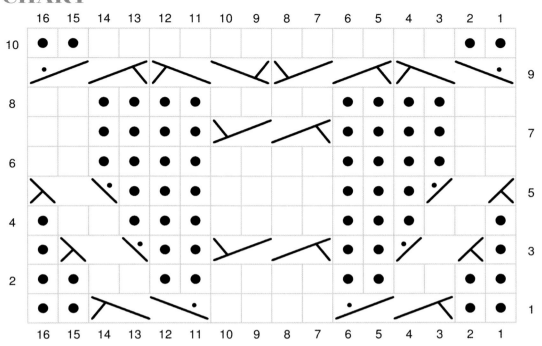

CHART PATTERN

Row 1 (RS): P2, 2/2 RPC, k4, 2/2 LPC, p2.

Row 2 (WS): K2, p2, k2, p4, k2, p2, k2.

Row 3: P1, 2/1 RPC, p2, C4B, p2, 2/1 LPC, p1.

Row 4: K1, p2, k3, p4, k3, p2, k1.

Row 5: 2/1 RPC, p3, k4, p3, 2/1 LPC.

Row 6: P2, k4, p4, k4, p2.

Row 7: K2, p4, C4B, p4, k2.

Row 8: P2, k4, p4, k4, p2.

Row 9: 2/2 LPC, C4B, C4F, 2/2 RPC.

Row 10: K2, p12, k2.

Legend		
☐		RS: Knit WS: Purl
●		RS: Purl WS: Knit
		C4B
		C4F
		2/2 RPC
		2/2 LPC
		2/1 RPC
		2/1 LPC

Magnolia Jumper

Embrace the chilly seasons in style with the Magnolia Jumper, the latest addition to my Magnolia collection. Designed as a cozy adaptation for the cooler months, this pattern is ideal for knitters seeking a fashionable and rewarding but still quick-to-knit project. Drawing inspiration from the natural beauty of magnolia flowers, this raglan design features an exquisite cable stitch motif on both the front and back sections. Resembling the petals of the majestic flower, the stitch adds an elegant touch to the overall design, whilst the bell sleeves, worked in smooth stockinette stitch, provide a graceful contrast to the intricate cables.

Construction Notes

This seamless jumper is worked entirely in the round in stockinette stitch and charted cables from the top down. You will first work the neck trim before working the yoke. You will then divide the body from the sleeves at the underarm point and continue to work the body in the round before knitting the sleeves in the round.

Skill Level

Intermediate

Sizing

XS (S, M, L, XL) (XXL, 3XL, 4XL, 5XL)

Finished bust: 37 (41, 44.8, 48.8, 53.6) (57.4, 61.4, 65.4, 69.2)" / 94 (104, 114, 124, 136) (146, 156, 166, 176) cm

Recommended ease: This jumper is designed with approximately 7.1–9.1 inches / 18–23 cm of positive ease

Sample shown is knit in Size S.

MATERIALS

Yarn

Super bulky weight, Cardigang, Chunky Merino Wool (100% merino wool), 87 yds (80 m) per 200-g skein, shown in Mauve on Over colorway

Any super bulky weight yarn can be used for this pattern as long as it matches gauge. A good substitute would be Wool and the Gang, Crazy Sexy Wool or Malabrigo, Rasta.

Yardage/Meterage

363 (390, 459, 547, 630) (667, 703, 784, 872) yds / 332 (357, 420, 500, 576) (610, 643, 717, 797) m

Needles

For body: US 19 (15 mm) 32- to 40-inch (80- to 100-cm) circular needle

For neck trim and bottom ribbing: US 17 (12 mm) 32- to 40-inch (80- to 100-cm) circular needle

Notions

Cable needle

Stitch markers

Tapestry needle

Scissors

Scrap yarn

GAUGE

8.5 sts x 10 rows = 4 inches (10 cm) in cable stitch (explained below) using larger needle

To Knit Gauge Swatch

CO 12 sts.

Row 1 (WS): P across.

Row 2 (RS): K2, C4B, k6.

Row 3: P across.

Row 4: K6, C4F, k2.

Work at least 10 rows.

SPECIAL TECHNIQUES

Magic Loop method (page 207)

Backwards Loop Cast On (page 212)

ABBREVIATIONS

1x1 rib(bing) - *Knit 1, purl 1*

BO - Bind off

BOR - Beginning of round

C4B - Cable 4 back (place 2 sts on cable needle and hold to **back** of work. K2, k2 from cable needle)

C4F - Cable 4 front (place 2 sts on cable needle and hold to **front** of work. K2, k2 from cable needle)

CO - Cast on

K - Knit

K2tog - Knit 2 stitches together

M1L - Make 1 left

M1R - Make 1 right

P - Purl

PM - Place marker

Rep - Repeat

RM - Remove marker

SM - Slip marker

Ssk - Slip, slip, knit 2 together through the back loops

St(s) - Stitch(es)

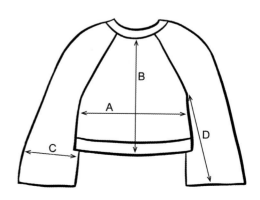

SIZING CHART

Size	XS	S	M	L	XL	XXL	3XL	4XL	5XL
To fit bust	28–30"/ 71–76 cm	32–34"/ 81–86 cm	36–38"/ 91.5–96.5 cm	40–42"/ 101.5–106.5 cm	44–46"/ 111.5–117 cm	48–50"/ 122–127 cm	52–54"/ 132–137 cm	56–58"/ 142–147 cm	60–62"/ 152–158 cm
(A) Width	18.5"/ 47 cm	20.5"/ 52 cm	22.4"/ 57 cm	24.4"/ 62 cm	26.8"/ 68 cm	28.7"/ 73 cm	30.7"/ 78 cm	32.7"/ 83 cm	34.6"/ 88 cm
(B) Length	15"/ 38 cm	15"/ 38 cm	15.5"/ 42 cm	15.5"/ 42 cm	18.1"/ 46 cm	19.7"/ 50 cm	19.7"/ 50 cm	21.3"/ 54 cm	22.8"/ 58 cm
(C) Sleeve Width	8.3"/ 21 cm	9.4"/ 24 cm	9.8"/ 25 cm	11"/ 28 cm	11.4"/ 29 cm	12.2"/ 31 cm	12.2"/ 31 cm	13.4"/ 34 cm	14.6"/ 37 cm
(D) Sleeve Length	13"/ 33 cm	13"/ 33 cm	13"/ 33 cm	14.2"/ 36 cm	14.2"/ 36 cm	14.2"/ 36 cm	15.4"/ 39 cm	15.4"/ 39 cm	15.4"/ 39 cm

MAGNOLIA JUMPER PATTERN

NECK TRIM

Using US 17 (12 mm) 32- to 40-inch (80- to 100-cm) circular needles and the Long Tail Cast On, CO 38 (38, 38, 38, 44) (44, 52, 52, 52) sts. Join in the round and PM to mark the BOR. *You will need to use the Magic Loop method (page 207).*

Rounds 1–5: *K1, p1*, rep ** until end of the round.

YOKE

Switch to US 19 (15 mm) 32- to 40-inch (80- to 100-cm) circular needles.

You will now place 3 additional markers to divide your stitches into 4 sections (front, sleeve 1, back, sleeve 2). Ensure your BOR marker can be easily distinguished from the other markers.

Setup round: K16 (16, 16, 16, 20) (20, 24, 24, 24), **PM**, k3 (3, 3, 3, 2) (2, 2, 2, 2), **PM**, k16 (16, 16, 16, 20) (20, 24, 24, 24), **PM**, k3 (3, 3, 3, 2) (2, 2, 2, 2).

Increase round: *K1, M1L, k to 1 st before marker, M1R, k1, SM*, rep ** until end of the round.

Restart your row count here. You will now begin to follow the charts (pages 43 to 46) for the front and back sections. The sleeves will be worked in stockinette stitch. *Begin with round 1 of the chart during Round 1 below where it says "work next round of Chart […]."*

Round 1: *Work next round of Chart A (A, A, A, B) (B, C, C, C), SM, k to marker, SM*, rep ** until end of the round.

BODY

You will now divide the sleeves from the body. Sizes M–5XL will cast on additional stitches for the underarms.

Sizes XS (S, -, -, -) (-, -, -, -) only

Next round: *K to marker, **RM**, place the next 27 (31, -, -, -) (-, -, -, -) sts on scrap yarn, SM*, rep ** until end of the round.

Sizes XS (S, -, -, -) (-, -, -, -) proceed to "All sizes continue."

Sizes - (-, M, L, XL) (XXL, 3XL, 4XL, 5XL) only

Cut working yarn, leaving a tail long enough to weave in later.

Next round: **RM**, place the last - (-, 31, 33, 34) (36, 38, 40, 42) sts from the previous round on scrap yarn, CO - (-, 2, 3, 3) (4, 3, 4, 5) new sts using the Long Tail Cast On and a new strand of yarn, k to marker, **RM**, place the next - (-, 31, 33, 34) (36, 38, 40, 42) sts on scrap yarn, CO - (-, 2, 3, 3) (4, 3, 4, 5) new sts using the Backwards Loop Cast On (page 212), **PM**, CO - (-, 2, 3, 3) (4, 3, 4, 5) new sts using the Backwards Loop Cast On, k to marker, **RM**, CO - (-, 2, 3, 3) (4, 3, 4, 5) new sts using the Backwards Loop Cast On, **PM** to mark the BOR.

Proceed to "All sizes continue."

All sizes continue

You should now have a **total** of 80 (88, 96, 104, 116) (124, 132, 140, 148) sts. Restart your row count here.

Round 2: *Work next round of Chart A (A, A, A, B) (B, C, C, C), SM, k1, M1L, k to 1 st before marker, M1R, k1, SM*, rep ** until end of the round.

Repeat rounds 1–2 until you have worked 23 (27, 27, 29, 31) (33, 35, 37, 39) rounds **total** of the chart. *Sizes XS (S, M, -, XL) (-, 3XL, 4XL, -) will not work the entire chart, so make sure you end on the correct round for your size.*

You should now have a **total** of 134 (150, 150, 158, 172) (180, 196, 204, 212) sts, with 40 (44, 44, 46, 52) (54, 60, 62, 64) sts for the front and back sections and 27 (31, 31, 33, 34) (36, 38, 40, 42) sts for each sleeve.

Sizes XS (-, M, -, -) (-, -, -, -) only

Round 1: Repeat round 1 (-, 3, -, -) (-, -, -, -) of Chart E (-, D, -, -) (-, -, -, -) until end of the round.

Round 2: Repeat round 2 (-, 4, -, -) (-, -, -, -) of Chart E (-, D, -, -) (-, -, -, -) until end of the round.

Round 3: Repeat round 3 (-, 1, -, -) (-, -, -, -) of Chart E (-, D, -, -) (-, -, -, -) until end of the round.

Round 4: Repeat round 4 (-, 2, -, -) (-, -, -, -) of Chart E (-, D, -, -) (-, -, -, -) until end of the round.

Rounds 5–8: Repeat rounds 1–4.

Rounds 9–11: Repeat rounds 1–3.

Sizes XS (-, M, -, -) (-, -, -, -) proceed to "All sizes continue."

Size S only

Rounds 1–4: *K2, rep corresponding round of Chart E until 2 sts before marker, k2, SM*, rep ** until end of the round.

Rounds 5–7: Repeat rounds 1–3.

Size S proceed to "All sizes continue."

Size L only

Rounds 1–4: *K2, rep corresponding round of Chart D until 2 sts before marker, k2, SM*, rep ** until end of the round.

Rounds 5–8: Repeat rounds 1–4.

Round 9: Repeat round 1.

Size L proceed to "All sizes continue."

Sizes - (-, -, -, XL) (-, 3XL, -, 5XL) only

Round 1: *K1, rep round - (-, -, -, 1) (-, 3, -, 1) of Chart - (-, -, -, E) (-, D, -, E) until 1 st before marker, k1, SM*, rep ** until end of the round.

Round 2: *K1, rep round - (-, -, -, 2) (-, 4, -, 2) of Chart - (-, -, -, E) (-, D, -, E) until 1 st before marker, k1, SM*, rep ** until end of the round.

Round 3: *K1, rep round - (-, -, -, 3) (-, 1, -, 3) of Chart - (-, -, -, E) (-, D, -, E) until 1 st before marker, k1, SM*, rep ** until end of the round.

Round 4: *K1, rep round - (-, -, -, 4) (-, 2, -, 4) of Chart - (-, -, -, E) (-, D, -, E) until 1 st before marker, k1, SM*, rep ** until end of the round.

Next - (-, -, -, 4) (-, 4, -, 8) rounds: Repeat rounds 1–4.

Next 3 rounds: Repeat rounds 1–3.

Sizes - (-, -, -, XL) (-, 3XL, -, 5XL) proceed to "All sizes continue."

Size - (-, -, -, -) (XXL, -, 4XL, -) only

Round 1: *K3, rep round - (-, -, -, -) (3, -, 1) of Chart - (-, -, -, -) (E, -, D, -) until 3 sts before marker, k3, SM*, rep ** until end of the round.

Round 2: *K3, rep round - (-, -, -, -) (4, -, 2) of Chart - (-, -, -, -) (E, -, D) until 3 sts before marker, k3, SM*, rep ** until end of the round.

Round 3: *K3, rep round - (-, -, -, -) (1, -, 3, -) of Chart - (-, -, -, -) (E, -, D, -) until 3 sts before marker, k3, SM*, rep ** until end of the round.

Round 4: *K3, rep round - (-, -, -, -) (2, -, 4, -) of Chart - (-, -, -, -) (E, -, D, -) until 3 sts before marker, k3, SM*, rep ** until end of the round.

Rounds 5–12: Repeat rounds 1–4.

Round 13: Repeat round 1.

Proceed to "All sizes continue."

All sizes continue

You should now have 67 (74, 80, 87, 97) (104, 110, 117, 124) sts.

Switch to US 17 (12 mm) 32- to 40-inch (80- to 100-cm) circular needles. Restart your row count here.

Sizes XS (-, -, L, XL) (-, -, 4XL, -) only

Round 1: K2tog, p1, *k1, p1*, rep ** until end of the round.

You should now have 66 (-, -, 86, 96) (-, -, 116, -) sts.

All sizes continue

Next 3 (4, 4, 3, 3) (4, 4, 3, 4) rounds: *K1, p1*, rep ** until end of the round.

BO all sts loosely in 1x1 rib pattern.

SLEEVES

Place one of the sections of 27 (31, 31, 33, 34) (36, 38, 40, 42) sts you left on scrap yarn onto your US 19 (15 mm) 32- to 40-inch (80- to 100-cm) circular needles.

Starting at the mid-underarm point, pick up 2 (2, 2, 3, 3) (4, 3, 4, 5) sts, k the next 27 (31, 31, 33, 34) (36, 38, 40, 42) sts, pick up 1 (1, 2, 3, 3) (4, 3, 4, 5) sts, PM to mark the BOR.

You should now have 30 (34, 35, 39, 40) (44, 44, 48, 52) sts.

Sizes S and M proceed to "All sizes continue."

Size XS only

Round 1: K1, M1L, k to 1 st before marker, M1R, k1.

Round 2: K across.

Rounds 3–4: Repeat rounds 1–2.

Size XS proceed to "All sizes continue."

All sizes continue

> **Note:** If you would like to add or subtract length to/from your jumper, do so here, keeping in mind the ribbing will add approximately 2.4 inches (6 cm).

You will now make decreases before working the ribbing.

Sizes XS (S, -, L, XL) (XXL, -, 4XL, 5XL) only

Next round: *K4, k2tog*, rep ** until last 2 (4, -, 2, 2) (4, -, 2, 4) sts, k to end of the round.

Sizes - (-, M, -, -) (-, 3XL, -, -) only

Next round: *K4, k2tog*, rep ** until end of the round.

Sizes - (-, -, L, XL) (XXL, 3XL, 4XL, 5XL) only

Round 1: K1, k2tog, k to last 3 sts, ssk, k1.

Round 2: K across.

Repeat the last 2 rounds - (-, -, 1, 1) (2, 2, 3, 3) **more** time(s).

Proceed to "All sizes continue."

All sizes continue

You should now have 34 (34, 35, 35, 36) (38, 38, 40, 44) sts.

Work in stockinette stitch until your sleeve measures approximately 13 (13, 13, 14.2, 14.2) (14.2, 15.4, 15.4, 15.4) inches / 33 (33, 33, 36, 36) (36, 39, 39, 39) cm from the underarm, or to desired length. *Make note of how many total rows you work so that you can work your second sleeve to match.*

BO all sts.

Repeat for the second sleeve.

FINISHING

Weave in all your loose ends.

Blocking super bulky yarn is not necessary. However, if you do wish to block your jumper, it is suggested that you use the spray blocking method (do *not* wet or steam block).

Legend	
☐	Knit
⟍⟋	C4B
⟋⟍	C4F
Γ	M1R, K1
Y	K1, M1L
▨	No Stitch

Charts A, B and C are on the following 3 pages.

CHART D

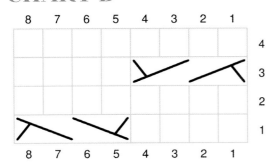

CHART D PATTERN

Round 1: K4, C4F.

Round 2: K across.

Round 3: C4B, k4.

Round 4: K across.

CHART E

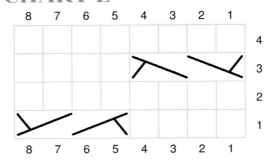

CHART E PATTERN

Round 1: K4, C4B.

Round 2: K across.

Round 3: C4F, k4.

Round 4: K across.

CHART A (SIZES XS–L)

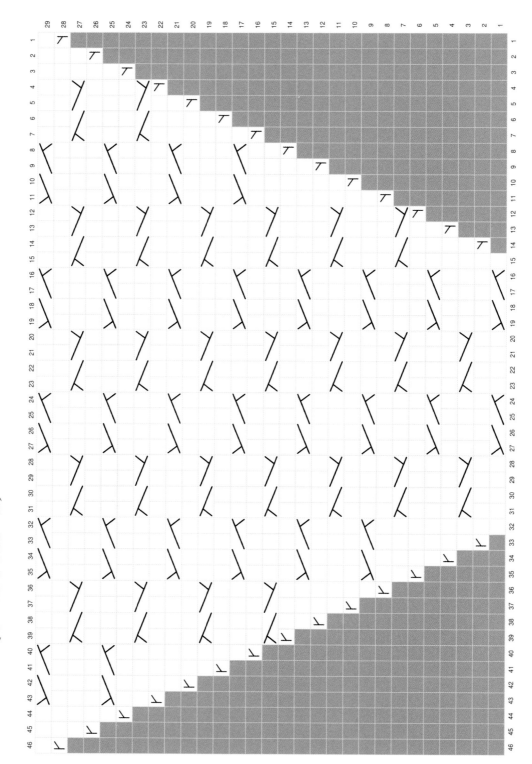

CHART B (SIZES XL–XXL)

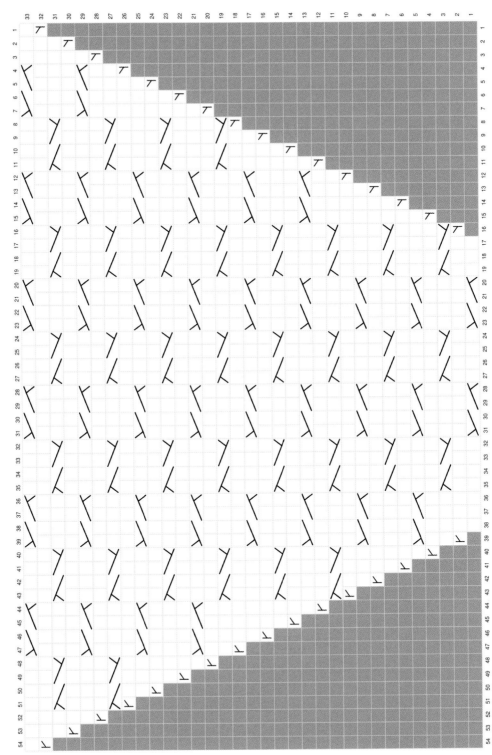

CHART C (SIZES 3XL–5XL)

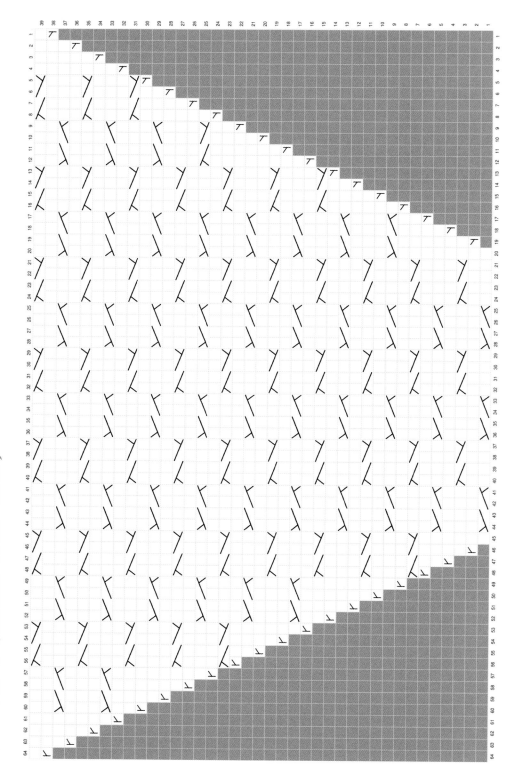

Orla Cardigan

This design holds a special place in my heart, as I knitted most of the sample in a tiny cabin nestled on a hill in the idyllic countryside of Victoria, Australia. Far removed from the distractions of social media and the bustling pace of city life, I had the privilege of immersing myself in the project and embracing the serenity of my natural surroundings. Each stitch became a moment of tranquility, and every row a gentle meditation. The result is my absolute dream cable cardigan that not only embodies my vision but also evokes cherished memories of that peaceful retreat. The cabin I stayed in was named Orla, so it felt only fitting that this design would share the same name. The pattern calls for bulky weight cotton yarn, which makes for a swift knitting experience, providing endless satisfaction as the cables intertwine like branches reaching towards the sky.

Construction Notes

This cardigan is worked mostly flat in charted cables from the bottom up. You will first work the back panel flat, followed by the front left and right panels. You will join the shoulder seams to create the neck hole using the Three Needle Bind Off method (page 207). To create the armholes, you will use the vertical Mattress stitch (page 209) to seam the sides together. The sleeves are worked in the round by picking up stitches along the armhole edges. You will finish by working the button band flat by picking up stitches along the inside edges.

Skill Level

Intermediate

Sizing

XS (S, M, L, XL) (XXL, 3XL, 4XL, 5XL)

Finished bust: 43.4 (47.2, 51.2, 56, 59) (63, 67, 71, 75.6)" / 110 (120, 130, 142, 150) (160, 170, 182, 192) cm, blocked

Recommended ease: This cardigan is designed with approximately 13.4–15.4 inches / 34–39 cm of positive ease

Sample shown is knit in Size S.

MATERIALS

Yarn

Bulky weight, Wool and the Gang, Big Love Cotton (100% Organic Cotton), 110 yds (100 m) per 100-g skein, shown in Eucalyptus Green colorway

Any bulky weight yarn can be used for this pattern as long as it matches gauge. A good substitute would be Katia, Homemade or Juniper Moon Farm, Bud.

Yardage/Meterage

708 (748, 849, 989, 1093) (1200, 1366, 1498, 1625) yds / 647 (684, 776, 904, 999) (1097, 1249, 1370, 1486) m

Needles

For body: US 10.5 (6.5 mm) 32- to 40-inch (80- to 100-cm) circular needle

For sleeves: US 10.5 (6.5 mm) 24- to 32-inch (60- to 80-cm) circular needle

For bottom ribbing and button band: US 9 (5.5 mm) 32- to 40-inch (80- to 100-cm) circular needle

For sleeve cuffs: US 9 (5.5 mm) 24-inch (60-cm) circular needle or DPNs

Notions

Buttons (can be 1.2" / 30 mm or larger) x 4 (4, 4, 5, 5) (5, 6, 6, 6)

Cable needle

Stitch marker

Tapestry needle

Scissors

Stitch holders

Measuring tape

GAUGE

12 sts x 16 rows = 4 inches (10 cm) in stockinette stitch using larger needle (blocked)

ABBREVIATIONS

1x1 rib(bing) - *Knit 1, purl 1*

BO - Bind off

BOR - Beginning of round

C4B - Cable 4 back (place 2 sts on cable needle and hold to **back** of work. K2, k2 from cable needle)

C4F - Cable 4 front (place 2 sts on cable needle and hold to **front** of work. K2, k2 from cable needle)

C8B - Cable 8 back (place 4 sts on cable needle and hold to **back** of work. K4, k4 from cable needle)

C8F - Cable 8 front (place 4 sts on cable needle and hold to **front** of work. K4, k4 from cable needle)

C10B - Cable 10 back (place 5 sts on cable needle and hold to **back** of work. K5, k5 from cable needle)

C10F - Cable 10 front (place 5 sts on cable needle and hold to **front** of work. K5, k5 from cable needle)

CO - Cast on

DPNs - Double pointed needles

K - Knit

K2tog - Knit 2 stitches together

LC - Left cross

P - Purl

P2tog - Purl 2 stitches together

PM - Place marker

RC - Right cross

Rep - Repeat

RS - Right side

Sl - Slip stitch

Ssk - Slip, slip, knit 2 stitches together through the back loops

Ssp - Slip, slip, purl 2 stitches together through the back loops

St(s) - Stitch(es)

Tbl - Through the back loop

WS - Wrong side

Wyib - With yarn held in back

Wyif - With yarn held in front

SIZING CHART

Size	XS	S	M	L	XL	XXL	3XL	4XL	5XL
To fit bust	28–30"/ 71–76 cm	32–34"/ 81–86 cm	36–38"/ 91.5– 96.5 cm	40–42"/ 101.5– 106.5 cm	44–46"/ 111.5– 117 cm	48–50"/ 122–127 cm	52–54"/ 132–137 cm	56–58"/ 142–147 cm	60–62"/ 152–158 cm
(A) Width	21.7"/ 55 cm	23.6"/ 60 cm	25.6"/ 65 cm	28"/ 71 cm	29.5"/ 75 cm	31.5"/ 80 cm	33.5"/ 85 cm	35.8"/ 91 cm	37.8"/ 96 cm
(B) Length	18.1"/ 46 cm	19.3"/ 49 cm	20.5"/ 52 cm	21.7"/ 55 cm	22.8"/ 58 cm	24"/ 61 cm	25.2"/ 64 cm	26.4"/ 67 cm	27.6"/ 70 cm
(C) Sleeve Width	7.9"/ 20 cm	7.9"/ 20 cm	7.9"/ 20 cm	9.4"/ 24 cm	9.4"/ 24 cm	9.4"/ 24 cm	11"/ 28 cm	11"/ 28 cm	11"/ 28 cm
(D) Sleeve Length	15"/ 38 cm	15"/ 38 cm	16.1"/ 41 cm	16.1"/ 41 cm	17.3"/ 44 cm	17.3"/ 44 cm	18.5"/ 47 cm	18.5"/ 47 cm	18.5"/ 47 cm

SPECIAL TECHNIQUES

Alternating Cable Cast On (page 208)

Magic Loop method (page 207)

Three Needle Bind Off (page 207)

Horizontal One Row Buttonhole (page 215)

Mattress stitch (page 209)

1/1 Left Cross

Place 1 st on cable needle and hold to **front** of work. K1, k1 from cable needle.

1/1 Right Cross

Place 1 st on cable needle and hold to **back** of work. K1, k1 from cable needle.

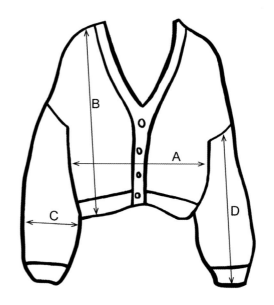

BACK PANEL

Using US 9 (5.5 mm) straight or 32- to 40-inch (80- to 100-cm) circular needles and the Alternating Cable Cast On (page 208), CO 82 (90, 98, 106, 112) (120, 128, 136, 144) sts.

Rows 1–9: *K1, p1*, rep ** until end of the row.

Switch to US 10.5 (6.5 mm) 32- to 40-inch (80- to 100-cm) circular needle. Restart your row count here.

Repeat the following 16 rows until you have worked 63 (67, 72, 77, 82) (87, 91, 96, 101) rows total. *You should end after row 15 (3, 8, 13, 2) (7, 11, 16, 5) of Chart B (page 60).*

> **Note:** When worked flat, odd (WS) rows of the chart are read from left to right, and even (RS) rows are read from right to left. On WS rows, the knit symbols on the chart are worked as purl sts and vice versa.

> **Note:** If you would like to add or subtract length to/from your cardigan, do so here, but ensure you still end after row 15 (3, 8, 13, 2) (7, 11, 16, 5) of Chart B or knit to your desired length, making note of what row of the chart you end after, as this will change which row you start with for the Back Shoulders. It is very important that you make note of how many rows you add or subtract so you can work the other panels to match.

Size XS only

Row 1 (WS): P4, k2, p2, k1, work corresponding row of Chart B (page 60), k1, p2, k2, p4.

Row 2 (RS): K4, p2, 1/1 LC, p1, work corresponding row of Chart B, p1, 1/1 RC, p2, k4.

Rows 3–16: Repeat rows 1–2.

Sizes - (S, -, L, XL) (-, -, -, -) only

Row 1 (WS): P- (3, -, 1, 4) (-, -, -, -), work corresponding row of Chart C (page 60) - (1, -, 2, 2) (-, -, -, -) time(s), work corresponding row of Chart B (page 60), work corresponding row of Chart A (page 59) - (1, -, 2, 2) (-, -, -, -) time(s), p- (3, -, 1, 4) (-, -, -, -).

Row 2 (RS): K- (3, -, 1, 4) (-, -, -, -), work corresponding row of Chart A - (1, -, 2, 2) (-, -, -, -) time(s), work corresponding row of Chart B, work corresponding row of Chart C - (1, -, 2, 2) (-, -, -, -) time(s), k- (3, -, 1, 4) (-, -, -, -).

Rows 3–16: Repeat rows 1–2.

Sizes - (-, M, -, -) (XXL, -, -, -) only

Row 1 (WS): P- (-, 3, -, -) (4, -, -, -), k1, p2, k1, work corresponding row of Chart C (page 60) - (-, 1, -, -) (2, -, -, -) time(s), work corresponding row of Chart B (page 60), work corresponding row of Chart A (page 59) - (-, 1, -, -) (2, -, -, -) time(s), k1, p2, k1, p- (-, 3, -, -) (4, -, -, -).

Row 2 (RS): K- (-, 3, -, -) (4, -, -, -), p1, 1/1 LC, p1, work corresponding row of Chart A - (-, 1, -, -) (2, -, -, -) time(s), work corresponding row of Chart B, work corresponding row of Chart C - (-, 1, -, -) (2, -, -, -) time(s), p1, 1/1 RC, p1, k- (-, 3, -, -) (4, -, -, -).

Rows 3–16: Repeat rows 1–2.

Row 2 (RS): K4, p1, k4, p1, work corresponding row of Chart D, work corresponding row of Chart A, work corresponding row of Chart B, work corresponding row of Chart C, work corresponding row of Chart E, p1, k4, p1, k4.

Row 3: Repeat row 1.

Row 4: K4, p1, C4F, p1, work corresponding row of Chart D, work corresponding row of Chart A, work corresponding row of Chart B, work corresponding row of Chart C, work corresponding row of Chart E, p1, C4B, p1, k4.

Rows 5–16: Repeat rows 1–4.

BACK SHOULDERS

You will now make decreases to shape the back neckline whilst continuing to work in pattern (including the 16-row repeat of non-charted edge stitches that have been established during the previous section).

> **A note on working in pattern:** As you decrease during this section, you will no longer always have complete full repeats of the Chart B pattern at the inner edges of the neckline. This means you will not always begin with stitch 1 (RS) or stitch 64 (WS) of Chart B when it says "work in pattern"; instead, you would start with the stitch that vertically matches the stitch column below it. If/when you reach a cable stitch and no longer have enough stitches to work that cable, simply knit those stitches instead. If it is helpful, place stitch markers between each chart section before you begin to decrease so that you can see where you are within the chart at any time.

You should be on row 16 (4, 9, 14, 3) (8, 12, 1, 6) of Chart B and the edge stitches.

Sizes - (-, -, -, -) (-, 3XL, 4XL, -) only

Row 1 (WS): P- (-, -, -, -) (-, 1, 5, -), k1, work corresponding row of Chart E (page 61), work corresponding row of Chart C (page 60), work corresponding row of Chart B (page 60), work corresponding row of Chart A (page 59), work corresponding row of Chart D (page 61), k1, p- (-, -, -, -) (-, 1, 5, -).

Row 2 (RS): K- (-, -, -, -) (-, 1, 5, -), p1, work corresponding row of Chart D, work corresponding row of Chart A, work corresponding row of Chart B, work corresponding row of Chart C, work corresponding row of Chart E, p1, k- (-, -, -, -) (-, 1, 5, -).

Rows 3–16: Repeat rows 1–2.

Size 5XL only

Row 1 (WS): P4, k1, p4, k1, work corresponding row of Chart E (page 61), work corresponding row of Chart C (page 60), work corresponding row of Chart B (page 60), work corresponding row of Chart A (page 59), work corresponding row of Chart D (page 61), k1, p4, k1, p4.

Setup row (RS (RS, WS, RS, WS) (RS, RS, WS, RS)): Work in pattern across 27 (29, 33, 37, 40) (43, 46, 49, 53) sts, BO 28 (32, 32, 32, 32) (34, 36, 38, 38) sts, work in pattern across the remaining 27 (29, 33, 37, 40) (43, 46, 49, 53) sts.

You will start with the back left (left, right, left, right) (left, left, right, left) shoulder, followed by the remaining shoulder. *You may leave the remaining shoulder stitches on the cord or place them on a stitch holder.*

You should be on row 1 (5, 10, 15, 4) (9, 13, 2, 7) of Chart B and the edge stitches.

Sizes XS (S, -, L, -) (XXL, 3XL, -, 5XL) only

Next row (WS): Work in pattern until last 3 sts, ssp, p1.

Next row (RS): K2, work in pattern until end of the row.

Cut yarn and place these 26 (28, -, 36, -) (42, 45, -, 52) left shoulder sts on a stitch holder. *You will come back to them later for the Shoulder Seams.*

Reattach yarn on the WS to the remaining 27 (29, -, 37, -) (43, 46, -, 53) right shoulder sts. *You should be on row 1 (5, -, 15, -) (9, 13, -, 7) of Chart B and the edge stitches.*

Next row (WS): P1, p2tog, work in pattern until end of the row.

Next row (RS): Work in pattern until last 2 sts, k2.

Cut yarn and place these 26 (28, -, 36, -) (42, 45, -, 52) right shoulder sts on a stitch holder. *You will come back to them later for the Shoulder Seams.*

Sizes - (-, M, -, XL) (-, -, 4XL, -) only

Next row (RS): Work in pattern until last 3 sts, k2tog, k1.

Next row (WS): P2, work in pattern until end of the row.

Cut yarn and place these - (-, 32, -, 39) (-, -, 48, -) right shoulder sts on a stitch holder. *You will come back to them later for the Shoulder Seams.*

Reattach yarn on the RS to the remaining - (-, 33, -, 40) (-, -, 49, -) left shoulder sts. *You should be on row - (-, 10, -, 4) (-, -, 2, -) of Chart B and the edge stitches.*

Next row (RS): K1, ssk, work in pattern until end of the row.

Next row (WS): Work in pattern until last 2 sts, p2.

Cut yarn and place these - (-, 32, -, 39) (-, -, 48, -) left shoulder sts on a stitch holder. *You will come back to them later for the Shoulder Seams.*

FRONT LEFT PANEL

Using US 9 (5.5 mm) straight or 24- to 32-inch (60- to 80-cm) circular needles and the Alternating Cable Cast On (page 208), CO 34 (37, 41, 45, 48) (51, 55, 58, 62) sts.

Sizes XS (-, -, -, XL) (-, -, 4XL, 5XL) only

Rows 1–9: *K1, p1*, rep ** until end of the row.

Sizes - (S, M, L, -) (XXL, 3XL, -, -) only

Row 1 (RS): *P1, k1*, rep ** until last st, p1.

Row 2 (WS): *K1, p1*, rep ** until last st, k1.

Rows 3–9: Repeat rows 1–2. You will end after a RS row.

All sizes continue

Switch to US 10.5 (6.5 mm) straight or 24- to 32-inch (60- to 80-cm) circular needles. Restart your row count here.

Repeat the following 8 rows until you have worked 35 (39, 43, 49, 53) (59, 59, 63, 69) rows **total**. *You should end after row 3 (7, 3, 1, 5) (3, 3, 7, 5) of Chart F (page 62).*

> **Note:** If you are adding length to your cardigan, work the number of rows you added to your Back Panel here in addition to the row count written above. If you are subtracting length from your cardigan, subtract the number of rows you subtracted from the Back Panel from the row count written above. Make note of what row of the chart you end after, as this will change which row you start with when you shape the front left neckline.

Sizes XS (S, M, -, -) (-, -, -, -) only

Row 1 (WS): P1 (2, 3, -, -) (-, -, -, -), k0 (0, 1, -, -) (-, -, -, -), work corresponding row of Chart F (page 62), k0 (0, 1, -, -) (-, -, -, -), p1 (3, 4, -, -) (-, -, -, -).

Row 2 (RS): K1 (3, 4, -, -) (-, -, -, -), p0 (0, 1, -, -) (-, -, -, -), work corresponding row of Chart F, p0 (0, 1, -, -) (-, -, -, -), k1 (2, 3, -, -) (-, -, -, -).

Rows 3–8: Repeat rows 1–2.

Sizes - (-, -, L, XL) (XXL, -, -, -) only

Row 1 (WS): P- (-, -, 2, 3) (4, -, -, -), k- (-, -, 1, 2) (2, -, -, -), p2, k1, work corresponding row of Chart F (page 62), k1, p2, k- (-, -, 1, 2) (2, -, -, -), p- (-, -, 3, 3) (5, -, -, -).

Row 2 (RS): K- (-, -, 3, 3) (5, -, -, -), p- (-, -, 1, 2) (2, -, -, -), 1/1 LC, p1, work corresponding row of Chart F, p1, 1/1 LC, p- (-, -, 1, 2) (2, -, -, -), k- (-, -, 2, 3) (4, -, -, -).

Rows 3–8: Repeat rows 1–2.

Size 3XL only

Row 1 (WS): P3, k2, p2, k1, work corresponding row of Chart F (page 62), k1, p2, *k2, p4*, rep ** until end of the row.

Row 2 (RS): K4, p2, k4, p2, 1/1 LC, p1, work corresponding row of Chart F, p1, 1/1 LC, p2, k3.

Row 3: Repeat row 1.

Row 4: K4, p2, C4F, p2, 1/1 LC, p1, work corresponding row of Chart F, p1, 1/1 LC, p2, k3.

Rows 5–8: Repeat rows 1–4.

Sizes - (-, -, -, -) (-, -, 4XL, 5XL) only

Row 1 (WS): P- (-, -, -, -) (-, -, 3, 4), k- (-, -, -, -) (-, -, 1, 2), p4, k2, p2, k1, work corresponding row of Chart F (page 62), k1, p2, k2, p4, k- (-, -, -, -) (-, -, 1, 2), p- (-, -, -, -) (-, -, 3, 4).

Row 2 (RS): K- (-, -, -, -) (-, -, 3, 4), p- (-, -, -, -) (-, -, 1, 2), k4, p2, 1/1 LC, p1, work corresponding row of Chart F, p1, 1/1 LC, p2, k4, p- (-, -, -, -) (-, -, 1, 2), k- (-, -, -, -) (-, -, 3, 4).

Row 3: Repeat row 1.

Row 4: K- (-, -, -, -) (-, -, 3, 4), p- (-, -, -, -) (-, -, 1, 2), C4F, p2, 1/1 LC, p1, work corresponding row of Chart F, p1, 1/1 LC, p2, C4F, p- (-, -, -, -) (-, -, 1, 2), k- (-, -, -, -) (-, -, 3, 4).

Rows 5–8: Repeat rows 1–4.

All sizes continue

You will now make decreases to shape the front left neckline, whilst continuing to work in pattern (including the 8-row repeat of non-charted edge stitches that have been established during the panel thus far). *You should be on row 4 (8, 4, 2, 6) (4, 4, 8, 6) of Chart F (page 62) and the edge stitches.*

> **Reminder:** If/when you reach a cable stitch and no longer have enough stitches to work that cable, simply knit those stitches instead.

Next row (RS): Work in pattern until last 3 sts, k2tog, k1.

Next row (WS): P2, work in pattern until end of the row.

Repeat the last 2 rows until you have worked them 8 (9, 9, 9, 9) (9, 10, 10, 10) times **total** (meaning 16 (18, 18, 18, 18) (18, 20, 20, 20) total rows). You should end after a WS row and have 26 (28, 32, 36, 39) (42, 45, 48, 52) sts. *You should end after row 3 (1, 5, 3, 7) (5, 7, 3, 1) of Chart F (page 62) and the edge stitches.*

You will now be working straight with no decreases. *You should be on row 4 (2, 6, 4, 8) (6, 8, 4, 2) of Chart F and the edge stitches.*

Next row (RS): Work in pattern until last 2 sts, k2.

Next row (WS): P2, work in pattern until end of the row.

Repeat the last 2 rows for 13 (11, 12, 11, 12) (11, 13, 14, 13) more rows. *You should end after row 2 (6, 3, 8, 5) (2, 6, 3, 8) of Chart F and the edge stitches.*

Cut yarn and place these 26 (28, 32, 36, 39) (42, 45, 48, 52) sts on a stitch holder. *You will come back to them later for the Shoulder Seams.*

FRONT RIGHT PANEL

Using US 9 (5.5 mm) straight or 24- to 32-inch (60- to 80-cm) circular needles and the Alternating Cable Cast On (page 208), CO 34 (37, 41, 45, 48) (51, 55, 58, 62) sts.

Sizes XS (-, -, -, XL) (-, -, 4XL, 5XL) only

Rows 1–9: *K1, p1*, rep ** until end of the row.

Sizes - (S, M, L, -) (XXL, 3XL, -, -) only

Row 1 (RS): *P1, k1*, rep ** until last st, p1.

Row 2 (WS): *K1, p1*, rep ** until last st, k1.

Rows 3–9: Repeat rows 1–2. You will end after a RS row.

All sizes continue

Switch to US 10.5 (6.5 mm) straight or 24- to 32-inch (60- to 80-cm) circular needles. Restart your row count here.

Repeat the following 8 rows until you have worked 35 (39, 43, 49, 53) (59, 59, 63, 69) rows **total**. *You should end after row 3 (7, 3, 1, 5) (3, 3, 7, 5) of Chart G (page 62).*

> **Note:** If you are adding length to your cardigan, work the number of rows you added to your Back Panel here in addition to the row count written above. If you are subtracting length from your cardigan, subtract the number of rows you subtracted from the Back Panel from the row count written above. Make note of what row of the chart you end after, as this will change which row you start with when you shape the front right neckline.

Sizes XS (S, M, -, -) (-, -, -, -) only

Row 1 (WS): P1 (3, 4, -, -) (-, -, -, -), k0 (0, 1, -, -) (-, -, -, -), work corresponding row of Chart G (page 62), k0 (0, 1, -, -) (-, -, -, -), p1 (2, 3, -, -) (-, -, -, -).

Row 2 (RS): K1 (2, 3, -, -) (-, -, -, -), p0 (0, 1, -, -) (-, -, -, -), work corresponding row of Chart G, p0 (0, 1, -, -) (-, -, -, -), k1 (3, 4, -, -) (-, -, -, -).

Rows 3–8: Repeat rows 1–2.

Sizes - (-, -, L, XL) (XXL, -, -, -) only

Row 1 (WS): P- (-, -, 3, 3) (5, -, -, -), k- (-, -, 1, 2) (2, -, -, -), p2, k1, work corresponding row of Chart G (page 62), k1, p2, k- (-, -, 1, 2) (2, -, -, -), p- (-, -, 2, 3) (4, -, -, -).

Row 2 (RS): K- (-, -, 2, 3) (4, -, -, -), p- (-, -, 1, 2) (2, -, -, -), 1/1 RC, p1, work corresponding row of Chart G, p1, 1/1 RC, p- (-, -, 1, 2) (2, -, -, -), k- (-, -, 3, 3) (5, -, -, -).

Rows 3–8: Repeat rows 1–2.

Size 3XL only

Row 1 (WS): P4, k2, p4, k2, p2, k1, work corresponding row of Chart G (page 62), k1, p2, k2, p3.

Row 2 (RS): K3, p2, 1/1 RC, p1, work corresponding row of Chart G, p1, 1/1 RC, *p2, k4*, rep ** until end of the row.

Row 3: Repeat row 1.

Row 4: K3, p2, 1/1 RC, p1, work corresponding row of Chart G (page 62), p1, 1/1 RC, p2, C4B, p2, k4.

Rows 5–8: Repeat rows 1–4.

Sizes - (-, -, -, -) (-, -, 4XL, 5XL) only

Row 1 (WS): P- (-, -, -, -) (-, -, 3, 4), k- (-, -, -, -) (-, -, 1, 2), p4, k2, p2, k1, work corresponding row of Chart G (page 62), k1, p2, k2, p4, k- (-, -, -, -) (-, -, 1, 2), p- (-, -, -, -) (-, -, 3, 4).

Row 2 (RS): K- (-, -, -, -) (-, -, 3, 4), p- (-, -, -, -) (-, -, 1, 2), k4, p2, 1/1 RC, p1, work corresponding row of Chart G, p1, 1/1 RC, p2, k4, p- (-, -, -, -) (-, -, 1, 2), k- (-, -, -, -) (-, -, 3, 4).

Row 3: Repeat row 1.

Row 4: K- (-, -, -, -) (-, -, 3, 4), p- (-, -, -, -) (-, -, 1, 2), C4B, p2, 1/1 RC, p1, work corresponding row of Chart G, p1, 1/1 RC, p2, C4B, p- (-, -, -, -) (-, -, 1, 2), k- (-, -, -, -) (-, -, 3, 4).

Rows 5–8: Repeat rows 1–4.

All sizes continue

You will now make decreases to shape the front right neckline whilst continuing to work in pattern (including the 8-row repeat of non-charted edge stitches that have been established in the panel thus far). *You should be on row 4 (8, 4, 2, 6) (4, 4, 8, 6) of Chart G (page 62) and the edge stitches.*

> **Reminder:** If/when you reach a cable stitch and no longer have enough sts to work that cable, simply knit those stitches instead.

Next row (RS): K1, ssk, work in pattern until end of the row.

Next row (WS): Work in pattern until last 2 sts, p2.

Repeat the last 2 rows until you have worked them 8 (9, 9, 9, 9) (9, 10, 10, 10) times total (meaning 16 (18, 18, 18, 18) (18, 20, 20, 20) total rows). You should end after a WS row and have 26 (28, 32, 36, 39) (42, 45, 48, 52) sts. *You should end after row 3 (1, 5, 3, 7) (5, 7, 3, 1) of Chart G and the edges stitches.*

You will now be working straight with no decreases. *You should be on row 4 (2, 6, 4, 8) (6, 8, 4, 2) of Chart G and the edge stitches.*

Next row (RS): K2, work in pattern until end of the row.

Next row (WS): Work in pattern until last 2 sts, p2.

Repeat the last 2 rows for 13 (11, 12, 11, 12) (11, 13, 14, 13) more rows. *You should end after row 2 (6, 3, 8, 5) (2, 6, 3, 8) of Chart G.*

Leave these 26 (28, 32, 36, 39) (42, 45, 48, 52) sts on your needle and do not cut the yarn. *Proceed to "Shoulder Seams."*

SHOULDER SEAMS

You will now be using the Three Needle Bind Off method (page 207) to join the shoulder seams.

1. Place the RS of your front and back panels together so that the outside edges line up.

2. Your front right (as worn) shoulder stitches should still be on your needle. Place the corresponding 26 (28, 32, 36, 39) (42, 45, 48, 52) sts left on hold for the back right shoulder onto the other needle. Make sure both needles are facing the same direction.

3. Insert a third needle (US 10.5 [6.5 mm] or smaller) knitwise into the first st of the panel that is facing you, then insert that same needle knitwise into the corresponding st of the other panel.

4. Continue, following the instructions for the Three Needle Bind Off method (page 207).

5. Repeat all steps for the other shoulder, using the corresponding front left and back left shoulder stitches left on hold.

SIDE SEAMS

1. Flip your work so that the RS are now facing out (your shoulder seams should be invisible).

2. Take a measuring tape and measure from the shoulder seam down. Place an interlocking stitch marker on the outside edge of your work at the 7.9 (7.9, 7.9, 9.4, 9.4) (9.4, 11, 11, 11) inch / 20 (20, 20, 24, 24) (24, 28, 28, 28) cm mark. Repeat this on both sides.

3. Use the Mattress stitch (page 209) to seam the sides, starting at the bottom.

4. Seam until you reach the stitch markers (you may now remove the markers).

SLEEVES

Using US 10.5 (6.5 mm) 24- to 32-inch (60- to 80-cm) circular needles, starting at the underarm point, pick up 48 (48, 48, 56, 56) (56, 60, 60, 60) sts, evenly spaced, around the armhole. PM to mark the BOR.

Repeat the following 8 rounds until you have worked 51 (51, 55, 55, 61) (61, 65, 65, 65) rounds **total**. *You should end after round 3 (3, 7, 7, 5) (5, 1, 1, 1) of the chart.*

> Note: When working in the round, the chart is read from right to left on every row.

> Note: If you would like to add or subtract length to/from your sleeve, do so here, but ensure you end after an odd-numbered round. Make note of how many total rows you work and which row of the chart after so that you can work your second sleeve to match.

Left Sleeve (as worn)

Rounds 1–8: K7 (7, 7, 11, 11) (11, 13, 13, 13), work corresponding round of Chart H (page 63), K7 (7, 7, 11, 11) (11, 13, 13, 13).

Right Sleeve (as worn)

Rounds 1–8: K7 (7, 7, 11, 11) (11, 13, 13, 13), work corresponding round of Chart I (page 63), K7 (7, 7, 11, 11) (11, 13, 13, 13).

Both Sleeves

You will now make decreases before working the sleeve cuffs.

Next round: *K2tog*, rep ** until end of the round.

You should now have 24 (24, 24, 28, 28) (28, 30, 30, 30) sts.

Switch to US 9 (5.5 mm) 24-inch (60-cm) circular needles or DPNs. *If using circular needles, you will need to use the Magic Loop method (page 207).*

Next 9 rounds: *K1, p1*, rep ** until end of the round.

BO all sts in 1x1 ribbing.

BUTTON BAND

Using US 9 (5.5 mm) 32- to 40-inch (80 to 100-cm) circular needles, starting from the bottom of the Front Right (as worn) Panel and working up to the right shoulder seam, pick up sts in the following pattern: *pick up 4 sts, skip 1 st*.

Working across the back neckline, pick up stitches in the following pattern: *pick up 3 sts, skip 1 st*.

Working from the left shoulder seam down the Front Left (as worn) Panel, pick up stitches in the following pattern: *pick up 4 sts, skip 1 st*.

Ensure you have an even number of stitches.

Rows 1–2: *K1, p1*, rep ** until end of the row.

You will now place stitch markers to mark where you will create the buttonholes on the right (as worn) side of the button band. Mark 4 (4, 4, 5, 5) (5, 6, 6, 6) spots where you will start each buttonhole. Your buttonholes should be evenly spaced. The top buttonhole should be close to where the shaping begins on the Front Right Panel, and the bottom hole should be approximately 2 inches (5 cm) from the bottom edge. Each buttonhole will comprise 3 stitches, and there should be approximately 6–7 stitches between each buttonhole.

Follow instructions for the Horizontal One Row Buttonhole (page 215) where it says "work buttonhole."

Row 3: *Work in 1x1 ribbing until marker, RM, work buttonhole*, rep ** until you have worked all buttonholes, work in 1x1 ribbing until end of the row.

Rows 4–6: *K1, p1*, rep ** until end of the row.

BO all sts in 1x1 ribbing.

FINISHING

Attach buttons along the left (as worn) side of the button band in line with buttonholes.

Weave in any remaining loose ends.

Wash and block (see Blocking 101 [page 216] or use your preferred blocking method).

CHART A

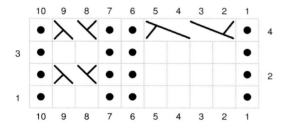

CHART A PATTERN

Row 1 (WS): K1, p2, k2, p4, k1.

Row 2 (RS): P1, k4, p2, 1/1 LC, p1.

Row 3: K1, p2, k2, p4, k1.

Row 4: P1, C4F, p2, 1/1 LC, p1.

Rows 5–16: Repeat rows 1–4.

Legend		
☐		RS: Knit WS: Purl
●		RS: Purl WS: Knit
		C4B
		C4F
		1/1 LC
		1/1 RC
		C8B
		C8F
		C10B
		C10F

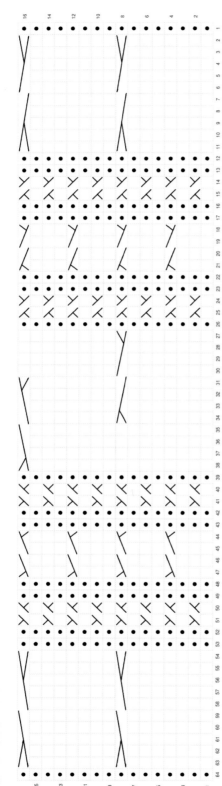

CHART B PATTERN

Row 1 (WS): K1, p10, k2, p2, k2, p4, k2, p2, k1, p12, k1, p2, k2, p4, k2, p2, k2, p10, k1.

Row 2 (RS): P1, k10, p2, 1/1 LC, p2, k4, p2, 1/1 LC, p1, k12, p1, 1/1 RC, p2, k4, p2, 1/1 RC, p2, k10, p1.

Row 3: K1, p10, k2, p2, k2, p4, k2, p2, k1, p12, k1, p2, k2, p4, k2, p2, k2, p10, k1.

Row 4: P1, k10, p2, 1/1 LC, p2, C4F, p2, 1/1 LC, p1, k12, p1, 1/1 RC, p2, C4B, p2, 1/1 RC, p2, k10, p1.

Rows 5–7: Repeat rows 1–3.

Row 8: P1, C10F, p2, 1/1 LC, p2, C4F, p2, 1/1 LC, p1, C8F, k4, p1, 1/1 RC, p2, C4B, p2, 1/1 RC, p2, C10B, p1.

Rows 9–15: Repeat rows 1–7.

Row 16: P1, C10F, p2, 1/1 LC, p2, C4F, p2, 1/1 LC, p1, k4, C8B, p1, 1/1 RC, p2, C4B, p2, 1/1 RC, p2, C10B, p1.

CHART C

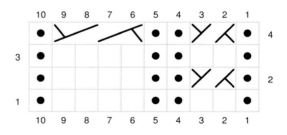

CHART C PATTERN

Row 1 (WS): K1, p4, k2, p2, k1.

Row 2 (RS): P1, 1/1 RC, p2, k4, p1.

Row 3: K1, p4, k2, p2, k1.

Row 4: P1, 1/1 RC, p2, C4B, p1.

Rows 5–16: Repeat rows 1–4.

CHART D

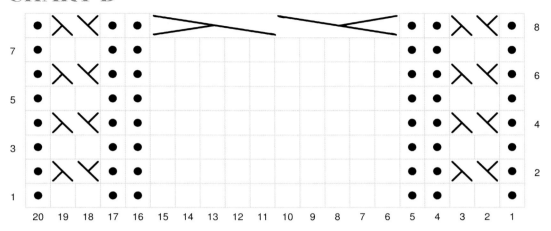

CHART E

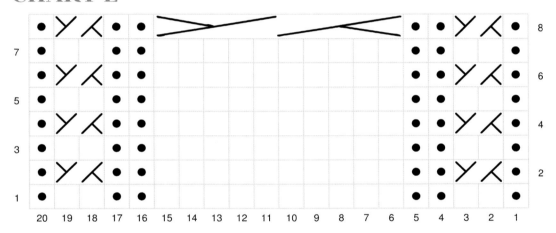

CHART D PATTERN

Row 1 (WS): K1, p2, k2, p10, k2, p2, k1.

Row 2 (RS): P1, 1/1 LC, p2, k10, p2, 1/1 LC, p1.

Rows 3–6: Repeat rows 1–2.

Row 7: K1, p2, k2, p10, k2, p2, k1.

Row 8: P1, 1/1 LC, p2, C10F, p2, 1/1 LC, p1.

Rows 9–16: Repeat rows 1–8.

CHART E PATTERN

Row 1 (WS): K1, p2, k2, p10, k2, p2, k1.

Row 2 (RS): P1, 1/1 RC, p2, k10, p2, 1/1 RC, p1.

Rows 3–6: Repeat rows 1–2.

Row 7: K1, p2, k2, p10, k2, p2, k1.

Row 8: P1, 1/1 RC, p2, C10B, p2, 1/1 RC, p1.

Rows 9–16: Repeat rows 1–8.

CHART F

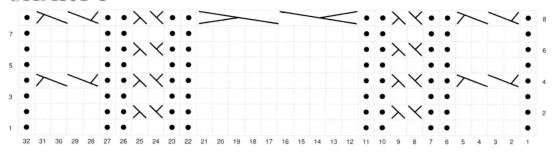

CHART G

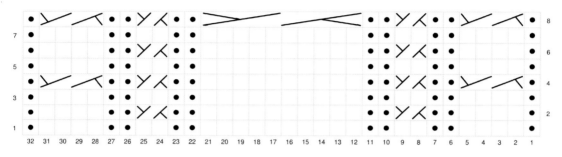

CHART F PATTERN

Row 1 (WS): K1, p4, k2, p2, k2, p10, k2, p2, k2, p4, k1.

Row 2 (RS): P1, k4, p2, 1/1 LC, p2, k10, p2, 1/1 LC, p2, k4, p1.

Row 3: K1, p4, k2, p2, k2, p10, k2, p2, k2, p4, k1.

Row 4: P1, C4F, p2, 1/1 LC, p2, k10, p2, 1/1 LC, p2, C4F, p1.

Rows 5–7: Repeat rows 1–3.

Row 8: P1, C4F, p2, 1/1 LC, p2, C10F, p2, 1/1 LC, p2, C4F, p1.

CHART G PATTERN

Row 1 (WS): K1, p4, k2, p2, k2, p10, k2, p2, k2, p4, k1.

Row 2 (RS): P1, k4, p2, 1/1 RC, p2, k10, p2, 1/1 RC, p2, k4, p1.

Row 3: K1, p4, k2, p2, k2, p10, k2, p2, k2, p4, k1.

Row 4: P1, C4B, p2, 1/1 RC, p2, k10, p2, 1/1 RC, p2, C4B, p1.

Rows 5–7: Repeat rows 1–3.

Row 8: P1, C4B, p2, 1/1 RC, p2, C10B, p2, 1/1 RC, p2, C4B, p1.

CHART H

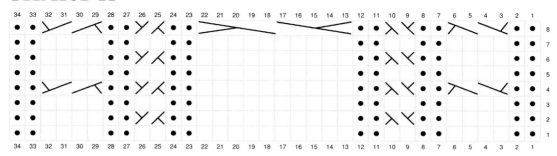

CHART I

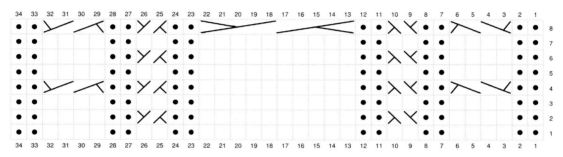

CHART H PATTERN

Round 1: P2, k4, p2, k2, p2, k10, p2, k2, p2, k4, p2.

Round 2: P2, k4, p2, 1/1 LC, p2, k10, p2, 1/1 RC, p2, k4, p2.

Round 3: P2, k4, p2, k2, p2, k10, p2, k2, p2, k4, p2.

Round 4: P2, C4F, p2, 1/1 LC, p2, k10, p2, 1/1 RC, p2, C4B, p2.

Rounds 5–7: Repeat rounds 1–3.

Round 8: P2, C4F, p2, 1/1 LC, p2, C10F, p2, 1/1 RC, p2, C4B, p2.

CHART I PATTERN

Round 1: P2, k4, p2, k2, p2, k10, p2, k2, p2, k4, p2.

Round 2: P2, k4, p2, 1/1 LC, p2, k10, p2, 1/1 RC, p2, k4, p2.

Round 3: P2, k4, p2, k2, p2, k10, p2, k2, p2, k4, p2.

Round 4: P2, C4F, p2, 1/1 LC, p2, k10, p2, 1/1 RC, p2, C4B, p2.

Rounds 5–7: Repeat rounds 1–3.

Round 8: P2, C4F, p2, 1/1 LC, p2, C10B, p2, 1/1 RC, p2, C4B, p2.

Totally Textured

You simply cannot go wrong with a good textured knit. I'm always on the hunt for new, interesting stitch patterns to incorporate into my designs, as I find textured projects to be super engaging and, I mean, the finished results speak for themselves. The patterns in this chapter are all designed to have basic construction to allow the fun and intricate stitch patterns to take center stage. The beauty of quick textured knitting projects is that the process isn't too tedious and it's not long before you're able to see the gorgeous patterns begin to take shape.

Producing an intricate-looking texture does not always require advanced stitches or techniques. The Miss Ziggy Vest (page 67) and Stairway to Heaven Vest (page 85) patterns are great for confident beginners, as the eye-catching textures are created using only knit and purl stitches. If you're interested in broadening your horizons and perhaps learning some new stitches or techniques, look no further than the Attention Deficit Jumper (page 101). This dynamic conglomerate of stitch patterns will keep you entertained from start to finish and is bound to help expand your knitting repertoire.

Miss Ziggy Vest

The Miss Ziggy Vest is a trans-seasonal adaptation of my Miss Ziggy Jumper pattern that is even quicker to knit up and will keep you cozy and stylish all year round. The standout feature of this pattern is the Chevron Seed stitch, which creates a playful zigzag effect using simple knits and purls. The resulting texture is not only visually appealing but also adds an extra dimension to the finished garment. The pattern incorporates a contrasting color for the ribbing, neck and sleeve trims, providing an additional element of interest to this eye-catching piece. Crafted with super bulky yarn and designed with a trendy, cropped fit, this vest works up in no time, making it an ideal choice for a fun weekend project that is sure to garner plenty of compliments when you wear it to work on Monday.

Construction Notes

This seamless vest is worked mostly in the round in a Chevron Seed stitch from the bottom up. You will first work the bottom section of the vest in the round, before splitting at the underarm point to work the back panel flat, followed by the front panel. You will join the shoulder seams to create the neck hole and armholes using the Three Needle Bind Off method (page 207). The neck and sleeve trims are worked in the round by picking up stitches along the neck hole/armhole edges.

Skill Level

Confident Beginner

Sizing

XS (S, M, L, XL) (XXL, 3XL, 4XL, 5XL)

Finished bust: 31.4 (36.2, 40.2, 44.8, 49.6) (54.4, 58.2, 63, 67.8)" / 80 (92, 102, 114, 126) (138, 148, 160, 172) cm

Recommended ease: This vest is designed with approximately 1.6–5.5 inches / 4–14 cm of positive ease

Sample shown is knit in Size S.

MATERIALS

Yarn

Super bulky weight, Cardigang, Chunky Merino Wool (100% merino wool), 87 yds (80 m) per 200-g skein, shown in Bubblegum (MC) and Purple Punch (CC) colorways

Any super bulky weight yarn can be used for this pattern as long as it matches gauge. A good substitute would be Wool and the Gang, Crazy Sexy Wool or Malabrigo, Rasta.

Yardage/Meterage

Yarn estimates are approximate and refer specifically to the recommended yarn.

2 (2, 2, 3, 3) (4, 4, 5, 6) skein(s) of MC

1 (1, 1, 1, 1) (1, 2, 2, 2) skein(s) of CC

Needles

For body: US 19 (15 mm) 32-inch (80-cm) circular needle

For bottom ribbing, neck and sleeve trims: US 17 (12 mm) 32-inch (80-cm) circular needle

Notions

Stitch markers

Tapestry needle

Scissors

Stitch holders

GAUGE

7 sts x 10 rows = 4 inches (10 cm) in Chevron Seed stitch (explained below) using larger needle

To Knit Gauge Swatch

1. CO 16 sts.
2. Work 2 horizontal repeats of the chart (page 74) for at least 10 rows.

Note: When worked flat, odd (RS) rows of the chart are read from right to left, and even (WS) rows are read from left to right. On WS rows, the knit symbols on the chart are worked as purl sts and vice versa.

ABBREVIATIONS

1x1 rib(bing) - *Knit 1, purl 1*

CC - Contrast color

CO - Cast on

BO - Bind off

BOR - Beginning of round

K - Knit

K2tog - Knit 2 stitches together

MC - Main color

P - Purl

P2tog - Purl 2 stitches together

PM - Place marker

Rep - Repeat

RS - Right side

Ssk - Slip, slip, knit 2 stitches together through the back loops

Ssp - Slip, slip, purl 2 stitches together through the back loops

St(s) - Stitch(es)

WS - Wrong side

SIZING CHART

Size	XS	S	M	L	XL	XXL	3XL	4XL	5XL
To fit bust	28–30"/ 71–76 cm	32–34"/ 81–86 cm	36–38"/ 91.5–96.5 cm	40–42"/ 101.5–106.5 cm	44–46"/ 111.5–117 cm	48–50"/ 122–127 cm	52–54"/ 132–137 cm	56–58"/ 142–147 cm	60–62"/ 152–158 cm
(A) Width	15.7"/ 40 cm	18.1"/ 46 cm	20.1"/ 51 cm	22.4"/ 57 cm	24.8"/ 63 cm	27.2"/ 69 cm	29.1"/ 74 cm	31.5"/ 80 cm	33.9"/ 86 cm
(B) Length	16.1"/ 41 cm	16.1"/ 41 cm	16.9"/ 43 cm	18.1"/ 46 cm	18.9"/ 48 cm	19.7"/ 50 cm	21.3"/ 54 cm	22.4"/ 57 cm	23.6"/ 60 cm
(C) Armhole Depth	8.7"/ 22 cm	8.7"/ 22 cm	8.7"/ 22 cm	9.4"/ 24 cm	9.4"/ 24 cm	9.4"/ 24 cm	10.2"/ 26 cm	10.2"/ 26 cm	10.2"/ 26 cm

SPECIAL TECHNIQUES

Magic Loop method (page 207)

Three Needle Bind Off (page 207)

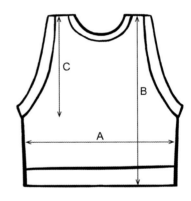

MISS ZIGGY VEST PATTERN

BOTTOM

Using US 17 (12 mm) 32-inch (80-cm) circular needles and the Long Tail Cast On, CO 56 (64, 72, 80, 88) (96, 104, 112, 120) sts in CC. Join in the round and PM to mark the BOR.

Rounds 1–5: *K1, p1*, rep ** until end of the round.

Switch to US 19 (15 mm) 32-inch (80-cm) circular needles and MC.

Setup round: K across.

Restart your row count here. Repeat the chart (page 74) (written instructions on page 70) until you have worked 14 (14, 16, 16, 18) (20, 22, 26, 28) rounds **total**. *You should end after round 2 (2, 4, 4, 2) (4, 2, 2, 4) of the chart.*

Note: When worked in the round, the chart is read from right to left on every row.

Note: If you would like to add or subtract length to/from your vest, do so here, but ensure you still end after round 2 (2, 4, 4, 2) (4, 2, 2, 4) of the chart, or knit to your desired length, making note of what row of the chart you end after, as this will change which row you start with for the Front and Back Panels.

Round 1: P1, k3, p1, k3.

Round 2: K1, p1, k5, p1.

Round 3: K2, p1, k3, p1, k1.

Round 4: K3, p1, k1, p1, k2.

BACK PANEL

You will now be working flat across **only the first 28 (32, 36, 40, 44) (48, 52, 56, 60) sts.** Leave the remaining stitches on the cord or place them on a stitch holder. *You will come back to them later for the Front Panel.*

You will now begin making decreases for the armholes. Restart your row count here, while continuing to follow the 4-row vertical repeat of the chart (page 74) where it says "work in pattern." *You should be on row 3 (3, 1, 1, 3) (1, 3, 3, 1) of the chart.*

Note: When worked flat, odd (RS) rows of the chart are read from right to left, and even (WS) rows are read from left to right. On WS rows, the knit symbols on the chart are worked as purl stitches and vice versa.

A note on working in pattern: As you decrease during this section, you will no longer always have complete 8-stitch repeats of the pattern at the outer edges of the panel. This means you will not always begin with stitch 1 (RS) or stitch 8 (WS) of the chart after the edge stitches when it says "work in pattern"; instead, start with the stitch that vertically matches the stitch column below it. If it is helpful, place stitch markers between each repeat before you begin to decrease so that you can see where you are within the 8-stitch motif at any time.

Row 1 (RS): K1, ssk, work in pattern until last 3 sts, k2tog, k1.

Row 2 (WS): P2, work in pattern until last 2 sts, p2.

Repeat rows 1–2 until you have worked them 6 (6, 7, 7, 8) (8, 9, 9, 10) times **total** (meaning 12 (12, 14, 14, 16) (16, 18, 18, 20) total rows). You should end after a WS row and have 16 (20, 22, 26, 28) (32, 34, 38, 40) sts. *You should end after row 2 (2, 2, 2, 2) (4, 4, 4, 4) of the chart.*

Work 6 (6, 4, 7, 5) (5, 5, 4, 3) rows in pattern (straight, no decreases). The first 2 stitches and last 2 stitches of each row should now be worked as their corresponding chart stitches, rather than the 2-stitch stockinette edges that were worked during the decreases. *You should end after row 4 (4, 2, 1, 3) (1, 1, 4, 3) of the chart.*

BACK SHOULDERS

You will now make decreases to shape the back neckline. *You should be on row 1 (1, 3, 2, 4) (2, 2, 1, 4) of the chart (page 74).*

Sizes XS (S, M, -, -) (-, -, 4XL, -) only

Setup row (RS): Work in pattern across 4 (5, 6, -, -) (-, -, 12, -) sts, BO 8 (10, 10, -, -) (-, -, 14, -) sts, work in pattern across the remaining 4 (5, 6, -, -) (-, -, 12, -) sts.

Next row (WS): Work in pattern until last 3 sts, ssp, p1.

Next row: K2, work in pattern until end of the row.

Cut yarn and place these 3 (4, 5, -, -) (-, -, 11, -) left shoulder sts on a stitch holder. *You will come back to them later for the Shoulder Seams.*

Reattach yarn on the WS to the remaining 4 (5, 6, -, -) (-, -, 12, -) right shoulder sts. *You should be on row 2 (2, 4, -, -) (-, -, 2, -) of the chart.*

Next row (WS): P1, p2tog, work in pattern until end of the row.

Next row (RS): Work in pattern until last 2 sts, k2.

Cut yarn and place these 3 (4, 5, -, -) (-, -, 11, -) right shoulder sts on a stitch holder. *You will come back to them later for the Shoulder Seams.*

Sizes - (-, -, L, XL) (XXL, 3XL, -, 5XL) only

Setup row (WS): Work in pattern across - (-, -, 8, 8) (10, 10, -, 13) sts, BO - (-, -, 10, 12) (12, 14, -, 14) sts, work in pattern across the remaining - (-, -, 8, 8) (10, 10, -, 13) sts.

Next row (RS): Work in pattern until last 3 sts, k2tog, k1.

Next row: P2, work in pattern until end of the row.

Cut yarn and place these - (-, -, 7, 7) (9, 9, -, 12) right shoulder sts on a stitch holder. *You will come back to them later for the Shoulder Seams.*

Reattach yarn on the RS to the remaining - (-, -, 8, 8) (10, 10, -, 13) left shoulder sts. *You should be on row - (-, -, 3, 1) (3, 3, -, 1) of the chart.*

Next row (RS): K1, ssk, work in pattern until end of the row.

Next row (WS): Work in pattern until last 2 sts, p2.

Cut yarn and place these - (-, -, 7, 7) (9, 9, -, 12) left shoulder sts on a stitch holder. *You will come back to them later for the Shoulder Seams.*

FRONT PANEL

You will now be working flat across the 28 (32, 36, 40, 44) (48, 52, 56, 60) sts you left on hold after the Bottom section. Reattach yarn on the RS.

Follow the Back Panel instructions for the armhole decrease rows, stopping before the straight rows.

You should end after a WS row and have 16 (20, 22, 26, 28) (32, 34, 38, 40) sts. *You should end after row 2 (2, 2, 2, 2) (4, 4, 4, 4) of the chart (page 74).*

Work 3 (3, 1, 4, 2) (2, 2, 1, 0) rows in pattern (straight, no decreases). The first 2 stitches and last 2 stitches of each row should now be worked as their corresponding chart stitches, rather than the 2-stitch stockinette edges that were worked during the decreases. *You should end after row 1 (1, 3, 2, 4) (2, 2, 1, 4) of the chart.*

FRONT SHOULDERS

You will now make decreases to shape the front neckline. *You should be on row 2 (2, 4, 3, 1) (3, 3, 2, 1) of the chart (page 74).*

Sizes XS (S, M, -, -) (-, -, 4XL, -) only

Setup row (WS): Work in pattern across 5 (6, 7, -, -) (-, -, 13, -) sts, BO 6 (8, 8, -, -) (-, -, 12, -) sts, work in pattern across the remaining 5 (6, 7, -, -) (-, -, 13, -) sts.

Row 1 (RS): Work in pattern until last 3 sts, k2tog, k1.

Row 2: P2, work in pattern until end of the row.

Rows 3–4: Repeat rows 1–2.

Row 5: Work in pattern until last 2 sts, k2.

Cut yarn and place these 3 (4, 5, -, -) (-, -, 11, -) left (as worn) shoulder sts on a stitch holder. *You will come back to them later for the Shoulder Seams.*

Reattach yarn on the RS to the remaining 5 (6, 7, -, -) (-, -, 13, -) right shoulder sts. *You should be on row 3 (3, 1, -, -) (-, -, 3, -) of the chart.*

Row 1 (RS): K1, ssk, work in pattern until end of the row.

Row 2 (WS): Work in pattern until last 2 sts, p2.

Rows 3–4: Repeat rows 1–2.

Row 5: K2, work in pattern until end of the row.

Leave these 3 (4, 5, -, -) (-, -, 11, -) sts on your needle and do not cut the yarn. *Proceed to "Shoulder Seams."*

Sizes - (-, -, L, XL) (XXL, 3XL, -, 5XL) only

Setup row (RS): Work in pattern across - (-, -, 9, 9) (11, 11, -, 14) sts, BO - (-, -, 8, 10) (10, 12, -, 12) sts, work in pattern across the remaining - (-, -, 9, 9) (11, 11, -, 14) sts.

Row 1 (WS): Work in pattern until the end of the row.

Row 2: K1, ssk, work in pattern until end of the row.

Row 3: Work in pattern until last 2 sts, p2.

Rows 4–5: Repeat rows 2–3.

Cut yarn and place these - (-, -, 7, 7) (9, 9, -, 12) right (as worn) shoulder sts on a stitch holder. *You will come back to them later for the Shoulder Seams.*

Reattach yarn on the WS to the remaining - (-, -, 9, 9) (11, 11, -, 14) left shoulder sts. *You should be on row - (-, -, 4, 2) (4, 4, -, 2) of the chart.*

Row 1 (WS): Work in pattern until end of the row.

Row 2 (RS): Work in pattern until last 3 sts, k2tog, k1.

Row 3: P2, work in pattern until end of the row.

Rows 4–5: Repeat rows 2–3.

Leave these - (-, -, 7, 7) (9, 9, -, 12) sts on your needle and do not cut the yarn. *Proceed to "Shoulder Seams."*

SHOULDER SEAMS

You will now be using the Three Needle Bind Off method (page 207) to join the shoulder seams.

1. Turn your work inside out and place the RS of your front and back panels together.

2. Your front right (right, right, left, left) (left, left, right, left) (as worn) shoulder stitches should still be on your needle. Place the corresponding 3 (4, 5, 7, 7) (9, 9, 11, 12) sts left on hold for the back right (right, right, left, left) (left, left, right, left) shoulder onto the other needle. Make sure both needles are facing the same direction.

3. Insert a third needle (US 19 [15 mm] or smaller) knitwise into the first st of the panel that is facing you, then insert that same needle knitwise into the corresponding st of the other panel.

4. Continue, following the instructions for the Three Needle Bind Off method (page 207).

5. Repeat all steps for the other shoulder, using the corresponding front and back shoulder stitches left on hold.

NECK TRIM

Flip your work so that the RS are now facing out (your shoulder seams should be invisible).

Using US 17 (12 mm) 32-inch (80-cm) circular needles and CC, pick up stitches in the following fashion:

1. Pick up 3 sts along the side of the back right shoulder.
2. Pick up 8 (10, 10, 10, 12) (12, 14, 14, 14) sts along the back neck.
3. Pick up 3 sts along the side of the back left shoulder.
4. Pick up 6 sts along the side of the front left (as worn) shoulder.
5. Pick up 6 (8, 8, 8, 10) (10, 12, 12, 12) sts along the front neck.
6. Pick up 6 sts along the side of the front right (as worn) shoulder.

You should now have 32 (36, 36, 36, 40) (40, 44, 44, 44) sts. PM to mark the BOR.

Rounds 1–2: *K1, p1*, rep ** until end of the round. *You will need to use the Magic Loop method (page 207).*

BO loosely in 1x1 rib pattern.

SLEEVE TRIMS

Using US 17 (12 mm) 32-inch (80-cm) circular needles and CC, starting at the underarm point, pick up stitches in the following fashion: *Pick up 4 sts, skip 1 st.* Make sure you have an even number of stitches. PM to mark the BOR.

Round 1: *K1, p1*, rep ** until end of the round. *You will need to use the Magic Loop method (page 207).*

BO all sts loosely in 1x1 rib pattern.

FINISHING

Weave in all your loose ends.

Blocking super bulky yarn is not necessary. However, if you do wish to block your vest, it is suggested that you use the spray blocking method (do *not* wet or steam block).

CHART

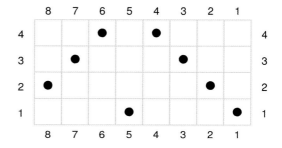

	Legend	
☐		RS: Knit WS: Purl
■		RS: Purl WS: Knit

CHART PATTERN WORKED FLAT

Row 1 (RS): P1, k3, p1, k3.

Row 2 (WS): K1, p5, k1, p1.

Row 3: K2, p1, k3, p1, k1.

Row 4: P2, k1, p1, k1, p3.

Bright Like a Diamond Cardigan

This was the very first piece I designed and worked on for this book, and it remains one of my absolute favorites. With its classic design and eye-catching texture, the Bright Like a Diamond Cardigan is bound to become a favorite of yours too. The standout feature of this cardigan is its unique Trellis stitch pattern. This seemingly intricate but surprisingly simple pattern creates a striking diamond-shaped texture that adds depth and visual interest to the finished piece. The cropped length of this cardigan makes it a great trans-seasonal piece that is perfect for layering, making it an ideal choice for both casual and dressy outfits.

Construction Notes

This seamless cardigan is worked in Trellis stitch from the bottom up. You will first work the bottom section of the cardigan flat, before splitting at the underarm point to work the front right panel, then the back panel, followed by the front left panel. You will join the shoulder seams to create the armholes using the Three Needle Bind Off method (page 207). The sleeves are worked in the round by picking up stitches along the armhole edges. You will finish by working the button band flat by picking up stitches along the inside edges. Instructions on how to adjust the body and sleeve length of your cardigan are included.

Skill Level

Advanced Beginner

Sizing

XS (S, M, L, XL) (XXL, 3XL, 4XL, 5XL)

Finished bust: 43.8 (46, 50.6, 52.6, 57.4) (59.4, 64.2, 66.2, 70.8)" / 111 (117, 129, 134, 146) (151, 163, 168, 180) cm

Recommended ease: This cardigan is designed with 12.2–14.2 inches / 31–36 cm of positive ease

Sample shown is knit in Size S.

MATERIALS

Yarn

Super bulky weight, Wool and the Gang, Crazy Sexy Wool (100% Wool), 87 yds (80 m) per 200-g skein, shown in Glow Up Cream colorway

Any super bulky weight yarn can be used for this pattern as long as it matches gauge. A good substitute would be Malabrigo, Rasta or Cardigang, Chunky Merino.

Yardage/Meterage

357 (372, 476, 538, 599) (639, 744, 783, 826) yds / 327 (340, 435, 492, 548) (584, 680, 716, 755) m

Needles

For body and sleeves: US 19 (15 mm) 32-inch (80-cm) circular needle

For ribbing: US 17 (12 mm) 32-inch (80-cm) circular needle

Notions

Stitch marker

Tapestry needle

Scissors

Stitch holders

Row counter (optional but highly recommended)

GAUGE

7 sts x 10 rows = 4 inches (10 cm) in stockinette stitch using larger needle

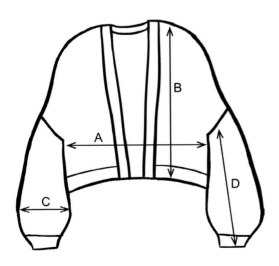

ABBREVIATIONS

1x1 rib(bing) - *Knit 1, purl 1*

BO - Bind off

BOR - Beginning of round

CO - Cast on

K - Knit

K2tog - Knit 2 stitches together

P - Purl

PM - Place marker

Sl wyif - Slip stitch purlwise with yarn held in front

St(s) - Stitch(es)

Rep - Repeat

RS - Right side

Uls - Under loose strand

WS - Wrong side

SPECIAL TECHNIQUES

Three Needle Bind Off (page 207)

Magic Loop method (page 207)

Knit Under Loose Strand

1. Insert right needle under the loose strand from front to back.

2. Knit the stitch normally, bringing the new stitch out from under the loose strand.

SIZING CHART

Size	XS	S	M	L	XL	XXL	3XL	4XL	5XL
To fit bust	28–30"/ 71–76 cm	32–34"/ 81–86 cm	36–38"/ 91.5–96.5 cm	40–42"/ 101.5–106.5 cm	44–46"/ 111.5–117 cm	48–50"/ 122–127 cm	52–54"/ 132–137 cm	56–58"/ 142–147 cm	60–62"/ 152–158 cm
(A) Width	21.9"/ 55.5 cm	23"/ 58.5 cm	25.3"/ 64.5 cm	26.3"/ 67 cm	28.7"/ 73 cm	29.7"/ 75.5 cm	32.1"/ 81.5 cm	33.1"/ 84 cm	35.4"/ 90 cm
(B) Length	15.4"/ 39 cm	15.4"/ 39 cm	18.1"/ 46 cm	18.1"/ 46 cm	20.9"/ 53 cm	20.9"/ 53 cm	23.6"/ 60 cm	23.6"/ 60 cm	26.4"/ 67 cm
(C) Sleeve Width	7.5"/ 19 cm	7.5"/ 19 cm	7.5"/ 19 cm	7.5"/ 19 cm	10"/ 25 cm	10"/ 25 cm	10"/ 25 cm	12"/ 31 cm	12"/ 31 cm
(D) Sleeve length	14.2"/ 36 cm	14.2"/ 36 cm	17.3"/ 44 cm	17.3"/ 44 cm	17.3"/ 44 cm	20.1"/ 51 cm	20.1"/ 51 cm	20.1"/ 51 cm	20.1"/ 51 cm

▬ BRIGHT LIKE A DIAMOND CARDIGAN PATTERN ▬

BOTTOM

Using US 17 (12 mm) 32-inch (80-cm) circular needles and the Long Tail Cast On, CO 69 (75, 81, 87, 93) (99, 105, 111, 117) sts.

Row 1 (WS): *K1, p1*, rep ** until last st, k1.

Row 2 (RS): *P1, k1*, rep ** until last st, p1.

Rows 3–6: Repeat rows 1–2.

Switch to US 19 (15 mm) 32-inch (80-cm) circular needles. Restart your row count here. You will repeat the following 8 rows until you have worked 21 (21, 29, 29, 27) (27, 35, 27, 35) rows total. *You should end after row 5 (5, 5, 5, 3) (3, 3, 3, 3).*

Note: I recommend you use a row counter to keep track of how many rows you have worked, as the slipped stitches make retrospectively counting rows difficult, so using a row counter will ensure you do not accidentally knit too many rows.

Note: If you would like to add or subtract length to/from your cardigan, do so here, but make sure you still end after row 5 (5, 5, 5, 3) (3, 3, 3, 3), or knit to your desired length, making note of what row of the pattern repeat you end after, as this will change which row you start with for the front and back panels.

Rows 1, 3, 5 & 7 (WS): P across.

Row 2 (RS): K2, *sl5 wyif, k1*, rep ** until last st, k1.

Row 4: K4, *k1 uls, k5*, rep ** until last 5 sts, k1 uls, k4.

Row 6: K1, sl3 wyif, k1, *sl5 wyif, k1*, rep ** until last 4 sts, sl3 wyif, k1.

Row 8: K1, *k1 uls, k5*, rep ** until last 2 sts, k1 uls, k1.

FRONT RIGHT PANEL

You will now be working across **only the first 15 (17, 18, 20, 21) (23, 24, 26, 27) sts.** Leave the remaining stitches on the cord or place them on a stitch holder. *You will come back to them later for the Back and Front Left Panels.*

Beginning at row 6 (6, 6, 6, 4) (4, 4, 4, 4), repeat the following 8 rows until you have worked 20 (20, 20, 20, 30) (30, 30, 38, 38) rows from the underarm separation. *All sizes should end after row 1.*

Rows 1, 3, 5 & 7 (WS): P across.

Row 2 (RS): K2, *sl5 wyif, k1*, rep ** until last st, k1.

Row 4: K4, *k1 uls, k5*, rep ** until last 5 sts, k1 uls, k4.

Row 6: K1, sl3 wyif, k1, *sl5 wyif, k1*, rep ** until last 4 sts, sl3 wyif, k1.

Row 8: K1, *k1 uls, k5*, rep ** until last 2 sts, k1 uls, k1.

Rows 1, 3, 5 & 7 (WS): P across.

Row 2 (RS): K2, *sl5 wyif, k1*, rep ** until last 3 sts, sl2 wyif, k1.

Row 4: K4, *k1 uls, k5*, rep ** until last st, k1 uls.

Row 6: K1, sl3 wyif, k1, *sl5 wyif, k1*, rep ** until end of the row.

Row 8: K1, *k1 uls, k5*, rep ** until last 4 sts, k1 uls, k3.

Rows 1, 3, 5 & 7 (WS): P across.

Row 2 (RS): K2, *sl5 wyif, k1*, rep ** until last 4 sts, sl3 wyif, k1.

Row 4: K4, *k1 uls, k5*, rep ** until last 2 sts, k1 uls, k1.

Row 6: K1, sl3 wyif, k1, *sl5 wyif, k1*, rep ** until last st, k1.

Row 8: K1, *k1 uls, k5*, rep ** until last 5 sts, k1 uls, k4.

Rows 1, 3, 5 & 7 (WS): P across.

Row 2 (RS): K2, *sl5 wyif, k1*, rep ** until end of the row.

Row 4: K4, *k1 uls, k5*, rep ** until last 4 sts, k1 uls, k3.

Row 6: K1, sl3 wyif, k1, *sl5 wyif, k1*, rep ** until last 3 sts, sl2 wyif, k1.

Row 8: K1, *k1 uls, k5*, rep ** until last st, k1 uls.

All sizes continue

Cut yarn and place these 15 (17, 18, 20, 21) (23, 24, 26, 27) sts on a stitch holder. *You will come back to them later for the Shoulder Seams.*

BACK PANEL

You will now be working across **only the next** 39 (41, 45, 47, 51) (53, 57, 59, 63) sts. Leave the remaining stitches on the cord or place them on a stitch holder. *You will come back to them later for the Front Left Panel.* Reattach yarn on the RS.

Beginning at row 6 (6, 6, 6, 4) (4, 4, 4, 4), repeat the following 8 rows until you have worked 19 (19, 19, 19, 29) (29, 29, 37, 37) rows from the underarm separation. *All sizes should end after row 8.*

Sizes XS (-, -, -, XL) (-, -, -, 5XL) only

Rows 1, 3, 5 & 7 (WS): P across.

Row 2 (RS): K1, sl3 wyif, k1, *sl5 wyif, k1*, rep ** until last 4 sts, sl3 wyif, k1.

Row 4: K1, *k1 uls, k5*, rep ** until last 2 sts, k1 uls, k1.

Row 6: K2, *sl5 wyif, k1*, rep ** until last st, k1.

Row 8: K4, *k1 uls, k5*, rep ** until last 5 sts, k1 uls, k4.

Sizes - (S, -, -, -) (XXL, -, -, -) only

Rows 1, 3, 5 & 7 (WS): P across.

Row 2 (RS): Sl2 wyif, k1, *sl5 wyif, k1*, rep ** until last 2 sts, sl2 wyif.

Row 4: K1 uls, k4, *k1 uls, k5*, rep ** until last 6 sts, k1 uls, k4, k1 uls.

Row 6: K1, sl4 wyif, k1, *sl5 wyif, k1*, rep ** until last 5 sts, sl4 wyif, k1.

Row 8: K2, *k1 uls, k5*, rep ** until last 3 sts, k1 uls, k2.

Sizes - (-, M, -, -) (-, 3XL, -, -) only

Rows 1, 3, 5 & 7 (WS): P across.

Row 2 (RS): K2, *sl5 wyif, k1*, rep ** until last st, k1.

Row 4: K4, *k1 uls, k5*, rep ** until last 5 sts, k1 uls, k4.

Row 6: K1, sl3 wyif, k1, *sl5 wyif, k1*, rep ** until last 4 sts, sl3 wyif, k1.

Row 8: K1, *k1 uls, k5*, rep ** until last 2 sts, k1 uls, k1.

Sizes - (-, -, L, -) (-, -, 4XL, -) only

Rows 1, 3, 5 & 7 (WS): P across.

Row 2 (RS): K1, sl4 wyif, k1, *sl5 wyif, k1*, rep ** until last 5 sts, sl4 wyif, k1.

Row 4: K2, *k1 uls, k5*, rep ** until last 3 sts, k1 uls, k2.

Row 6: Sl2 wyif, k1, *sl5 wyif, k1*, rep ** until last 2 sts, sl2 wyif.

Row 8: K1 uls, k4, *k1 uls, k5*, rep ** until last 6 sts, k1 uls, k4, k1 uls.

All sizes continue

You should now be on a WS row.

Next row: P15 (17, 18, 20, 21) (23, 24, 26, 27), BO9 (7, 9, 7, 9) (7, 9, 7, 9), p to the end of the row.

You have now split your two shoulder sections.

Cut yarn and place both sections of the remaining 30 (34, 36, 40, 42) (46, 48, 52, 54) shoulder sts on stitch holders. *You will come back to them later for the Shoulder Seams.*

FRONT LEFT PANEL

Reattach yarn on the RS to the remaining 15 (17, 18, 20, 21) (23, 24, 26, 27) sts.

Beginning at row 6 (6, 6, 6, 4) (4, 4, 4, 4), repeat the following 8 rows until you have worked 20 (20, 20, 20, 30) (30, 30, 38, 38) rows from the underarm separation. *All sizes should end after row 1.*

Sizes XS (-, -, -, XL) (-, -, -, 5XL) only

Rows 1, 3, 5 & 7 (WS): P across.

Row 2 (RS): K2, *sl5 wyif, k1*, rep ** until last st, k1.

Row 4: K4, *k1 uls, k5*, rep ** until last 5 sts, k1 uls, k4.

Row 6: K1, sl3 wyif, k1, *sl5 wyif, k1*, rep ** until last 4 sts, sl3 wyif, k1.

Row 8: K1, *k1 uls, k5*, rep ** until last 2 sts, k1 uls, k1.

Sizes - (S, -, -, -) (XXL, -, -, -) only

Rows 1, 3, 5 & 7 (WS): P across.

Row 2 (RS): K1, sl2 wyif, k1, *sl5 wyif, k1*, rep ** until last st, k1.

Row 4: K1, k1 uls, k4, *k1 uls, k5*, rep ** until last 5 sts, k1 uls, k4.

Row 6: K1, *sl5 wyif, k1*, rep ** until last 4 sts, sl3 wyif, k1.

Row 8: K3, *k1 uls, k5*, rep ** until last 2 sts, k1 uls, k1.

Sizes - (-, M, -, -) (-, 3XL, -, -) only

Rows 1, 3, 5 & 7 (WS): P across.

Row 2 (RS): K1, sl3 wyif, k1, *sl5 wyif, k1*, rep ** until last st, k1.

Row 4: K1, *k1 uls, k5*, rep ** until last 5 sts, k1 uls, k4.

Row 6: K2, *sl5 wyif, k1*, rep ** until last 4 sts, sl3 wyif, k1.

Row 8: K4, *k1 uls, k5*, rep ** until last 2 sts, k1 uls, k1.

Sizes - (-, -, L, -) (-, -, 4XL, -) only

Rows 1, 3, 5 & 7 (WS): P across.

Row 2 (RS): K1, *sl5 wyif, k1*, rep ** until last st, k1.

Row 4: K3, *k1 uls, k5*, rep ** until last 5 sts, k1 uls, k4.

Row 6: K1, sl2 wyif, k1, *sl5 wyif, k1*, rep ** until last 4 sts, sl3 wyif, k1.

Row 8: K1, k1 uls, k4, *k1 uls, k5*, rep ** until last 2 sts, k1 uls, k1.

All sizes continue

Leave these 15 (17, 18, 20, 21) (23, 24, 26, 27) sts on your needle and do not cut the yarn.

SHOULDER SEAMS

You will be using the Three Needle Bind Off method (page 207) to join the shoulder seams.

1. Turn your work inside out and place the RS of your front and back panels together.

2. Your front left shoulder stitches should still be on your needle. Place the corresponding 15 (17, 18, 20, 21) (23, 24, 26, 27) sts left on hold for the back left shoulder onto the other needle. Make sure both needles are facing the same direction.

3. Insert a third needle (US 19 [15 mm] or smaller) knitwise into the first st of the panel that is facing you, then insert that same needle knitwise into the corresponding st of the other panel.

4. Continue, following the instructions for the Three Needle Bind Off method (page 207).

5. Repeat all steps for the other shoulder, using the corresponding front right and back right shoulder stitches left on hold.

SLEEVES

Flip your work so that the RS are now facing out (your shoulder seams should be invisible). You will now be working the sleeves in the round. *You may need to use the Magic Loop method (page 207).*

Using US 19 (15 mm) needles, starting at the underarm, pick up 36 (36, 36, 36, 42) (42, 42, 48, 48) sts, evenly spaced, around the armhole. PM to mark the BOR.

Repeat the following 8 rounds until you have worked 32 (32, 40, 40, 40) (48, 48, 48, 48) rounds total. *You should end on round 8.*

Note: If you would like to add or subtract length to/from your sleeve, do so here, but make sure you still end on round 8. Keep in mind the sleeve cuff will add approximately 3.2–3.9 inches (8–10 cm). Make note of how many total rows you work so that you can work your second sleeve to match.

Rounds 1, 3 & 5: K across.

Round 2: *Sl5 wyif, k1*, rep ** until end of the round.

Round 4: K2, *k1 uls, k5*, rep ** until last 4 sts, k1 uls, k3.

Round 6: K3, *sl5 wyif, k1*, rep ** until last 3 sts, sl3 wyif.

Round 7: Sl2 wyif, k across.

Round 8: *K5, k1 uls*, rep ** until end of the round.

You will now make decreases before working the sleeve cuffs.

Sizes XS (S, M, L, -) (-, -, -, -) only

Next 2 rounds: *K2tog, k1*, rep ** until end of the round.

Sizes - (-, -, -, XL) (XXL, 3XL, -, -) only

Next round: *K2tog, k1, k2tog, k2*, rep ** until end of the round.

Next round: *K2tog, k1*, rep ** until end of the round.

Sizes - (-, -, -, -) (-, -, 4XL, 5XL) only

Next round: *K2tog*, rep ** until end of the round.

All sizes continue

You should now have 16 (16, 16, 16, 20) (20, 20, 24, 24) sts.

Switch to US 17 (12 mm) 32-inch (80-cm) circular needles. *You will need to use the Magic Loop method (page 207) to work the sleeve cuff.*

Next 7 (7, 7, 7, 8) (8, 8, 9, 9) rounds: *K1, p1*, rep ** until end of the round.

BO all sts in 1x1 rib pattern.

BUTTON BAND

Using US 17 (12 mm) 32-inch (80-cm) circular needles, starting from the bottom of the Front Right Panel, working up and across the back neckline, then back down the Front Left Panel, pick up stitches in the following pattern: *pick up 4 sts, skip 1 st*, ensuring you end up with an even number of stitches.

Next 3 (2, 3, 2, 3) (2, 3, 2, 3) rows: *K1, p1*, rep ** until end of the row.

BO all sts in 1x1 rib pattern.

FINISHING

Weave in all your loose ends.

Blocking super bulky yarn is not necessary. However, if you do wish to block your cardigan, it is suggested that you use the spray blocking method (do *not* wet or steam block).

Stairway to Heaven Vest

I've long wanted to design something inspired by a staircase, and when I came across the Diagonal Rib stitch, with its subtle yet intricate texture created by a simple combination of knits and purls, I knew it was the perfect stitch to bring my vision to life. The Stairway to Heaven Vest is a timeless, fitted and cropped piece that offers versatility for any wardrobe. It can be layered with other pieces or worn comfortably on its own. The textured design truly shines when worked up in either a variegated or solid colorway, allowing the exquisite stitch pattern to take center stage.

This design is very special to me, because it allowed me to dip my toes into the wonderful world of yarn dyeing, thanks to my amazing friend Chloe from Wool and Works. Chloe and I developed the colorway used for the sample and hand-dyed the yarn together, which was an incredibly enlightening and fun experience. I gained even more of an appreciation for how much work goes into dyeing yarn by hand, and it made the experience of knitting the sample vest even more rewarding.

Construction Notes

This seamless vest is worked mostly in the round in a Diagonal Rib stitch from the bottom up. You will first work the bottom section of the vest in the round, before splitting at the underarm point to work the back panel flat, followed by the front panel. You will join the shoulder seams to create the neck hole and armholes using the Three Needle Bind Off method (page 207). The neck and sleeve trims are worked in the round by picking up stitches along the neck hole/armhole edges.

Skill Level

Confident Beginner

Sizing

XS (S, M, L, XL) (XXL, 3XL, 4XL, 5XL)

Finished bust: 32.2 (36.2, 41, 44.8, 49.6) (53.4, 56, 59.8, 64.6)" / 82 (92, 104, 114, 126) (136, 142, 152, 164) cm, blocked

Recommended ease: This vest is designed with approximately 2.4–4.3 inches / 6–11 cm of positive ease

Sample shown is knit in Size S.

MATERIALS

Yarn

Bulky weight, Wool and Works, Chunky Singles (80% Superwash Merino, 20% Nylon), 77 yds (70 m) per 100-g skein, shown in Jaime's Rose Garden colorway

Any bulky weight yarn can be used for this pattern as long as it matches gauge. A good substitute would be Wool and the Gang, Lil' Crazy Sexy Wool or Qing Fiber, Big Merino Chunky.

Yardage/Meterage

232 (260, 316, 371, 428) (481, 542, 612, 696) yds / 212 (238, 289, 339, 391) (440, 496, 560, 636) m

Needles

For body: US 10.5* (7 mm) 32- to 40-inch (80- to 100-cm) circular needle

For sleeve and neck trims: US 10 (6 mm) 24- to 32-inch (60- to 80-cm) circular needle

There is no direct US equivalent to 7 mm needles; US 10.5 (6.5 mm) is the closest size

Notions

Stitch marker

Tapestry needle

Scissors

Stitch holders

GAUGE

11 sts x 17 rows = 4 inches (10 cm) in left Diagonal Rib stitch (explained below) using larger needle (blocked)

To Knit Gauge Swatch

1. CO 18 sts.
2. Work 3 horizontal repeats of the chart (page 93) for at least 17 rows.

Note: When worked flat, odd (RS) rows of the chart are read from right to left, and even (WS) rows are read from left to right. On WS rows, the knit symbols on the chart are worked as purl stitches and vice versa.

ABBREVIATIONS

1x1 rib(bing) - *Knit 1, purl 1*

BO - Bind off

BOR - Beginning of round

CO - Cast on

K - Knit

K2tog - Knit 2 stitches together

P - Purl

P2tog - Purl 2 stitches together

PM - Place marker

Rep - Repeat

RS - Right side

Ssk - Slip, slip, knit 2 stitches together through the back loops

Ssp - Slip, slip, purl 2 stitches together through the back loops

St(s) - Stitch(es)

WS - Wrong side

SIZING CHART

Size	XS	S	M	L	XL	XXL	3XL	4XL	5XL
To fit bust	28–30"/ 71–76 cm	32–34"/ 81–86 cm	36–38"/ 91.5–96.5 cm	40–42"/ 101.5–106.5 cm	44–46"/ 111.5–117 cm	48–50"/ 122–127 cm	52–54"/ 132–137 cm	56–58"/ 142–147 cm	60–62"/ 152–158 cm
(A) Width	16.1"/ 41 cm	18.1"/ 46 cm	20.5"/ 52 cm	22.4"/ 57 cm	24.8"/ 63 cm	26.7"/ 68 cm	28"/ 71 cm	29.9"/ 76 cm	32.3"/ 82 cm
(B) Length	15.7"/ 40 cm	15.7"/ 40 cm	16.9"/ 43 cm	18.1"/ 46 cm	18.9"/ 48 cm	19.7"/ 50 cm	21.3"/ 54 cm	22.4"/ 57 cm	23.6"/ 60 cm
(C) Armhole Depth	8.7"/ 22 cm	8.7"/ 22 cm	8.7"/ 22 cm	9.8"/ 25 cm	9.8"/ 25 cm	10.6"/ 27 cm	10.6"/ 27 cm	11.8"/ 30 cm	11.8"/ 30 cm

SPECIAL TECHNIQUES

Three Needle Bind Off (page 207)

Magic Loop method (page 207)

Stretchy Bind Off (page 211)

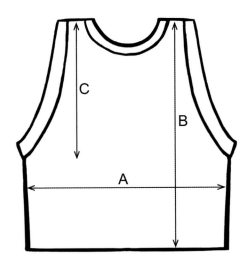

BOTTOM

Using US 10.5* (7mm) 32- to 40-inch (80- to 100-cm) circular needles and the Long Tail Cast On, CO 90 (102, 114, 126, 138) (150, 156, 168, 180) sts. Join in the round and PM to mark the BOR.

Repeat the chart (page 93) (written instructions below) until you have worked 30 (30, 36, 36, 40) (40, 46, 46, 50) rounds total. *You should end after round 6 (6, 12, 12, 4) (4, 10, 10, 2) of the chart.*

> Note: If you would like to add or subtract length to/from your vest, do so here, but ensure you still end after round 6 (6, 12, 12, 4) (4, 10, 10, 2) of the chart, or knit to your desired length, making note of what row of the chart you end after, as this will change which row you start with for the front and back panels.

> Note: When worked in the round, the chart is read from right to left on every row.

Rounds 1–4: *P2, k4*, rep ** until end of the round.

Rounds 5–8: *K2, p2, k2*, rep ** until end of the round.

Rounds 9–12: *K4, p2*, rep ** until end of the round.

BACK PANEL

You will now be working flat across **only the first 45 (51, 57, 63, 69) (75, 78, 84, 90) sts.** Leave the remaining stitches on the cord or place them on a stitch holder. *You will come back to them later for the Front Panel.*

You will now begin making decreases for the armholes. Restart your row count here, while continuing to follow the 12-row vertical repeat of the chart (page 93) where it says "work in pattern." *You should be on row 7 (7, 1, 1, 5) (5, 11, 11, 3) of the chart.*

> Note: When worked flat, odd (RS) rows of the chart are read from right to left, and even (WS) rows are read from left to right. On WS rows, the knit symbols on the chart are worked as purl stitches and vice versa.

> A note on working in pattern: As you decrease during this section, you will no longer always have complete 6-stitch repeats of the pattern at the outer edges of the panel. This means you will not always begin with stitch 1 (RS) or stitch 6 (WS) of the chart after the edge stitches when it says "work in pattern"; instead, start with the stitch that vertically matches the stitch column below it. If it is helpful, place stitch markers between each repeat before you begin to decrease so that you can see where you are within the 6-stitch motif at any time, and remember that the 2 columns of purl stitches move 2 stitches to the left every 4 rows when viewed on the RS.

Row 1 (RS): K1, ssk, work in pattern until last 3 sts, k2tog, k1.

Row 2 (WS): P2, work in pattern until last 2 sts, p2.

Repeat rows 1–2 until you have worked them 9 (9, 9, 9, 10) (10, 10, 10, 11) times total (meaning 18 (18, 18, 18, 20) (20, 20, 20, 22) total rows). You should end after a WS row and have 27 (33, 39, 45, 49) (55, 58, 64, 68) sts. *You should end after row 12 (12, 6, 6, 12) (12, 6, 6, 12) of the chart.*

Work 17 (17, 17, 21, 19) (22, 23, 28, 27) rows in pattern (straight, no decreases). The first 2 stitches and last 2 stitches of each row should now be worked as their corresponding chart stitches, rather than the 2-stitch stockinette edges that were worked during the decreases. *You should end after row 5 (5, 11, 3, 7) (10, 5, 10, 3) of the chart.*

BACK SHOULDERS

You will now make decreases to shape the back neckline. *You should be on row 6 (6, 12, 4, 8) (11, 6, 11, 4) of the chart.*

Sizes XS (S, M, L, XL) (-, 3XL, -, 5XL) only

Row 1 (WS): Work in pattern across 6 (9, 12, 15, 16) (-, 19, -, 23) sts, turn.

Row 2 (RS): K1, ssk, work in pattern until end of the row.

Row 3: Work in pattern until last 2 sts, p2.

Cut yarn and place these 5 (8, 11, 14, 15) (-, 18, -, 22) left shoulder sts on a stitch holder. *You will come back to them later for the Shoulder Seams.*

Place the middle 15 (15, 15, 15, 17) (-, 20, -, 22) sts on another stitch holder. *You will come back to them later for the Neck Trim.*

Reattach yarn on the WS to the remaining 6 (9, 12, 15, 16) (-, 19, -, 23) right shoulder sts. *You should be on row 6 (6, 12, 4, 8) (-, 6, -, 4) of the chart (page 93).*

Row 1 (WS): Work in pattern until end of the row.

Row 2 (RS): Work in pattern until last 3 sts, k2tog, k1.

Row 3: P2, work in pattern until end of the row.

Cut yarn and place these 5 (8, 11, 14, 15) (-, 18, -, 22) sts on a stitch holder. *You will come back to them later for the Shoulder Seams.*

Sizes - (-, -, -, -) (XXL, -, 4XL, -) only

Row 1 (RS): Work in pattern across - (-, -, -, -) (19, -, 22, -) sts, turn.

Row 2 (WS): P1, p2tog, work in pattern until end of the row.

Row 3: Work in pattern until last 2 sts, k2.

Cut yarn and place these - (-, -, -, -) (18, -, 21, -) right shoulder sts on a stitch holder. *You will come back to them later for the Shoulder Seams.*

Place the middle - (-, -, -, -) (17, -, 20, -) sts on another stitch holder. *You will come back to them later for the Neck Trim.*

Reattach yarn on the RS to the remaining - (-, -, -, -) (19, -, 22, -) left shoulder sts. *You should be on row - (-, -, -, -) (11, -, 11, -) of the chart (page 93).*

Row 1 (RS): Work in pattern until end of the row.

Row 2 (WS): Work in pattern until last 3 sts, ssp, p1.

Row 3: K2, work in pattern until end of the row.

Cut yarn and place these - (-, -, -, -) (18, -, 21, -) sts on a stitch holder. *You will come back to them later for the Shoulder Seams.*

FRONT PANEL

You will now be working flat across the 45 (51, 57, 63, 69) (75, 78, 84, 90) sts you left on hold after the Bottom section. Reattach yarn on the RS.

Follow the Back Panel instructions for the armhole decrease rows, stopping before the straight rows.

You should end after a WS row and have 27 (33, 39, 45, 49) (55, 58, 64, 68) sts. *You should end after row 12 (12, 6, 6, 12) (12, 6, 6, 12) of the chart.*

Work 12 (12, 12, 16, 14) (17, 18, 23, 22) rows in pattern (straight, no decreases). The first 2 stitches and last 2 stitches of each row should now be worked as their corresponding chart stitches rather than the 2-stitch stockinette edges that were worked during the decreases. *You should end after row 12 (12, 6, 10, 2) (5, 12, 5, 10) of the chart.*

FRONT SHOULDERS

You will now make decreases to shape the front neckline. *You should be on row 1 (1, 7, 11, 3) (6, 1, 6, 11) of the chart.*

Sizes XS (S, M, L, XL) (-, 3XL, -, 5XL) only

Row 1 (RS): Work in pattern across 8 (11, 14, 17, 18) (-, 21, -, 25) sts, turn.

Row 2 (WS): P1, p2tog, work in pattern until end of the row.

Row 3: Work in pattern until last 2 sts, k2.

Rows 4–7: Repeat rows 2–3.

Row 8: P2, work in pattern until end of the row.

Cut yarn and place these 5 (8, 11, 14, 15) (-, 18, -, 22) left (as worn) shoulder sts on a stitch holder. *You will come back to them later for the Shoulder Seams.*

Place the middle 11 (11, 11, 11, 13) (-, 16, -, 18) sts on another stitch holder. *You will come back to them later for the Neck Trim.*

Reattach yarn on the RS to the remaining 8 (11, 14, 17, 18) (-, 21, -, 25) right (as worn) shoulder sts. *You should be on row 1 (1, 7, 11, 3) (-, 1, -, 11) of the chart.*

Row 1 (RS): Work in pattern until end of the row.

Row 2 (WS): Work in pattern until last 3 sts, ssp, p1.

Row 3: K2, work in pattern until end of the row.

Rows 4–7: Repeat rows 2–3.

Row 8: Work in pattern until last 2 sts, p2.

Leave these 5 (8, 11, 14, 15) (-, 18, -, 22) sts on your needle and do not cut the yarn. *Proceed to "Shoulder Seams."*

Sizes - (-, -, -, -) (XXL, -, 4XL, -) only

Row 1 (WS): Work in pattern across - (-, -, -, -) (21, -, 24, -) sts, turn.

Row 2 (RS): K1, ssk, work in pattern until end of the row.

Row 3: Work in pattern until last 2 sts, p2.

Rows 4–7: Repeat rows 2–3.

Row 8: K2, work in pattern until end of the row.

Cut yarn and place these - (-, -, -, -) (18, -, 21, -) right (as worn) shoulder sts on a stitch holder. *You will come back to them later for the Shoulder Seams.*

Place the middle - (-, -, -, -) (13, -, 16, -) sts on another stitch holder. *You will come back to them later for the Neck Trim.*

Reattach yarn on the WS to the remaining - (-, -, -, -) (21, -, 24, -) left (as worn) shoulder sts. *You should be on row - (-, -, -, -) (6, -, 6, -) of the chart.*

Row 1 (WS): Work in pattern until end of the row.

Row 2 (RS): Work in pattern until last 3 sts, k2tog, k1.

Row 3: P2, work in pattern until end of the row.

Rows 4–7: Repeat rows 2–3.

Row 8: Work in pattern until last 2 sts, k2.

Leave these - (-, -, -, -) (18, -, 21, -) sts on your needle and do not cut the yarn. *Proceed to "Shoulder Seams."*

SHOULDER SEAMS

You will now be using the Three Needle Bind Off method (page 207) to join the shoulder seams.

1. Turn your work inside out and place the RS of your front and back panels together.

2. Your front left (left, left, left, left) (right, left, right, left) (as worn) shoulder stitches should still be on your needle. Place the corresponding 5 (8, 11, 14, 15) (18, 18, 21, 22) sts left on hold for the back left (left, left, left, left) (right, left, right, left) shoulder onto the other needle. Make sure both needles are facing the same direction.

3. Insert a third needle (US 10.5* [7 mm] or smaller) knitwise into the first st of the panel that is facing you, then insert that same needle knitwise into the corresponding st of the other panel.

4. Continue, following the instructions for the Three Needle Bind Off method (page 207).

5. Repeat all steps for the other shoulder, using the corresponding front and back shoulder stitches left on hold.

NECK TRIM

Flip your work so that the RS are facing out and your shoulder seams are invisible.

Using US 10 (6 mm) 24- to 32-inch (60- to 80-cm) circular needles, pick up stitches in the following fashion:

1. Pick up 3 sts along the side of the back right shoulder.
2. Pick up and knit the 15 (15, 15, 15, 17) (17, 20, 20, 22) live sts from the stitch holder at the back neck.
3. Pick up 3 sts along the side of the back left shoulder.
4. Pick up 8 sts along the side of the front left (as worn) shoulder.
5. Pick up and knit the 11 (11, 11, 11, 13) (13, 16, 16, 18) live sts from the stitch holder at the front neck.
6. Pick up 8 sts along the side of the front right (as worn) shoulder.

You should now have 48 (48, 48, 48, 52) (52, 58, 58, 62) sts. PM to mark the BOR.

Rounds 1–3: *K1, p1*, rep ** until end of the round. *You may need to use the Magic Loop method (page 207).*

BO using the Stretchy Bind Off method (page 211).

SLEEVE TRIMS

Using US 10 (6 mm) 24- to 32-inch (60- to 80-cm) circular needles and starting at the underarm point, pick up stitches in the following fashion: *Pick up 3 sts, skip 1 st.* Make sure you have an even number of stitches.

Rounds 1–3: *K1, p1*, rep ** until end of the round. *You may need to use the Magic Loop method (page 207).*

BO loosely in 1x1 rib pattern.

FINISHING

Weave in all your loose ends.

Wash and block (see Blocking 101 [page 216] or use your preferred blocking method).

CHART PATTERN WORKED FLAT

Row 1 (RS): *P2, k4*, rep ** until end of the row.

Row 2 (WS): *P4, k2*, rep ** until end of the row.

Rows 3–4: Repeat rows 1–2.

Row 5: *K2, p2, k2*, rep ** until end of the row.

Row 6: *P2, k2, p2*, rep ** until end of the row.

Rows 7–8: Repeat rows 5–6.

Row 9: *K4, p2*, rep ** until end of the row.

Row 10: *K2, p4*, rep ** until end of the row.

Rows 11–12: Repeat rows 9–10.

CHART

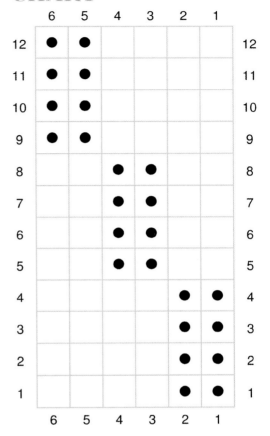

Legend		
	☐	RS: Knit WS: Purl
	⊡	RS: Purl WS: Knit

Cassie Cardigan

Inspired by my beautiful dog Cassie, this cardigan embodies all the qualities that make Cassie, both the dog and the design, extremely loveable. Just like Cassie's soft, fluffy fur, this knitting project promises a cozy embrace and undeniable cuteness. Designed with beginners in mind, the Cassie Cardigan is a simple yet eye-catching piece that showcases the beautiful Fisherman's Rib stitch. This stitch creates a stunning, intricate texture that belies its ease of execution. The double-knitted button band adds a clean, polished finish to the edges, which not only enhances the cardigan's aesthetic appeal but also presents an enjoyable challenge for beginners seeking to level up their skills. Working a single strand of chunky mohair yarn with large needles produces a lightweight, airy fabric that stretches with ease—perfect for those crisp spring and summer evenings.

Construction Notes

This seamless cardigan is worked in Fisherman's Rib stitch from the bottom up. You will first work the bottom section of the cardigan flat, before splitting at the underarm point to work the front left panel, then the back panel, followed by the front right panel. You will join the shoulder seams to create the armholes using the Three Needle Bind Off method (page 207). The sleeves are worked in the round by picking up stitches along the armhole edges. You will finish by working the double-knitted button band flat by picking up stitches along the inside edges. Instructions on how to adjust the body and sleeve length of your cardigan are included.

Skill Level

Advanced Beginner

Sizing

XS (S, M, L, XL) (XXL, 3XL, 4XL, 5XL)

Finished bust: 42.6 (46.4, 50.4, 54.4, 58.2) (62.2, 66.2, 70, 74.8)" / 108 (118, 128, 138, 148) (158, 168, 178, 190) cm, blocked

Recommended ease: This cardigan is designed with approximately 12.6–14.6 inches / 32–37 cm of positive ease

Sample shown is knit in Size M.

MATERIALS

Yarn

Aran weight, Wool and the Gang, Take Care Mohair (78% Mohair, 13% Wool, 9% Polyamide), 109 yds (100 m) per 50-g skein, shown in Lime Sherbert colorway

Any Aran weight fluffy yarn can be used for this pattern as long as it matches gauge. A good substitute would be Hip Knit Shop, Fluff or Cardigang, Chunky Mohair.

Yardage/Meterage

437 (459, 488, 559, 638) (677, 757, 821, 890) yds / 400 (420, 446, 511, 584) (619, 692, 751, 814) m

Needles

For body: US 11 (8 mm) 32- to 40-inch (80- to 100-cm) circular needle

For sleeves: US 11 (8 mm) 24- to 32-inch (60- to 80-cm) circular needle

For sleeve cuffs: US 8 (5 mm) 16- to 24-inch (40- to 60-cm) circular needle or DPNs

For button band: US 8 (5 mm) 32- to 40-inch (80- to 100-cm) circular needle

Notions

Stitch marker

Tapestry needle

Scissors

Stitch holders

GAUGE

8 sts x 18 rows* = 4 inches (10 cm) in Fisherman's Rib stitch using larger needle (blocked). *Fisherman's Rib stitch is notoriously stretchy so be mindful of this when measuring gauge.*

When counting rows in Fisherman's Rib stitch, it is important to note that two rows will appear as one row.

ABBREVIATIONS

1x1 rib(bing) - *Knit 1, purl 1*

BO - Bind off

BOR - Beginning of round

CO - Cast on

DPNs - Double pointed needles

K - Knit

K1b - Knit 1 below

K2tog - Knit 2 stitches together

P - Purl

P1b - Purl 1 below

PM - Place marker

Rep - Repeat

RM - Remove marker

RS - Right side

St(s) - Stitch(es)

WS - Wrong side

SIZING CHART

Size	XS	S	M	L	XL	XXL	3XL	4XL	5XL
To fit bust	28–30"/ 71–76 cm	32–34"/ 81–86 cm	36–38"/ 91.5–96.5 cm	40–42"/ 101.5–106.5 cm	44–46"/ 111.5–117 cm	48–50"/ 122–127 cm	52–54"/ 132–137 cm	56–58"/ 142–147 cm	60–62"/ 152–158 cm
(A) Width	21.3"/ 54 cm	23.2"/ 59 cm	25.2"/ 64 cm	27.2"/ 69 cm	29.1"/ 74 cm	31.1"/ 79 cm	33.1"/ 84 cm	35"/ 89 cm	37.4"/ 95 cm
(B) Length	16.5"/ 42 cm	17.3"/ 44 cm	17.3"/ 44 cm	18.1"/ 46 cm	18.9"/ 48 cm	20.1"/ 51 cm	20.8"/ 53 cm	21.7"/ 55 cm	22.4"/ 57 cm
(C) Sleeve Width	7.9"/ 20 cm	7.9"/ 20 cm	7.9"/ 20 cm	9.4"/ 24 cm	9.4"/ 24 cm	9.4"/ 24 cm	11"/ 28 cm	11"/ 28 cm	11"/ 28 cm
(D) Sleeve Length	17.3"/ 44 cm	17.3"/ 44 cm	18.1"/ 46 cm	18.1"/ 46 cm	18.1"/ 46 cm	18.9"/ 48 cm	18.9"/ 48 cm	19.7"/ 50 cm	19.7"/ 50 cm

SPECIAL TECHNIQUES

Three Needle Bind Off (page 207)

Magic Loop method (page 207)

Double Knitting (https://www.jaimecreates. me/book/tutorials)

Italian Cast On (https://www.jaimecreates. me/book/tutorials)

Grafting (page 214)

Stretchy Bind Off (page 211)

Knit 1 Below

Insert the right needle into the center of the stitch below the first stitch on the left needle; knit this stitch normally.

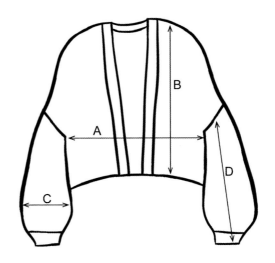

BOTTOM

Using US 11 (8 mm) 32- to 40-inch (80- to 100-cm) circular needles and the Long Tail Cast On, CO 75 (83, 91, 99, 107) (115, 123, 131, 139) sts.

Setup row (WS): *K1, p1*, rep ** until last st, k1.

Row 1 (RS): *P1, k1b*, rep ** until last st, p1.

Row 2 (WS): K1, *p1, k1b*, rep ** until last 2 sts, p1, k1.

Repeat rows 1–2 until you have worked 39 (43, 43, 41, 43) (49, 45, 49, 53) rows total. *You should end after a RS row.*

> **Note:** If you would like to add length to your cardigan, do so here, but make sure to end after a RS row.

FRONT LEFT PANEL

You will now be working across **only the first 15 (17, 19, 21, 23) (25, 27, 29, 31) sts.** Leave the remaining stitches on the cord or place them on a stitch holder. *You will come back to them later for the Back and Front Right Panels.*

Row 1 (WS): K1, *p1, k1b*, rep ** until last 2 sts, p1, k1.

Row 2 (RS): *P1, k1b*, rep ** until last st, p1.

Repeat rows 1–2 until you have worked 36 (36, 36, 44, 44) (44, 50, 50, 50) rows from the underarm separation. *You should end after a RS row.*

Cut yarn and place these 15 (17, 19, 21, 23) (25, 27, 29, 31) sts on a stitch holder. *You will come back to them later for the Shoulder Seams.*

BACK PANEL

You will now be working across **only the next 45 (49, 53, 57, 61) (65, 69, 73, 77) sts.** Leave the remaining stitches on the cord or place them on a stitch holder. *You will come back to them later for the Front Right Panel. Reattach yarn on the WS.*

Row 1 (WS): *P1, k1b*, rep ** until last st, p1.

Row 2 (RS): K1, *P1, k1b*, rep ** until last 2 sts, p1, k1.

Repeat rows 1–2 until you have worked 35 (35, 35, 43, 43) (43, 49, 49, 49) rows from the underarm separation. *You should end after a WS row.*

BACK SHOULDERS

Count 15 (17, 19, 21, 23) (25, 27, 29, 31) sts in from the right edge (RS facing you) and PM.

Next row (RS): K1, *P1, k1b*, rep ** until 2 sts before marker, p1, k1, **RM**, BO 15, *P1, k1b*, rep ** until last 2 sts, p1, k1.

You should now have 15 (17, 19, 21, 23) (25, 27, 29, 31) sts for each shoulder.

Cut yarn and place your 30 (34, 38, 42, 46) (50, 54, 58, 62) left and right shoulder sts on two stitch holders. *You will come back to them later for the Shoulder Seams.*

FRONT RIGHT PANEL

Reattach yarn on the WS to the remaining 15 (17, 19, 21, 23) (25, 27, 29, 31) sts.

Row 1 (WS): K1, *p1, k1b*, rep ** until last 2 sts, p1, k1.

Row 2 (RS): *P1, k1b*, rep ** until last st, p1.

Repeat rows 1–2 until you have worked 36 (36, 36, 44, 44) (44, 50, 50, 50) rows **from the underarm separation**. *You should end after a RS row.*

Leave these 15 (17, 19, 21, 23) (25, 27, 29, 31) sts on your needle and do not cut the yarn. *Proceed to "Shoulder Seams."*

SHOULDER SEAMS

You will now be using the Three Needle Bind Off method (page 207) to join the shoulder seams.

1. Place the RS of your front and back panels together.

2. Your front right (as worn) shoulder stitches should still be on your needle. Place the corresponding 15 (17, 19, 21, 23) (25, 27, 29, 31) sts left on hold for the back right shoulder onto the other needle. Make sure both needles are facing the same direction.

3. Insert a third needle (US 11 [8 mm] or smaller) knitwise into the first st of the panel that is facing you, then insert that same needle knitwise into the corresponding st of the other panel.

4. Continue, following the instructions for the Three Needle Bind Off method (page 207).

5. Repeat all steps for the other shoulder, using the corresponding front left and back left shoulder stitches left on hold.

SLEEVES

Flip your work so that the RS are now facing out (your shoulder seams should be invisible).

Using US 11 (8 mm) 24- to 32-inch (60- to 80-cm) circular needles, starting at the underarm point, pick up 34 (34, 34, 38, 38) (38, 44, 44, 44) sts, evenly spaced, around the armhole. PM to mark the BOR. *You may need to use the Magic Loop method (page 207).*

Setup round: *K1, p1*, rep ** until end of the round.

Round 1: *K1b, p1*, rep ** until end of the round.

Round 2: *K1, p1b*, rep ** until end of the round.

Repeat rounds 1–2 until you have worked 68 (68, 72, 72, 72) (76, 76, 80, 80) rounds total.

> **Note:** If you would like to add length to your sleeve, do so here, but keep in mind that the sleeve cuff will add approximately 2.4 inches (6 cm). Make note of how many total rows you work so that you can work your second sleeve to match.

You will now make decreases before working the sleeve cuffs.

Next round: *K1, k2tog*, rep ** until last st, k1.

Next round: *K1, k2tog*, rep ** until last 2 sts, k2.

All sizes continue

You should now have 23 (23, 23, 26, 26) (26, 30, 30, 30) sts.

Switch to US 8 (5 mm) 16- to 24-inch (40- to 60-cm) circular needle or DPNs. *If using circular needles, you will need to use the Magic Loop method (page 207). Restart your row count here.*

Round 1: K2tog, p1, *k1, p1*, rep ** until end of the round.

You should now have 22 (22, 22, -, -) (-, -, -, -) sts.

All sizes continue

Next 8 (8, 8, 9, 9) (9, 9, 9, 9) rounds: *K1, p1*, rep ** until end of the round.

BO all sts in 1x1 rib pattern or using the Stretchy Bind Off method (page 211).

BUTTON BAND

1. Using US 8 (5 mm) 32- to 40-inch (80- to 100-cm) circular needles, starting from the bottom of the Front Right Panel (as worn) and working up to the right shoulder seam, pick up stitches in the following pattern: *pick up 3 sts, skip 1 st*.

2. Working across the back neckline, pick up all bound off stitches.

3. Working from the left shoulder seam down the Front Left Panel, pick up stitches in the following pattern: *pick up 3 sts, skip 1 st*.

4. Cut yarn, leaving a tail long enough to weave in.

5. Using the Italian Cast On method, CO 7 sts onto the other needle (on the edge of the Front Right Panel). *For a video tutorial on the Italian Cast On, visit the following page on my site: https://www.jaimecreates.me/book/tutorials.*

6. Work in double knitting across all stitches until you have worked the entire button band. *For a video tutorial on double knitting, visit the following page on my site: https://www.jaimecreates.me/book/tutorials.*

7. Cut the working yarn, leaving a tail that is 2–3 times longer than the width of the button band.

8. BO the button band by following the instructions for Grafting (page 214).

FINISHING

Weave in any remaining loose ends.

Wash and block (see Blocking 101 [page 216] or use your preferred blocking method).

Attention Deficit Jumper

As someone with ADHD, keeping my hands occupied is essential to staying focused. Knitting has been my saving grace in this department since before I was even diagnosed. However, monotony often creeps in, especially when working on larger projects with repetitive stitch patterns, which can lead to boredom, lack of motivation and an ever-growing pile of unfinished projects. This is why I'm thrilled to bring you the Attention Deficit Jumper, a captivating knit that promises to keep your hands busy and your mind engaged from start to finish. With five main stitch patterns used throughout, monotony becomes a thing of the past, as each section introduces a new and exciting adventure, ensuring that you'll always have something fresh and intriguing to work on. Not only will you stay engaged, but you'll also hopefully learn some new techniques and expand your knitting repertoire along the way. With a slouchy, oversized, semi-cropped fit, this jumper can be dressed up or down and is suitable for both a fun night out or a cozy night in.

Construction Notes

This seamless jumper is worked mostly in the round in a variety of different written and/or charted stitch patterns from the bottom up. You will first work the bottom section of the jumper in the round, before splitting at the underarm point to work the back panel flat, followed by the front panel. You will join the shoulder seams to create the neck and armholes using the Three Needle Bind Off method (page 207). The neck trim and sleeves are worked in the round by picking up stitches along the neck hole/armhole edges.

Skill Level

Intermediate

Sizing

XS (S, M, L, XL) (XXL, 3XL, 4XL, 5XL)

Finished bust: 44.9 (47.2, 51.2, 56.7, 59.8) (66.1, 69.3, 71.7, 78)" / 114 (120, 130, 144, 152) (168, 176, 182, 198) cm, blocked

Recommended ease: This jumper is designed with approximately 13.2–17 inches / 33.5–43 cm of positive ease

Sample shown is knit in Size S.

MATERIALS

Yarn

Aran weight, Wool and the Gang, Feeling Good Yarn (70% Baby Alpaca, 7% Merino, 23% Recycled Nylon), 142 yds (130 m) per 50-g skein, **held double**, shown in Buttercup Yellow colorway

Any Aran weight yarn (held double) or bulky weight yarn (held single) can be used for this pattern as long as it matches gauge. A good substitute would be Sandnes Garn, Kos or Drops, Air (both held double).

Yardage/Meterage

Yarn estimates are approximate and refer specifically to the recommended yarn held double.

1055 (1180, 1317, 1577, 1717) (1963, 2186, 2333, 2594) yds / 965 (1079, 1204, 1442, 1570) (1795, 1999, 2133, 2372) m

Needles

For body: US 11 (8 mm) 32- to 40-inch (80- to 100-cm) circular needle

For sleeves: US 11 (8 mm) 24-inch (60-cm) circular needle

For bottom ribbing: US 10 (6 mm) 32- to 40-inch (80- to 100-cm) circular needle

For neck trim: US 10 (6 mm) 24-inch (60-cm) circular needle

For sleeve cuffs: US 10 (6 mm) 16-inch (40-cm) circular needle or DPNs

Notions

Stitch marker

Tapestry needles

Scissors

Stitch holders

GAUGE

10.5 sts x 17 rows = 4 inches (10 cm) in stockinette stitch using larger needle (blocked)

ABBREVIATIONS

1x1 rib(bing) - *Knit 1, purl 1*

BO - Bind off

BOR - Beginning of round

CO - Cast on

K - Knit

K2tog - Knit 2 stitches together

K4b - Knit 4 below

LC - Left cross

P - Purl

PM - Place marker

RC - Right cross

Rep - Repeat

RS - Right side

Sl wyib - Slip stitch purlwise with yarn held in back

Sl wyif - Slip stitch purlwise with yarn held in front

Ssk - Slip, slip, knit 2 stitches together through the back loops

St(s) - Stitch(es)

Uls - Under loose strand

WS - Wrong side

SPECIAL TECHNIQUES

Alternating Cable Cast On (page 208)

Three Needle Bind Off (page 207)

Magic Loop method (page 207)

Adding Elastic (page 213)

Knit 4 Below

Drop the first stitch on the left needle off of the needle.

Unravel this stitch 4 times. This will create 4 horizontal ladders between the needles.

Insert the right needle in the remaining live stitch under the horizontal ladders (this will be in the 5th row down).

Knit this stitch, catching the 4 horizontal ladders behind the stitch.

Knit Under Loose Strand

Insert right needle under the loose strand from front to back.

Knit the stitch normally, bringing the new stitch out from under the loose strand.

1/1 Left Cross

Place 1 st on cable needle and hold to **front** of work. K1, k1 from cable needle.

1/2 Left Cross

Place 1 st on cable needle and hold to **front** of work. K2, k1 from cable needle.

1/1 Right Cross

Place 1 st on cable needle and hold to **back** of work. K1, k1 from cable needle.

1/2 Right Cross

Place 2 sts on cable needle and hold to **back** of work. K1, k2 from cable needle.

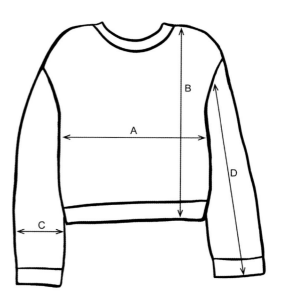

SIZING CHART

Size	XS	S	M	L	XL	XXL	3XL	4XL	5XL
To fit bust	28–30"/ 71–76 cm	32–34"/ 81–86 cm	36–38"/ 91.5–96.5 cm	40–42"/ 101.5–106.5 cm	44–46"/ 111.5–117 cm	48–50"/ 122–127 cm	52–54"/ 132–137 cm	56–58"/ 142–147 cm	60–62"/ 152–158 cm
(A) Width	22.4"/ 57 cm	23.6"/ 60 cm	25.6"/ 65 cm	28.3"/ 72 cm	29.9"/ 76 cm	33.1"/ 84 cm	34.6"/ 88 cm	35.8"/ 91 cm	39"/ 99 cm
(B) Length	17.3"/ 44 cm	18.5"/ 47 cm	19.7"/ 50 cm	20.9"/ 53 cm	22"/ 56 cm	23.2"/ 59 cm	24.4"/ 62 cm	25.6"/ 65 cm	26.8"/ 68 cm
(C) Sleeve Width	7.9"/ 20 cm	7.9"/ 20 cm	7.9"/ 20 cm	9.4"/ 24 cm	9.4"/ 24 cm	9.4"/ 24 cm	11"/ 28 cm	11"/ 28 cm	11.8"/ 30 cm
(D) Sleeve Length	15.7" / 40 cm	17.3" / 44 cm	17.3" / 44 cm	18.5" / 47 cm	18.5" / 47 cm	19.7" / 50 cm	19.7" / 50 cm	19.7" / 50 cm	19.7" / 50 cm

ATTENTION DEFICIT JUMPER PATTERN

BOTTOM

Using US 10 (6 mm) 32- to 40-inch (80- to 100-cm) circular needles and the Alternating Cable Cast On (page 208), CO 120 (128, 136, 152, 160) (176, 184, 192, 208) sts. Join in the round and PM to mark the BOR.

Rounds 1–8: *K1, p1*, rep ** until end of the round.

Switch to US 11 (8 mm) 32- to 40-inch (80- to 100-cm) circular needles.

Setup round: *P1, k1*, rep ** until end of the round.

Restart your row count here. You will now begin working in Alternating Welted Leaf stitch.

Rounds 1–10: Rep corresponding round of the Alternating Welted Leaf Stitch Chart (page 115) until end of the round. *You should repeat the chart 15 (16, 17, 19, 20) (22, 23, 24, 26) times per round.*

> Note: When worked in the round, the chart is read from right to left on every row.

Work 2 rounds of Moss stitch as follows:

Next round: *K1, p1*, rep ** until end of the round.

Next round: *P1, k1*, rep ** until end of the round.

Restart your row count here. You will now begin working in Diamond Mesh stitch.

Sizes XS (-, -, -, -) (-, -, 4XL, -) only

Rounds 1–12: Rep corresponding round of the Diamond Mesh stitch chart (page 116) until end of the round. You should repeat the chart 20 (-, -, -, -) (-, -, 32, -) times per round.

Sizes - (S, -, L, -) (XXL, -, -, -) only

Rounds 1–5: K1, rep corresponding round of the Diamond Mesh stitch chart (page 116) - (21, -, 25, -) (29, -, -, -) times, k1.

Round 6: K all sts.

Rounds 7–11: K1, rep corresponding round of the chart - (21, -, 25, -) (29, -, -, -) times, k1.

Round 12: K all sts.

Sizes - (-, M, -, XL) (-, 3XL, -, 5XL) only

Round 1–4: K1, sl1 wyib, rep corresponding round of the Diamond Mesh stitch chart (page 116) - (-, 22, -, 26) (-, 30, -, 34) times, sl1 wyib, k1.

Round 5: 1/1 RC, rep round 5 of the chart - (-, 22, -, 26) (-, 30, -, 34) times, 1/1 LC.

Round 6: K all sts.

Rounds 7–10: Sl1 wyib, k1, rep corresponding round of the chart - (-, 22, -, 26) (-, 30, -, 34) times, k1, sl1 wyib.

Round 11: 1/1 LC, rep round 11 of the chart - (-, 22, -, 26) (-, 30, -, 34) times, 1/1 RC.

Round 12: K all sts.

Sizes - (-, -, -, -) (XXL, 3XL, 4XL, 5XL) only

Rounds 13–24: Repeat rounds 1–12 (follow instructions for your respective size).

All sizes continue

Work 2 rounds of Moss stitch as follows:

Next round: *K1, p1*, rep ** until end of the round.

Next round: *P1, k1*, rep ** until end of the round.

Restart your row count here. You will now begin working in Slip Stitch Rib stitch.

Sizes XS (-, -, -, -) (-, -, 4XL, -) only

Round 1: *K1, p2*, rep ** until end of the round.

Round 2: *Sl1 wyib, p2*, rep ** until end of the round.

Round 3: *K1, p2*, rep ** until end of the round.

Repeat rounds 2–3 until you have worked them 2 (-, -, -, -) (-, -, 7, -) times **total**. *You should have worked 5 (-, -, -, -) (-, -, 15, -) total rounds in this pattern.*

Round 1: *K1, p2*, rep ** until last 2 sts, k1, p1.

Round 2: *Sl1 wyib, p2*, rep ** until last 2 sts, sl1 wyib, p1.

Round 3: *K1, p2*, rep ** until last 2 sts, k1, p1.

Repeat rounds 2–3 until you have worked them - (3, -, 7, -) (6, -, -, -) times **total**. *You should have worked - (7, -, 15, -) (13, -, -, -) total rounds in this pattern.*

Sizes - (-, M, -, XL) (-, 3XL, -, 5XL) only

Round 1: *K1, p2*, rep ** until last 4 sts, k1, p3.

Round 2: *Sl1 wyib, p2*, rep ** until last 4 sts, sl1 wyib, p3.

Round 3: *K1, p2*, rep ** until last 4 sts, k1, p3.

Repeat rounds 2–3 until you have worked them - (-, 7, -, 9) (-, 5, -, 10) times **total**. *You should have worked - (-, 15, -, 19) (-, 11, -, 21) total rounds in this pattern.*

BACK PANEL

You will now be working flat across **only the first 60 (64, 68, 76, 80) (88, 92, 96, 104) sts.** Leave the remaining stitches on the cord or place them on a stitch holder. *You will come back to them later for the Front Panel.*

Work 2 rows of Moss stitch as follows:

Next row (RS): *K1, p1*, rep ** until end of the row.

Next row (WS): *P1, k1*, rep ** until end of the row.

You will now begin working in Gulls and Garter stitch. Sizes XS (-, M, L, -) (-, 3XL, -, -) will work off Chart A (page 116), and sizes - (S, -, -, XL) (XXL, -, 4XL, 5XL) will work off Chart B (page 117).

> **Note:** When worked flat, odd (RS) rows of each chart are read from right to left, and even (WS) rows are read from left to right.

Setup row (RS): K across.

Restart your row count here.

Sizes XS (-, M, L, -) (-, 3XL, -, -) only

Row 1 (WS): Rep row 1 of Gulls and Garter stitch chart A (page 116) 7 (-, 8, 9, -) (-, 11, -, -) times, k4.

Row 2 (RS): K4, rep row 2 of Gulls and Garter stitch chart A until end of the row.

Row 3: Rep row 3 of Chart A 7 (-, 8, 9, -) (-, 11, -, -) times, k4.

Row 4: K4, rep row 4 of Chart A until end of the row.

Repeat rows 1–4 until you have worked them 4 (-, 4, 5, -) (-, 7, -, -) times **total**. *You should have worked 16 (-, 16, 20, -) (-, 28, -, -) total rows in this pattern.*

Rows 1–5: Work in stockinette stitch, starting with a purl (WS) row.

Row 6: K2, k4b, *k3, k4b*, rep ** until last st, k1.

Rows 7–10: Work in stockinette stitch, starting with a purl (WS) row.

BACK SHOULDERS

You will now make decreases to shape the back neckline, whilst continuing to work in Bubble stitch.

You will start with the back left shoulder, followed by the back right shoulder.

Row 11 (WS): P22 (23, 25, 29, 30) (34, 36, 37, 41) sts, turn.

Sizes XS (-, -, -, XL) (XXL, -, -, -) only
Row 12 (RS): K1, ssk, k3, *k4b, k3*, rep ** until end of the row.

Row 13: P across.

Size S only
Row 12 (RS): K1, ssk, *k4b, k3*, rep ** until end of the row.

Row 13: P across.

Sizes - (-, M, L, -) (-, -, 4XL, 5XL) only
Row 12 (RS): K1, ssk, k2, *k4b, k3*, rep ** until end of the row.

Row 13: P across.

Size 3XL only
Row 12 (RS): K1, ssk, k1, *k4b, k3*, rep ** until end of the row.

Row 13: P across.

Sizes - (S, -, -, XL) (XXL, -, 4XL, 5XL) only
Rows 1–4: Rep corresponding row of Gulls and Garter stitch chart B (page 117) until end of the row. *You should repeat the chart - (8, -, -, 10) (11, -, 12, 13) times per row.* Repeat rows 1–4 until you have worked them - (4, -, -, 5) (5, -, 8, 8) times **total**. *You should have worked - (16, -, -, 20) (20, -, 32, 32) total rows in this pattern.*

All sizes continue
Work 2 rows of Moss stitch as follows:

Next row (WS): *K1, p1*, rep ** until end of the row.

Next row (RS): *P1, k1*, rep ** until end of the row.

Restart your row count here. You will now begin working in Bubble stitch.

All sizes continue

Cut yarn and place these 21 (22, 24, 28, 29) (33, 35, 36, 40) left shoulder sts on a stitch holder. *You will come back to them later for the Shoulder Seams.*

Place the middle 16 (18, 18, 18, 20) (20, 20, 22, 22) sts on another stitch holder. *You will come back to them later for the Neck Trim.*

Reattach yarn on the WS to the remaining 22 (23, 25, 29, 30) (34, 36, 37, 41) right shoulder sts.

Sizes XS (-, -, -, XL) (XXL, -, -, -) only

Row 11 (WS): P across.

Row 12 (RS): K1, *k3, k4b*, rep ** until the last 5 sts, k2, k2tog, k1.

Row 13: P across.

Size S only

Row 11 (WS): P all sts.

Row 12 (RS): K1, *k3, k4b*, rep ** until the last 6 sts, k3, k2tog, k1.

Row 13: P across.

Sizes - (-, M, L, -) (-, -, 4XL, 5XL) only

Row 11 (WS): P across.

Row 12 (RS): K1, *k3, k4b*, rep ** until the last 4 sts, k1, k2tog, k1.

Row 13: P across.

Size 3XL only

Row 11 (WS): P across.

Row 12 (RS): K1, *k3, k4b*, rep ** until the last 3 sts, k2tog, k1.

Row 13: P across.

All sizes continue

Cut yarn and place these 21 (22, 24, 28, 29) (33, 35, 36, 40) right shoulder sts on a stitch holder. *You will come back to them later for the Shoulder Seams.*

FRONT PANEL

You will now be working flat across the 60 (64, 68, 76, 80) (88, 92, 96, 104) sts you left on hold after the Bottom section. Reattach yarn on the RS.

Follow instructions for the Back Panel up until the beginning of the Bubble stitch section.

FRONT SHOULDERS

Restart your row count here. You will now make decreases to shape the front neck, whilst beginning to work in Bubble stitch.

Row 1 (WS): P across.

You will start with the front left (as worn) shoulder, followed by the front right (as worn) shoulder.

Row 2 (RS): K25 (26, 28, 32, 33) (37, 39, 40, 44) sts, turn.

Sizes XS (-, -, -, XL) (XXL, -, -, -) only

Row 3 (WS): P across.

Row 4 (RS): K to last 3 sts, k2tog, k1.

Row 5: P across.

Row 6: K2, *k4b, k3*, rep ** until the last 6 sts, k4b, k2, k2tog, k1.

Row 7: P across.

Rows 8–11: Repeat rows 4–5.

Row 12: K1, *k3, k4b*, rep ** until the last 4 sts, k4.

Row 13: P across.

Size S only

Row 3 (WS): P across.

Row 4 (RS): K to last 3 sts, k2tog, k1.

Row 5: P across.

Row 6: K2, *k4b, k3* rep ** until the last 3 sts, k2tog, k1.

Row 7: P across.

Rows 8–11: Repeat rows 4–5.

Row 12: K1, *k3, k4b* rep ** until the last st, k1.

Row 13: P across.

Sizes - (-, M, L, -) (-, -, 4XL, 5XL) only

Row 3 (WS): P across.

Row 4 (RS): K to last 3 sts, k2tog, k1.

Row 5: P across.

Row 6: K2, *k4b, k3*, rep ** until last 5 sts, k4b, k1, k2tog, k1.

Row 7: P across.

Rows 8–11: Repeat rows 4–5.

Row 12: K1, *k3, k4b*, rep ** until the last 3 sts, k3.

Row 13: P across.

Size 3XL only

Row 3 (WS): P across.

Row 4 (RS): K to last 3 sts, k2tog, k1.

Row 5: P across.

Row 6: K2, *k4b, k3*, rep ** until the last 4 sts, k4b, k2tog, k1.

Row 7: P across.

Rows 8–11: Repeat rows 4–5.

Row 12: K1, *k3, k4b*, rep ** until the last 2 sts, k2.

Row 13: P across.

All sizes continue

Cut yarn and place these 21 (22, 24, 28, 29) (33, 35, 36, 40) left shoulder sts on a stitch holder. *You will come back to them later for the Shoulder Seams.*

Place the middle 10 (12, 12, 12, 14) (14, 14, 16, 16) sts on another stitch holder. *You will come back to them later for the Neck Trim.*

Reattach yarn on the RS to the remaining 25 (26, 28, 32, 33) (37, 39, 40, 44) right shoulder sts.

Sizes XS (-, -, -, XL) (XXL, -, -, -) only

Row 2 (RS): K across.

Row 3 (WS): P across.

Row 4: K1, ssk, k to the end of the row.

Row 5: P across.

Row 6: K1, ssk, *k3, k4b*, rep ** until the last st, k1.

Row 7: P across.

Rows 8–11: Repeat rows 4–5.

Row 12: K5, *k4b, k3*, rep ** until the end of the row.

Row 13: P across.

Size S only

Row 2 (RS): K across.

Row 3 (WS): P across.

Row 4: K1, ssk, k to the end of the row.

Row 5: P across.

Row 6: K1, ssk, *k4b, k3*, rep ** until the last 2 sts, k4b, k1.

Row 7: P across.

Rows 8–11: Repeat rows 4–5.

Row 12: K2, *k4b, k3*, rep ** until the end of the row.

Row 13: P across.

Sizes - (-, M, L, -) (-, -, 4XL, 5XL) only

Row 2 (RS): K across.

Row 3 (WS): P across.

Row 4: K1, ssk, k to the end of the row.

Row 5: P across.

Row 6: K1, ssk, k2, *k4b, k3*, rep ** until the last 2 sts, k4b, k1.

Row 7: P across.

Rows 8–11: Repeat rows 4–5.

Row 12: K1, *k3, k4b*, rep ** until the last 3 sts, k3.

Row 13: P across.

Size 3XL only

Row 2 (RS): K across.

Row 3 (WS): P across.

Row 4: K1, ssk, k to the end of the row.

Row 5: P across.

Row 6: K1, ssk, k1, *k4b, k3*, rep ** until the last 2 sts, k4b, k1.

Row 7: P across.

Rows 8–11: Repeat rows 4–5.

Row 12: *K3, k4b*, rep ** until the last 3 sts, k3.

Row 13: P across.

All sizes continue

Leave these 21 (22, 24, 28, 29) (33, 35, 36, 40) sts on your needle and do not cut the yarn.

SHOULDER SEAMS

You will now be using the Three Needle Bind Off method (page 207) to join the shoulder seams.

1. Turn your work inside out and place the RS of your front and back panels together.

2. Your front right (as worn) shoulder stitches should still be on your needle. Place the corresponding 21 (22, 24, 28, 29) (33, 35, 36, 40) sts left on hold for the back right shoulder onto the other needle. Make sure both needles are facing the same direction.

3. Insert a third needle (US 11 [8 mm] or smaller) knitwise into the first st of the panel that is facing you, then insert that same needle knitwise into the corresponding st of the other panel.

4. Continue, following the instructions for the Three Needle Bind Off method (page 207).

5. Repeat all steps for the other shoulder, using the corresponding front left and back left shoulder stitches left on hold.

NECK TRIM

Flip your work so that the RS are facing out and your shoulder seams are invisible.

Using US 10 (6 mm) 24-inch (60-cm) circular needles, pick up stitches in the following fashion:

1. Pick up 4 sts along the side of the back right shoulder.

2. Pick up and knit the 16 (18, 18, 18, 20) (20, 20, 22, 22) live sts from the stitch holder at the back neck.

3. Pick up 4 sts along the side of the back left shoulder.

4. Pick up 10 sts along the side of the front left (as worn) shoulder.

5. Pick up and knit the 10 (12, 12, 12, 14) (14, 14, 16, 16) live sts from the stitch holder at the front neck.

6. Pick up 10 sts along the side of the front right (as worn) shoulder.

You should now have 54 (58, 58, 58, 62) (62, 62, 66, 66) sts. PM to mark the BOR.

Rounds 1–6: *K1, p1*, rep ** until end of the round.

BO loosely in 1x1 rib pattern.

SLEEVES

Using US 11 (8 mm) 24-inch (60-cm) circular needles, starting at the underarm point, pick up 48 (48, 48, 56, 56) (56, 64, 64, 64) sts, evenly spaced, around the armhole. PM to mark the BOR.

You will start by working in Bubble stitch.

Rounds 1–12: Rep corresponding round of the Bubble stitch chart (page 117) until end of the round. *You should repeat the chart 12 (12, 12, 14, 14) (14, 16, 16, 16) times per round.*

Note: When worked in the round, the chart is read from right to left on every row.

Work 2 rounds of Moss stitch as follows:

Next round: *K1, p1*, rep ** until end of the round.

Next round: *P1, k1*, rep ** until end of the round.

Restart your row count here. You will now be working in Gulls and Garter stitch.

Rounds 1–4: Rep corresponding round of the Gulls and Garter stitch chart A on page 116 (written instructions below) until end of round. *You should repeat the chart 6 (6, 6, 7, 7) (7, 8, 8, 8) times per round.*

Round 1: K5, p3.

Round 2: Sl5 wyif, k3.

Round 3: K5, p3.

Round 4: K2, k1 uls, k5.

Repeat rounds 1–4 until you have worked them 3 (4, 4, 4, 4) (5, 5, 5, 5) times total. *You should have worked 12 (16, 16, 16, 16) (20, 20, 20, 20) total rounds in this pattern.*

Work 2 rounds of Moss stitch as follows:

Next round: *K1, p1*, rep ** until end of the round.

Next round: *P1, k1*, rep ** until end of the round.

Restart your row count here. You will now be working in Slip Stitch Rib stitch.

Round 1: *K1, p2*, rep ** until end of the round.

Round 2: *Sl1 wyib, p2*, rep ** until end of the round.

Round 3: *K1, p2*, rep ** until end of the round.

Repeat rounds 2–3 until you have worked them 3 (3, 3, -, -) (-, -, -, -) times **total**. *You should have worked 7 (7, 7, -, -) (-, -, -, -) total rounds in this pattern.*

Round 1: *K1, p2*, rep ** until last 2 sts, k1, p1.

Round 2: *Sl1 wyib, p2*, rep ** until last 2 sts, sl1, p1.

Round 3: *K1, p2*, rep ** until last 2 sts, k1, p1.

Repeat rounds 2–3 until you have worked them - (-, -, 3, 3) (4, -, -, -) times **total**. *You should have worked - (-, -, 7, 7) (9, -, -, -) total rounds in this pattern.*

Round 1: *K1, p2*, rep ** until last 4 sts, k1, p3.

Round 2: *Sl1 wyib, p2*, rep ** until last 4 sts, sl1, p3.

Round 3: *K1, p2*, rep ** until last 4 sts, k1, p3.

Repeat rounds 2–3 until you have worked them - (-, -, -, -) (-, 4, 4, 4) times **total**. *You should have worked - (-, -, -, -) (-, 9, 9, 9) total rounds in this pattern.*

All sizes continue

Work 2 rounds of Moss stitch as follows:

Next round: *K1, p1*, rep ** until end of the round.

Next round: *P1, k1*, rep ** until end of the round.

Restart your row count here. You will now begin working in Diamond Mesh stitch.

Rounds 1–12: Rep corresponding round of the Diamond Mesh stitch chart (page 116) until end of round. *You should repeat the chart 8 (8, 8, -, -) (-, -, -, -) times per round.*

Rounds 1–5: K1, rep corresponding round of the Diamond Mesh stitch chart (page 116) - (-, -, 9, 9) (9, -, -, -) times, k1.

Round 6: K across.

Rounds 7–11: K1, rep corresponding round of the chart - (-, -, 9, 9) (9, -, -, -) times, k1.

Round 12: K across.

Rounds 1–4: K1, sl1 wyib, rep corresponding round of the Diamond Mesh stitch chart (page 116) - (-, -, -, -) (-, 10, 10, 10) times, sl1 wyib, k1.

Round 5: 1/1 RC, rep corresponding round of the chart - (-, -, -, -) (-, 10, 10, 10) times, 1/1 LC.

Round 6: K across.

Rounds 7–10: Sl1 wyib, k1, rep corresponding round of the chart - (-, -, -, -) (-, 10, 10, 10) times, k1, sl1 wyib.

Round 11: 1/1 LC, rep corresponding round of the chart - (-, -, -, -) (-, 10, 10, 10) times, 1/1 RC.

Round 12: K across.

All sizes continue

Work 2 rounds of Moss stitch as follows:

Next round: *K1, p1*, rep ** until end of the round.

Next round: *P1, k1*, rep ** until end of the round.

Restart your row count here. You will now begin working in Alternating Welted Leaf stitch.

Rounds 1–10: Rep corresponding round of the Alternating Welted Leaf stitch chart (page 115) until end of round. *You should repeat the chart 6 (6, 6, 7, 7) (7, 8, 8, 8) times per round.*

Work 2 rounds of Moss stitch as follows:

Next round: *K1, p1*, rep ** until end of the round.

Next round: *P1, k1*, rep ** until end of the round.

You will now make decreases before working the sleeve cuffs.

Next round: *K2tog, k2*, rep ** until end of the round.

You should now have 36 (36, 36, 42, 42) (42, 48, 48, 48) sts.

Switch to US 10 (6 mm) 16-inch (40-cm) circular needles or DPNs *(or use Magic Loop method [page 207] if using longer cord).*

Next 7 rounds: *K1, p1*, rep ** until end of the round.

BO in 1x1 rib pattern.

FINISHING

Weave in any remaining loose ends.

Wash and block (see Blocking 101 [page 216] or use your preferred blocking method).

You may wish to add a thin elastic thread to your neck trim. This ensures the neck trim keeps its shape and doesn't stretch with wear. Follow the instructions for Adding Elastic (page 213).

ALTERNATING WELTED LEAF STITCH PATTERN

Rounds 1–2: K across.

Round 3: K4, p4.

Round 4: P1, k4, p3.

Round 5: P2, k4, p2.

Round 6: P3, k4, p1.

Round 7: K3, p4, k1.

Round 8: K2, p4, k2.

Round 9: K1, p4, k3.

Round 10: P4, k4.

Legend	
☐	RS: Knit WS: Purl
⊡	RS: Purl WS: Knit
1/2 RC symbol	1/2 RC
1/2 LC symbol	1/2 LC
V	Sl wyib
⅄	Sl wyif
⋀	K1 uls
⟨4⟩	K4b

ALTERNATING WELTED LEAF STITCH CHART

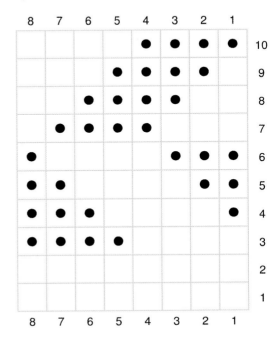

DIAMOND MESH STITCH CHART

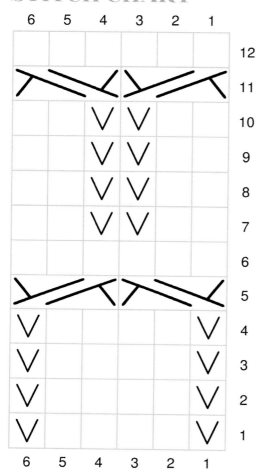

GULLS AND GARTER STITCH CHART A

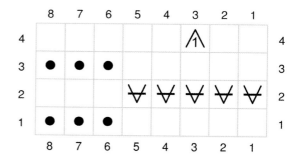

GULLS AND GARTER STITCH CHART A PATTERN WORKED FLAT

Row 1 (WS): K3, p5.

Row 2 (RS): Sl5 wyif, k3.

Row 3: K3, p5.

Row 4: K2, k1 uls, k5.

DIAMOND MESH STITCH CHART PATTERN

Rounds 1–4: Sl1 wyib, k4, sl1 wyib.

Round 5: 1/2 LC, 1/2 RC.

Round 6: K across.

Rounds 7–10: K2, sl2 wyib, k2.

Round 11: 1/2 RC, 1/2 LC.

Round 12: K across.

GULLS AND GARTER STITCH CHART B

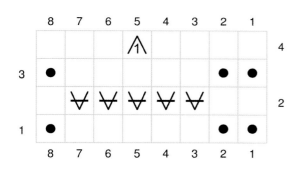

GULLS AND GARTER STITCH CHART B PATTERN

Row 1 (WS): K1, p5, k2.

Row 2 (RS): K2, sl5 wyif, k1.

Row 3: K1, p5, k2.

Row 4: K4, k1 uls, k3.

BUBBLE STITCH CHART

Rounds 1–5: K across.

Round 6: K3, k4b.

Rounds 7–11: K across.

Round 12: K1, k4b, k2.

A Splash of Color

The patterns in this chapter showcase a multitude of simple yet effective colorwork techniques including intarsia, duplicate stitch and more that are sure to get your creative juices flowing and will hopefully inspire you to add a splash of color into your future projects.

I first ventured into colorwork during the early days of the pandemic, and it was at this point that my approach to knitting transformed completely as I began to view my makes as wearable art. Even though I wasn't used to wearing an abundance of color, something was telling me I needed to push beyond my comfort zone and allow my creativity to run wild. It wasn't long before my closet was overflowing with bright-colored knits, and I have truly never looked back.

My goal with this chapter was to create a collection of wearable colorwork designs that are both easy and fun to knit, as these were the types of projects that made me fall in love with colorwork all those years ago. When knitting these patterns, I encourage you to embrace your personal style, but also to not be afraid to take some risks and step outside the confines of your typical color palette. These patterns are perfect for mixing and matching colors to create a handmade masterpiece that is totally unique to you.

Somewhere Over the Raglan Jumper

Worked entirely in the round, the Somewhere Over the Raglan Jumper embraces the magic of a quick, seamless colorwork project. It's like clicking your heels together and finding yourself in a knitting paradise! With colors changing every second row, you'll never get tired, and if you're new to raglan knitting, this pattern will guide you along the yellow brick road to success. Follow your own personal rainbow and choose the colors that speak to you. From muted pastels to electric neons, the options are as limitless as your imagination. With its folded collar for extra warmth and its delightful stripes, this wonderfully whimsical design will have you feeling like a true knitting wizard. Crafted with bulky yarn and designed to have a cropped fit, the Somewhere Over the Raglan Jumper will be taking shape faster than you can say, "There's no place like home."

Construction Notes

This seamless striped jumper is worked entirely in the round in stockinette stitch from the top down. You will first work the folded neck trim before working the yoke. You will then divide the body from the sleeves at the underarm point and continue to work the body in the round before knitting the sleeves in the round. You will be changing colors every second row throughout all stockinette sections. To avoid weaving in so many ends, follow the instructions for the Weavin' Stephen technique (page 212) to learn how to weave in ends as you go. Follow the instructions for Jogless Stripes (page 211) to avoid jogs when knitting your stripes in the round.

Skill Level

Advanced Beginner

Sizing

XS (S, M, L, XL) (XXL, 3XL, 4XL, 5XL)

Finished bust: 41 (45.6, 48.8, 52.8, 57.4) (62.2, 66.2, 69.2, 74)" / 104 (116, 124, 134, 146) (158, 168, 176, 188) cm, blocked

Recommended ease: This jumper is designed with 11.8–14.2 inches / 30–36 cm of positive ease

Sample shown is knit in Size S.

MATERIALS

Yarn

Bulky weight, Wool and the Gang, Alpachino Merino (60% Merino Wool, 40% Baby Alpaca), 110 yds (100 m) per 100-g skein, shown in Cameo Rose (A), Lilac Punch (B), Bubblegum Pink (C), Chalk Yellow (D) and Pink Sherbet (E) colorways

Any bulky weight yarn can be used for this pattern as long as it matches gauge. A good substitute would be Drops, Andes or Wool and Works, Chunky Merino.

Yardage/Meterage

Yarn estimates are approximate and refer specifically to the recommended yarn.

2 (2, 2, 3, 3) (3, 3, 3, 3) skeins of Color A

1 (1, 2, 2, 2) (2, 2, 2, 2) skein(s) of Color B

1 (2, 2, 2, 2) (2, 2,2, 2) skein(s) of Color C

1 (1, 2, 2, 2) (2, 3, 3, 3) skein(s) of Color D

1 (2, 2, 2, 2) (2, 3, 3, 3) skein(s) of Color E

Needles

For body: US 11 (8 mm) 32- to 40-inch (80- to 100-cm) circular needle

For sleeves: US 11 (8 mm) 24-inch (60-cm) circular needle

For neckline and sleeve cuffs: US 10 (6 mm) 16- to 24-inch (40- to 60-cm) circular needle

For bottom ribbing: US 10 (6 mm) 32- to 40-inch (80- to 100-cm) circular needle

Notions

Scrap yarn

(Optional) US G/6–J/10 (4–6 mm) crochet hook (if using crocheted Provisional Cast On method)

Additional circular needle for folded neckline

Stitch markers

Tapestry needle

Scissors

GAUGE

10 sts x 15-16 rows = 4 inches (10 cm) in stockinette stitch using larger needle (blocked)

ABBREVIATIONS

1x1 rib(bing) - *Knit 1, purl 1*

BO - Bind off

BOR - Beginning of round

K - Knit

K2tog - Knit 2 stitches together

M1L - Make 1 left

M1R - Make 1 right

P - Purl

PM - Place marker

Rep - Repeat

RM - Remove marker

SM - Slip marker

St(s) - Stitch(es)

SIZING CHART

Size	XS	S	M	L	XL	XXL	3XL	4XL	5XL
To fit bust	28–30"/ 71–76 cm	32–34"/ 81–86 cm	36–38"/ 91.5– 96.5 cm	40–42"/ 101.5– 106.5 cm	44–46"/ 111.5– 117 cm	48–50"/ 122–127 cm	52–54"/ 132–137 cm	56–58"/ 142–147 cm	60–62"/ 152–158 cm
(A) Width	20.5"/ 52 cm	22.8"/ 58 cm	24.4"/ 62 cm	26.4"/ 67 cm	28.7"/ 73 cm	31.1"/ 79 cm	33.1"/ 84 cm	34.6"/ 88 cm	37"/ 94 cm
(B) Length	14.2"/ 36 cm	15"/ 38 cm	15.7"/ 40 cm	16.5"/ 42 cm	17.7"/ 45 cm	19"/ 48 cm	20.1"/ 51 cm	21.3"/ 54 cm	22.8"/ 58 cm
(C) Sleeve Width	7.9"/ 20 cm	7.9"/ 20 cm	8.7"/ 22 cm	9.4"/ 24 cm	9.4"/ 24 cm	10.2"/ 26 cm	11"/ 28 cm	11"/ 28 cm	11.8"/ 30 cm
(D) Sleeve Length	17.3"/ 44 cm	18.5"/ 47 cm	18.5"/ 47 cm	18.5"/ 47 cm	18.5"/ 47 cm	19.7"/ 50 cm	19.7"/ 50 cm	19.7"/ 50 cm	19.7"/ 50 cm

SPECIAL TECHNIQUES

Provisional Cast On (https://www.jaimecreates.me/book/tutorials)

Weavin' Stephen (page 212)

Jogless Stripes (page 211)

Tubular Bind Off (page 209)

Magic Loop method (page 207)

Backwards Loop Cast On (page 212)

Adding Elastic (page 213)

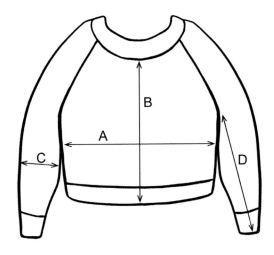

NECK TRIM

Using scrap yarn in a similar weight and contrasting color to your Color A, provisionally cast on 60 (60, 60, 64, 64) (64, 68, 68, 68) sts. *For a video tutorial on the Provisional Cast-On, visit the following page on my site: https://www.jaimecreates. me/book/tutorials.*

Using US 10 (6 mm) 16- to 24-inch (40- to 60-cm) circular needles and Color A, knit all provisionally cast on stitches. Join in the round and PM to mark the BOR.

Rounds 1–16: *K1, p1*, rep ** until end of the round.

You will now create and secure the foldover neckline hem.

Place your provisionally cast on stitches onto an additional circular needle. Fold your work in half so that your working needle with your live stitches and your additional needle with the provisionally cast on stitches are aligned, with the working needle facing you.

Knit 1 live st from your working needle together with 1 st from the additional needle, as if you were working a k2tog. Repeat this until you reach the BOR. You should now have all your stitches on your US 10 (6 mm) circular needle, and your neckline should be completely sealed shut.

YOKE

Switch to Color B and your US 11 (8 mm) 32- to 40-inch (80- to 100-cm) circular needle. *You may need to use the Magic Loop method (page 207) for the first few rounds.*

You will now place 3 additional markers to divide your stitches into 4 sections (front, sleeve 1, back, sleeve 2). Ensure your BOR marker can be easily distinguished from the other markers.

Setup round: K20 (20, 20, 21, 21) (21, 22, 22, 22), **PM**, k10 (10, 10, 11, 11) (11, 12, 12, 12), **PM**, k20 (20, 20, 21, 21) (21, 22, 22, 22), **PM**, k10 (10, 10, 11, 11) (11, 12, 12, 12).

Increase round: *K1, M1L, k to 1 st before marker, M1R, k1, SM*, rep ** until end of the round.

Switch to your next color (in this case it is Color C).

Next round: K all sts, slipping markers as they appear.

Repeat the last 2 rounds, taking care to switch colors every 2nd round, until you have worked 26 (28, 32, 34, 36) (38, 40, 40, 44) rounds **total**, including the setup round. *You will end after an increase round.*

You should now have a total of 164 (172, 188, 200, 208) (216, 228, 228, 244) sts, with 46 (48, 52, 55, 57) (59, 62, 62, 66) sts for the front and back sections, and 36 (38, 42, 45, 47) (49, 52, 52, 56) sts for each sleeve.

BODY

You will now divide the sleeves from the body. *Remember to switch colors before working this next round.*

Next round: RM, place the *last* 36 (38, 42, 45, 47) (49, 52, 52, 56) sts from the previous round on scrap yarn, CO 3 (5, 5, 6, 8) (10, 11, 13, 14) new sts using the Long Tail Cast On, k to marker, RM, place the next 36 (38, 42, 45, 47) (49, 52, 52, 56) sts on scrap yarn, RM, CO 6 (10, 10, 12, 16) (20, 22, 26, 28) new sts using the Backwards Loop Cast On (page 212), k to marker, RM, CO 3 (5, 5, 6, 8) (10, 11, 13, 14) new sts using the Backwards Loop Cast On, PM to mark the BOR.

You should now have 104 (116, 124, 134, 146) (158, 168, 176, 188) sts on your needles and two sections of 36 (38, 42, 45, 47) (49, 52, 52, 56) sts on scrap yarn.

Work 21 (23, 23, 23, 26) (28, 31, 36, 38) rounds in stockinette stitch, taking care to switch colors every 2nd round.

> **Note:** If you would like to add or subtract length to/from your jumper, do so here, keeping in mind that the bottom ribbing will add approximately 1.6 inches (4 cm).

Switch to your US 10 (6 mm) 32- to 40-inch (80- to 100-cm) circular needle. Do not switch colors before working the bottom ribbing.

Next 7 rounds: *K1, p1*, rep ** until end of the round.

BO all sts using the Tubular Bind Off (page 209).

SLEEVES

Place one of the sections of 36 (38, 42, 45, 47) (49, 52, 52, 56) sts you left on scrap yarn onto your US 11 (8 mm) 24-inch (60-cm) circular needle.

Using your next color, starting at the mid-underarm point, pick up 3 (5, 5, 6, 8) (10, 11, 13, 14) sts, k the next 36 (38, 42, 45, 47) (49, 52, 52, 56) sts, pick up 3 (5, 5, 6, 8) (10, 11, 13, 14) sts, PM to mark the BOR.

You should now have 42 (48, 52, 57, 63) (69, 74, 78, 84) sts.

Size XS proceed to "All sizes continue."

Sizes - (S, M, L, XL) (-, 3XL, 4XL, -) only

Next round: K1, k2tog, k to last 3 sts, ssk, k1.

Next round: K across.

Repeat the last 2 rounds until you have worked them - (3, 3, 4, 5) (-, 1, 1, -) time(s) **total** (meaning – (6, 6, 8, 10) (-, 2, 2, -) total rounds).

Sizes - (S, M, L, -) (-, -, -, -) proceed to "All sizes continue."

Sizes - (-, -, -, XL) (XXL, 3XL, 4XL, 5XL) only

Next round: K1, k2tog, k1, k2tog, k to last 6 sts, ssk, k1, ssk, k1.

Next round: K across.

Repeat the last 2 rounds until you have worked them - (-, -, -, 1) (4, 4, 5, 6) time(s) **total** (meaning – (-, -, -, 2) (8, 8, 10, 12) total rounds).

Proceed to "All sizes continue."

All sizes continue

You should now have 42 (42, 46, 49, 49) (53, 56, 56, 60) sts.

Work in stockinette stitch, taking care to switch colors every 2nd row, until your sleeve measures approximately 15.7 (16.9, 16.9, 16.9 16.9) (18.1, 18.1, 18.1, 18.1) inches / 40 (43, 43, 43, 43) (46, 46, 46, 46) cm from the underarm, or to desired length. *Keep in mind the sleeve cuff will add approximately 1.6 inches (4 cm). Make note of how many total rows you work so that you can work your second sleeve to match.*

You will now make decreases for the sleeve cuff.

Switch to your next color (even if you are not up to a color change row).

Sizes XS (S, M, -, -) (-, -, -, -) only

Next round: K1, *k2tog*, rep ** until last st, k1.

Sizes - (-, -, L, XL) (XXL, -, -, -) only

Next round: *K2tog*, rep until last st, k1.

Sizes - (-, -, -, -) (-, 3XL, 4XL, 5XL) only

Next round: *K2tog*, rep ** until end of the round.

All sizes continue

You should now have 22 (22, 24, 25, 25) (27, 28, 28, 30) sts.

Switch to US 10 (6 mm) 16- to 24-inch (40- to 60-cm) circular needle. *You may need to use the Magic Loop method (page 207) to work the sleeve cuffs.*

Sizes - (-, -, L, XL) (XXL, -, -, -) only

Next round: K2tog, p1, *k1, p1*, rep ** until end of the round.

You should now have - (-, -, 24, 24) (26, -, -, -) sts.

All sizes continue

Next 7 (7, 7, 6, 6) (6, 7, 7, 7) rounds: *K1, p1*, rep ** until end of the round.

BO all sts using the Tubular Bind Off (page 209).

Repeat for the second sleeve.

FINISHING

Weave in any remaining loose ends.

Wash and block (see Blocking 101 [page 216] or use your preferred blocking method).

You may wish to add a thin elastic thread to your neck trim. This ensures the neck trim keeps its shape and doesn't stretch with wear. Follow the instructions for Adding Elastic (page 213).

Kaleidoscope Cardigan

The Kaleidoscope Cardigan is a beginner-friendly pattern with a basic construction that offers an opportunity to explore the art of blending multiple strands of yarn, which creates a breathtaking marbled effect reminiscent of a watercolor painting. The best part? Each Kaleidoscope Cardigan you knit will be a totally unique creation, tailored to your personal color palette. You'll be amazed at how quickly your project takes shape just by holding three strands of worsted weight yarn together. The basic stockinette stitch allows the colors to take center stage, showcasing the vibrant interplay of shades and hues. Whether you opt for a harmonious combination or a bold contrast, the Kaleidoscope Cardigan guarantees an awe-inspiring result that will turn heads and keep you cozy all season long.

Construction Notes

This seamless cardigan is worked in stockinette stitch from the bottom up with three strands of worsted weight yarn held together. You will first work the bottom section of the cardigan flat, before splitting at the underarm point to work the front right panel, then the back panel, followed by the front left panel. You will join the shoulder seams to create the armholes using the Three Needle Bind Off method (page 207). The sleeves are worked in the round by picking up stitches along the armhole edges. You will finish by working the button band flat by picking up stitches along the inside edges. Instructions on how to adjust the body and sleeve length of your cardigan are included.

Skill Level

Confident Beginner

Sizing

XS (S, M, L, XL) (XXL, 3XL, 4XL, 5XL)

Finished bust: 41 (44.8, 48.8, 52.8, 56.6) (60.6, 64.6, 68.6, 73.2)" / 104 (114, 124, 134, 144) (154, 164, 174, 186) cm, blocked

Recommended ease: This cardigan is designed with approximately 11–13 inches / 28–33 cm of positive ease

Sample shown is knit in Size S.

MATERIALS

Yarn

Worsted weight, Malabrigo, Rios (100% Superwash Merino Wool), 210 yds (192 m) per 100-g skein, **held triple**, shown in Water Green, Aquamarine and Almond Blossom colorways

Any worsted weight yarn (held triple) can be used for this pattern as long as it matches gauge.

You will need to hold three strands together, each in a different color.

Yardage/Meterage

1508 (1705, 1890, 2188, 2385) (2520, 2941, 3259, 3533) yds / 1379 (1559, 1728, 2001, 2181) (2304, 2689, 2980, 3231) m **total**

You will need approximately 503 (568, 630, 729, 795) (840, 980, 1086, 1178) yds / 460 (520, 576, 667, 727) (768, 896, 993, 1077) m of each color

Needles

For body: US 13 (9 mm), 32- to 40-inch (80- to 100-cm) circular needle

For sleeves: US 13 (9 mm), 24- to 32-inch (60- to 80-cm) circular needle

For bottom ribbing and button band: US 10.5* (7 mm), 32- to 40-inch (80- to 100-cm) circular needle

For sleeve cuffs: US 10.5* (7 mm), 24-inch (60-cm) circular needle or DPNs

*There is no direct US equivalent to 7 mm needles; US 10.5 (6.5 mm) is the closest size

Notions

Buttons (can be 0.6" / 16 mm or larger) x 5 (5, 5, 6, 6) (6, 7, 7, 7)

Stitch marker

Tapestry needle

Scissors

Stitch holders

GAUGE

9.5 sts x 16 rows = 4 inches (10 cm) in stockinette stitch using larger needle (blocked)

ABBREVIATIONS

1x1 rib(bing) - *Knit 1, purl 1*

BO - Bind off

BOR - Beginning of round

CO - Cast on

K - Knit

K2tog - Knit 2 stitches together

P - Purl

PM - Place marker

Rep - Repeat

RS - Right side

Ssk - Slip, slip, knit 2 stitches together through the back loops

St(s) - Stitch(es)

WS - Wrong side

SIZING CHART

Size	XS	S	M	L	XL	XXL	3XL	4XL	5XL
To fit bust	28–30"/ 71–76 cm	32–34"/ 81–86 cm	36–38"/ 91.5–96.5 cm	40–42"/ 101.5–106.5 cm	44–46"/ 111.5–117 cm	48–50"/ 122–127 cm	52–54"/ 132–137 cm	56–58"/ 142–147 cm	60–62"/ 152–158 cm
(A) Width	20.5"/ 52 cm	22.4"/ 57 cm	24.4"/ 62 cm	26.4"/ 67 cm	28.3"/ 72 cm	30.3"/ 77 cm	32.3"/ 82 cm	34.3"/ 87 cm	36.6"/ 93 cm
(B) Length	16.5"/ 42 cm	17.3"/ 44 cm	18.1"/ 46 cm	18.9"/ 48 cm	20.1"/ 51 cm	20.9"/ 53 cm	21.7"/ 55 cm	22.8"/ 58 cm	23.6"/ 60 cm
(C) Sleeve Width	7.9"/ 20 cm	7.9"/ 20 cm	7.9"/ 20 cm	9.4"/ 24 cm	9.4"/ 24 cm	9.4"/ 24 cm	11"/ 28 cm	11"/ 28 cm	11"/ 28 cm
(D) Sleeve Length	15"/ 38 cm	16.1"/ 41 cm	16.1"/ 41 cm	16.1"/ 41 cm	16.1"/ 41 cm	17.3"/ 44 cm	17.3"/ 44 cm	17.3"/ 44 cm	17.3"/ 44 cm

SPECIAL TECHNIQUES

Alternating Cable Cast On (page 208)

Magic Loop method (page 207)

Three Needle Bind Off (page 207)

Tubular Bind Off (page 209)

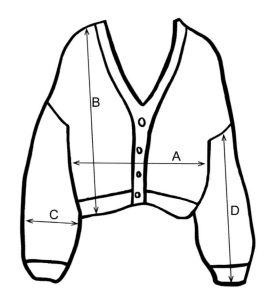

BOTTOM

Using US 10.5* (7 mm) 32- to 40-inch (80- to 100-cm) circular needles and the Alternating Cable Cast On (page 208), CO 93 (104, 115, 124, 130) (139, 150, 157, 168) sts. Remember that you are using 3 strands of worsted weight yarn, held together.

Sizes XS (-, M, -, -) (XXL, -, 4XL, -) only

Row 1 (RS): *P1, k1*, rep ** until last st, p1.

Row 2 (WS): *K1, p1*, rep ** until last st, k1.

Rows 3–8: Repeat rows 1–2.

Sizes - (S, -, L, XL) (-, 3XL, -, 5XL) only

Row 1 (RS): *K1, p1*, rep ** until end of the row.

Rows 2–8: Repeat row 1.

All sizes continue

Switch to US 13 (9 mm) 32- to 40-inch (80- to 100-cm) circular needles. Restart your row count here.

Starting with a RS (knit) row, work 28 (32, 36, 34, 38) (40, 38, 42, 46) rows in stockinette stitch. *You should end after a WS row.*

> **Note:** If you would like to add length to your cardigan, do so here, but make sure you end after a WS row.

FRONT RIGHT PANEL

You will now be working across **only the first 22 (25, 28, 30, 31) (33, 36, 37, 40) sts.** Leave the remaining stitches on the cord or place them on a stitch holder. *You will come back to them later for the Back and Front Left Panels.*

Starting with a RS row, work 2 rows in stockinette stitch.

You will now make decreases to shape the front right (as worn) neckline.

Row 1 (RS): K1, ssk, k to end of the row.

Row 2 (WS): P across.

Repeat rows 1–2 until you have worked them 5 (5, 5, 6, 6) (6, 7, 7, 7) times **total** (meaning 10 (10, 10, 12, 12) (12, 14, 14, 14) total rows). You should end after a WS row and have 17 (20, 23, 24, 25) (27, 29, 30, 33) sts.

Starting with a RS row, work 18 (18, 18, 22, 22) (22, 26, 26, 26) straight rows in stockinette stitch with no decreases. *You should end after a WS row.*

Cut yarn and place these 17 (20, 23, 24, 25) (27, 29, 30, 33) sts on a stitch holder. *You will come back to them later for the Shoulder Seams.*

BACK PANEL

You will now be working across only the next 49 (54, 59, 64, 68) (73, 78, 83, 88) sts. Leave the remaining stitches on the cord or place them on a stitch holder. *You will come back to them later for the Front Left Panel.* Reattach yarn on the RS.

Starting with a RS row, work 29 (29, 29, 35, 35) (35, 41, 41, 41) rows in stockinette stitch. *You should end after a RS row.*

BACK SHOULDERS

Next row (WS): P17 (20, 23, 24, 25) (27, 29, 30, 33), BO 15 (14, 13, 16, 18) (19, 20, 23, 22), p to end of the row.

Cut yarn and place each set of 17 (20, 23, 24, 25) (27, 29, 30, 33) back shoulder sts on separate stitch holders. *You will come back to them later for the Shoulder Seams.*

FRONT LEFT PANEL

Reattach yarn on the RS to the remaining 22 (25, 28, 30, 31) (33, 36, 37, 40) sts.

Starting with a RS row, work 2 rows in stockinette stitch.

You will now make decreases to shape the front left (as worn) neckline.

Row 1 (RS): K to last 3 sts, k2tog, k1.

Row 2 (WS): P across.

Repeat rows 1–2 until you have worked them 5 (5, 5, 6, 6) (6, 7, 7, 7) times **total** (meaning 10 (10, 10, 12, 12) (12, 14, 14, 14) total rows). You should end after a WS row and have 17 (20, 23, 24, 25) (27, 29, 30, 33) sts.

Starting on a RS row, work 18 (18, 18, 22, 22) (22, 26, 26, 26) straight rows in stockinette stitch with no decreases. *You should end after a WS row.*

Leave these 17 (20, 23, 24, 25) (27, 29, 30, 33) sts on your needle and do not cut the yarn. *Proceed to "Shoulder Seams."*

SHOULDER SEAMS

You will now be using the Three Needle Bind Off method (page 207) to join the shoulder seams.

1. Place the RS of your front and back panels together.

2. Your front left (as worn) shoulder stitches should still be on your needle. Place the corresponding 17 (20, 23, 24, 25) (27, 29, 30, 33) sts left on hold for the back left shoulder onto the other needle. Make sure both needles are facing the same direction.

3. Insert a third needle (US 13 [9 mm] or smaller) knitwise into the first st of the panel that is facing you, then insert that same needle knitwise into the corresponding st of the other panel.

4. Continue, following the instructions for the Three Needle Bind Off method (page 207).

5. Repeat all steps for the other shoulder, using the corresponding front left and back left shoulder stitches left on hold.

BUTTON BAND

Using US 10.5* (7 mm) 32- to 40-inch (80- to 100-cm) circular needles, starting from the bottom of the Front Right (as worn) Panel, working up and across the back neckline, then back down the Front Left (as worn) Panel, pick up stitches in the following pattern: *Pick up 4 sts, skip 1 st*, ensuring you end up with an even number of stitches.

Rows 1–3: *K1, p1*, rep ** until end of the row.

BO all sts loosely in 1x1 rib pattern.

You will notice there are no buttonholes on the right (as worn) side of the button band. This is because the yarn is quite thick, so your buttons should easily fit between your stitches as they are.

SLEEVES

Flip your work so that the RS are now facing out (your shoulder seams should be invisible).

Using US 13 (9 mm) 24- to 32-inch (60- to 80-cm) circular needles, starting at the underarm point, pick up 48 (48, 48, 52, 52) (52, 56, 56, 56) sts, evenly spaced, around the armhole. PM to mark the BOR. *You may need to use the Magic Loop method (page 207).*

Work 51 (56, 56, 56, 56) (61, 61, 61, 61) rounds in stockinette stitch, or until you reach your desired length. *Keep in mind that the sleeve cuff will add approximately 2.4 inches (6 cm) and that your sleeve will lengthen after blocking. Make note of how many total rows you work so that you can work your second sleeve to match.*

You will now make decreases before working the sleeve cuffs.

Next round: *K2tog*, rep ** until end of the round.

You should now have 24 (24, 24, 26, 26) (26, 28, 28, 28) sts.

Switch to US 10.5* (7 mm) 24-inch (60-cm) circular needles or DPNs. *If using circular needles, you will need to use the Magic Loop method (page 207).*

Next 8 rounds: *K1, p1*, rep ** until end of the round.

BO all sts using the Tubular Bind Off (page 209).

FINISHING

Attach 5 (5, 5, 6, 6) (6, 7, 7, 7) buttons, evenly spaced, along the left (as worn) side of the button band.

Weave in any remaining loose ends.

Wash and block (see Blocking 101 [page 216] or use your preferred blocking method).

V-Stripy Vest

This stylish and comfortable vest features a classic V-neck design and colorful stripes that are sure to make you stand out from the crowd. This design boasts a casual, oversized fit with minimal shaping, making it an ideal layering piece for any season. Choosing your color palette is the best part—whether you prefer bold and bright colors or a more subtle palette, the V-Stripy Vest can be customized to suit your personal style. It also presents a fantastic opportunity for zero-waste creativity. By using up your leftover scraps from previous projects, perhaps even some from other patterns in this book, you can reduce waste and create something beautiful and practical simultaneously.

Construction Notes

This seamless striped vest is worked mostly in the round in stockinette stitch from the bottom up. You will first work the bottom section of the vest in the round, before splitting at the underarm point to work the back panel flat, followed by the front panel where you will shape the V-neck. You will join the shoulder seams to create the neck hole and armholes using the Three Needle Bind Off method (page 207). The neck and sleeve trims are worked in the round by picking up stitches along the neck hole/armhole edges. The bottom edge remains as is with no ribbing to create a rolled edge. Follow the instructions for Jogless Stripes (page 211) to avoid jogs when knitting your stripes in the round.

Skill Level

Confident Beginner

Sizing

XS (S, M, L, XL) (XXL, 3XL, 4XL, 5XL)

Finished bust: 36.2 (39.4, 44, 47.2, 52) (55.2, 59.8, 63, 67.8)" / 92 (100, 112, 120, 132) (140, 152, 160, 172) cm

Recommended ease: This vest is designed with 6.2–8.2 inches / 16–21 cm of positive ease

Sample shown is knit in Size S.

MATERIALS

Yarn

Super bulky weight, Wool and the Gang, Crazy Sexy Wool (100% Wool), 87 yds (80 m) per 200-g skein, shown in Chalk Yellow (A), Pink Lemonade (B), Ivory White (C), Lilac Powder (D) and Paradise Peach (E) colorways

Any super bulky weight yarn can be used for this pattern as long as it matches gauge. A good substitute would be Cardigang, Chunky Merino or Malabrigo, Rasta.

Yardage/Meterage

Yarn estimates are approximate and refer specifically to the recommended yarn.

1 (1, 1, 1, 2) (2, 2, 3, 3) skein(s) of Color A

1 (1, 1, 2, 2) (2, 2, 2, 2) skein(s) of Color B

1 (1, 1, 1, 1) (1, 1, 2, 2) skein(s) of Color C

1 (1, 1, 1, 1) (1, 1, 2, 2) skein(s) of Color D

1 (1, 1, 1, 1) (1, 1, 2, 2) skein(s) of Color E

Needles

For body: US 19 (15 mm) 32-inch (80-cm) circular needle

For V-neck and sleeve trims: US 17 (12 mm) 32-inch (80-cm) circular needle

Notions

Stitch marker

Tapestry needles

Scissors

Stitch holders

GAUGE

7 sts x 10 rows = 4 inches (10 cm) in stockinette stitch using larger needle

ABBREVIATIONS

1x1 ribbing - *Knit 1, Purl 1*

BO - Bind off

BOR - Beginning of round

CO - Cast on

K - Knit

K2tog - Knit 2 stitches together

P - Purl

P2tog - Purl 2 stitches together

PM - Place marker

Rep - Repeat

RS - Right side

RM - Repeat marker

S2KP - Slip 2 stitches together knitwise, knit 1, pass slipped stitches over

Ssk - Slip, slip, knit 2 stitches together through the back loops

Ssp - Slip, slip, purl 2 stitches together through the back loops

St(s) - Stitch(es)

WS - Wrong side

SPECIAL TECHNIQUES

Jogless Stripes (page 211)

Three Needle Bind Off (page 207)

Magic Loop method (page 207)

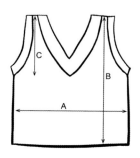

SIZING CHART

Size	XS	S	M	L	XL	XXL	3XL	4XL	5XL
To fit bust	28–30"/ 71–76 cm	32–34"/ 81–86 cm	36–38"/ 91.5–96.5 cm	40–42"/ 101.5–106.5 cm	44–46"/ 111.5–117 cm	48–50"/ 122–127 cm	52–54"/ 132–137 cm	56–58"/ 142–147 cm	60–62"/ 152–158 cm
(A) Width	18.1"/ 46 cm	19.7"/ 50 cm	22"/ 56 cm	23.6"/ 60 cm	26"/ 66 cm	27.6"/ 70 cm	29.9"/ 76 cm	31.5"/ 80 cm	33.9"/ 86 cm
(B) Length	17.3"/ 44 cm	18.5"/ 47 cm	19.7"/ 50 cm	20.9"/ 53 cm	22"/ 56 cm	23.2"/ 59 cm	24.4"/ 62 cm	25.6"/ 65 cm	26.4"/ 67 cm
(C) Armhole Depth	7.9" / 20 cm	7.9" / 20 cm	7.9" / 20 cm	7.9" / 20 cm	9.8" / 25 cm	9.8" / 25 cm	9.8" / 25 cm	11" / 28 cm	11" / 28 cm

V-STRIPY VEST PATTERN

BOTTOM

Using US 19 (15 mm) 32-inch (80-cm) circular needles and the Long Tail Cast On, CO 64 (70, 78, 84, 92) (98, 106, 112, 120) sts in Color A. Join in the round and PM to mark the BOR.

Work 6 (7, 7, 7, 7) (8, 8, 8, 8) rounds in stockinette stitch.

Switch to Color B.

> A note on changing colors: When introducing a new color, the first row you work will show up as a row of the previous color. To prevent confusion and ensure accuracy when counting how many rows you have worked with the current color before switching to the next color, count the live stitches that are on your needles as a row.

Work 5 (6, 6, 7, 6) (7, 7, 7, 7) rounds in stockinette stitch.

Switch to Color C.

Work 3 (3, 3, 4, 3) (4, 5, 4, 5) rounds in stockinette stitch.

Switch to Color D.

Work 4 (5, 6, 6, 6) (6, 6, 6, 7) rounds in stockinette stitch.

Switch to Color E.

Work 2 (2, 3, 3, 3) (3, 4, 4, 4) rounds in stockinette stitch.

Switch to Color A.

Work 4 (4, 5, 5, 5) (5, 6, 6, 6) rounds in stockinette stitch.

Switch to Color B.

Work 3 (3, 3, 4, 4) (4, 4, 4, 5) rounds in stockinette stitch.

BACK PANEL

You will now be working flat across **only the first 32 (35, 39, 42, 46) (49, 53, 56, 60) sts.** Leave the remaining stitches on the cord or place them on a stitch holder. *You will come back to them later for the Front Panel.*

Starting with a RS row, work 2 rows in stockinette stitch.

Switch to Color C.

Restart your row count here. You will now begin making decreases for the armholes. The decrease sequence is as follows:

Row 1 (RS): K1, ssk, k to last 3 sts, k2tog, k1.

Row 2 (WS): P across.

Repeat rows 1–2 until you have worked them 6 (7, 7, 7, 8) (8, 9, 9, 9) times **total** (meaning 12 (14, 14, 14, 16) (16, 18, 18, 18) total rows), switching colors in the following fashion:

5 (6, 6, 6, 6) (6, 7, 7, 7) rows in Color C.

3 (3, 3, 3, 4) (4, 4, 4, 4) rows in Color D.

4 (5, 5, 5, 6) (6, 6, 6, 6) rows in Color E.

You should end after a WS row and have 20 (21, 25, 28, 30) (33, 35, 38, 42) sts on the needles.

Work 3 (1, 1, 1, 2) (4, 2, 5, 5) straight rows in stockinette stitch with no decreases. *Sizes XL–5XL will switch to Color A on the second row.*

BACK SHOULDERS

You will now make decreases to shape the back neckline.

Sizes XS (S, M, L, -) (-, -, 4XL, 5XL) only

Row 1 (WS): P5 (5, 7, 9, -) (-, -, 13, 15), turn.

Sizes XS–L switch to Color A on the next row.

Row 2 (RS): K1, ssk, k2 (2, 4, 6, -) (-, -, 10, 12).

Row 3: P4 (4, 6, 8, -) (-, -, 12, 14).

Cut yarn and place these 4 (4, 6, 8, -) (-, -, 12, 14) left shoulder sts on a stitch holder. *You will come back to them later for the Shoulder Seams.*

Place the next 10 (11, 11, 10, -) (-, -, 12, 12) sts on a different stitch holder. *You will come back to them later for the Neck Trim.*

Reattach yarn using Color E (E, E, E, -) (-, -, A, A) on the WS to work the remaining 5 (5, 7, 9, -) (-, -, 13, 15) right shoulder sts.

Row 1 (WS): P5 (5, 7, 9, -) (-, -, 13, 15), turn.

Sizes XS–L switch to Color A on the next row.

Row 2 (RS): K2 (2, 4, 6, -) (-, -, 10, 12), k2tog, k1.

Row 3: P4 (4, 6, 8, -) (-, -, 12, 14).

Cut yarn and place these 4 (4, 6, 8, -) (-, -, 12, 14) right shoulder sts on a stitch holder. *You will come back to them later for the Shoulder Seams.*

Sizes - (-, -, -, XL) (XXL, 3XL, -, -) only

Row 1 (RS): K- (-, -, -, 10) (11, 11, -, -), turn.

Row 2 (WS): P1, p2tog, p- (-, -, -, 7) (8, 8, -, -).

Row 3: K- (-, -, -, 9) (10, 10, -, -).

Cut yarn and place these - (-, -, -, 9) (10, 10, -, -) right shoulder sts on a stitch holder. *You will come back to them later for the Shoulder Seams.*

Place the next - (-, -, -, 10) (11, 13, -, -) sts on a different stitch holder. *You will come back to them later for the Neck Trim.*

Reattach yarn using Color A on the RS to work the remaining - (-, -, -, 10) (11, 11, -, -) sts for the left shoulder.

Row 1 (RS): K- (-, -, -, 10) (11, 11, -, -), turn.

Row 2 (WS): P- (-, -, -, 7) (8, 8, -, -), ssp, p1.

Row 3: K- (-, -, -, 9) (10, 10, -, -).

Cut yarn and place these - (-, -, -, 9) (10, 10, -, -) left shoulder sts on a stitch holder. *You will come back to them later for the Shoulder Seams.*

FRONT PANEL

You will now be working flat across the 32 (35, 39, 42, 46) (49, 53, 56, 60) sts you left on hold after the bottom section.

Reattach yarn using Color B on the RS.

Starting with a RS row, work 2 rows in stockinette stitch.

Switch to Color C.

Restart your row count here. You will now begin making decreases for the armholes and the V-neck, **continuing to switch colors in the same fashion as you did for the back piece.**

Size XS only

Row 1 (RS): K1, ssk, k13, turn.

Row 2 (WS): P across.

Row 3: K1, ssk, k to last 3 sts, k2tog, k1.

Row 4: P across.

Repeat rows 3–4 until you have worked them 5 times **total** (meaning 10 total rows) and have 5 sts.

Next row (RS): K to last 3 sts, k2tog, k1.

Next row (WS): P across.

Work 4 straight rows in stockinette stitch with no decreases.

Cut yarn and place these 4 front left (as worn) shoulder sts on a stitch holder. *You will come back to them later for the Shoulder Seams.*

Reattach yarn using Color C on the WS to the remaining 16 front right (as worn) sts.

Row 1 (RS): K to last 3 sts, k2tog, k1.

Row 2 (WS): P across.

Row 3: K1, ssk, k to last 3 sts, k2tog, k1.

Row 4: P across.

Repeat rows 3–4 until you have worked them 5 times **total** (meaning 10 total rows) and have 5 sts.

Next row (RS): K1, ssk, k to end of the row.

Next row (WS): P across.

Work 4 straight rows in stockinette stitch with no decreases.

Leave these 4 sts on your needle and do not cut the yarn. *Proceed to "Shoulder Seams."*

Sizes - (S, M, -, -) (-, -, -, -) only

Setup row (RS): K1, ssk, k- (14, 16, -, -) (-, -, -, -), BO 1, k- (14, 16, -, -) (-, -, -, -), k2tog, k1.

You will now be working across only the - (16, 18, -, -) (-, -, -, -) front right (as worn) sts before the bound off middle stitch. Leave the remaining stitches on the cord or place them on a stitch holder. *You will come back to them later for the left side.*

Row 1 (WS): P across.

Row 2 (RS): K1, ssk, k to last 3 sts, k2tog, k1.

Row 3: P across.

Repeat rows 2–3 until you have worked them 6 times **total** (meaning 12 total rows) and have - (4, 6, -, -) (-, -, -, -) sts.

Work 4 straight rows in stockinette stitch with no decreases.

Cut yarn and place these - (4, 6, -, -) (-, -, -, -) front right (as worn) sts on a stitch holder. *You will come back to them later for the Shoulder Seams.*

Reattach yarn using Color C on the WS to the remaining - (16, 18, -, -) (-, -, -, -) front left (as worn) sts next to the middle stitch you bound off.

Row 1 (WS): P across.

Row 2 (RS): K1, ssk, k to last 3 sts, k2tog, k1.

Row 3: P across.

Repeat rows 2–3 until you have worked them 6 times **total** (meaning 12 total rows) and have - (4, 6, -, -) (-, -, -, -) sts.

Work 4 straight rows in stockinette stitch with no decreases.

Leave these - (4, 6, -, -) (-, -, -, -) sts on your needle and do not cut the yarn. *Proceed to "Shoulder Seams."*

Size L only

Row 1 (RS): K1, ssk, k18, turn.

Row 2 (WS): P across.

Row 3: K1, ssk, k to last 3 sts, k2tog, k1.

Row 4: P across.

Repeat rows 3–4 until you have worked them 6 times **total** (meaning 12 total rows) and have 8 sts.

Work 6 straight rows in stockinette stitch with no decreases.

Cut yarn and place these 8 front left (as worn) shoulder sts on a stitch holder. *You will come back to them later for the Shoulder Seams.*

Reattach yarn using Color C on the WS to the remaining 18 front right (as worn) sts.

Row 1 (RS): K to last 3 sts, k2tog, k1.

Row 2 (WS): P across.

Row 3: K1, ssk, k to last 3 sts, k2tog, k1.

Row 4: P across.

Repeat rows 3–4 until you have worked them 6 times **total** (meaning 12 total rows) and have 8 sts.

Work 6 straight rows in stockinette stitch with no decreases.

Leave these 8 sts on your needle and do not cut the yarn. *Proceed to "Shoulder Seams."*

Sizes - (-, -, -, XL) (-, -, 4XL, 5XL) only
Row 1 (RS): K1, ssk, k- (-, -, -, 20) (-, -, 25, 27), turn.

Row 2 (WS): P across.

Row 3: K1, ssk, k to last 3 sts, k2tog, k1.

Row 4: P across.

Repeat rows 3–4 until you have worked them - (-, -, -, 6) (-, -, 7, 7) times **total** (meaning – (-, -, -, 12) (-, -, 14, 14) total rows) and have - (-, -, -, 10) (-, -, 13, 15) sts.

Next row (RS): K1, ssk, k to end of the row.

Next row (WS): P across.

Work - (-, -, -, 7) (-, -, 8, 8) straight rows in stockinette stitch with no decreases.

Cut yarn and place these - (-, -, -, 9) (-, -, 12, 14) front left (as worn) shoulder sts on a stitch holder. *You will come back to them later for the Shoulder Seams.*

Reattach yarn using Color C on the WS to the remaining - (-, -, -, 23) (-, -, 28, 30) front right (as worn) sts.

Row 1 (RS): K to last 3 sts, k2tog, k1.

Row 2 (WS): P across.

Row 3: K1, ssk, k to last 3 sts, k2tog, k1.

Row 4: P across.

Repeat rows 3–4 until you have worked them - (-, -, -, 6) (-, -, 7, 7) times **total** (meaning – (-, -, -, 12) (-, -, 14, 14) total rows) and have - (-, -, -, 10) (-, -, 13, 15) sts.

Next row (RS): K to last 3 sts, k2tog, k1.

Next row (WS): P across.

Work - (-, -, -, 7) (-, -, 8, 8) straight rows in stockinette stitch with no decreases.

Leave these - (-, -, -, 9) (-, -, 12, 14) sts on your needle and do not cut the yarn. *Proceed to "Shoulder Seams."*

Sizes - (-, -, -, -) (XXL, 3XL, -, -) only
Setup row (RS): K1, ssk, k- (-, -, -, -) (21, 23, -, -), BO 1, k- (-, -, -, -) (21, 23, -, -), k2tog, k1.

You will now be working across only the - (-, -, -, -) (21, 23, -, -) front right (as worn) sts before the bound off middle stitch. Leave the remaining stitches on the cord or place them on a stitch holder. *You will come back to them later for the left side.*

Row 1 (WS): P across.

Row 2 (RS): K1, ssk, k to last 3 sts, k2tog, k1.

Row 3: P across.

Repeat rows 2–3 until you have worked them - (-, -, -, -) (6, 7, -, -) times **total** (meaning – (-, -, -, -) (12, 14, -, -) total rows) and have - (-, -, -, -) (11, 11, -, -) sts.

Next row (RS): K1, ssk, k to end of the row.

Next row (WS): P across.

Work - (-, -, -, -) (7, 5, -, -) straight rows in stockinette stitch with no decreases.

Cut yarn and place these - (-, -, -, -) (10, 10, -, -) front right (as worn) sts on a stitch holder. *You will come back to them later for the Shoulder Seams.*

Reattach yarn using Color C on the WS to the remaining - (-, -, -, -) (21, 23, -, -) front left (as worn) sts next to the middle stitch you bound off.

Row 1 (WS): P across.

Row 2 (RS): K1, ssk, k to last 3 sts, k2tog, k1.

Row 3: P across.

Repeat rows 2–3 until you have worked them - (-, -, -, -) (6, 7, -, -) times **total** (meaning – (-, -, -, -) (12, 14, -, -) total rows) and have - (-, -, -, -) (11, 11, -, -) sts.

Next row (RS): K to the last 3 sts, k2tog, k1.

Next row (WS): P across.

Work - (-, -, -, -) (7, 5, -, -) straight rows in stockinette stitch with no decreases.

Leave these - (-, -, -, -) (10, 10, -, -) sts on your needle and do not cut the yarn. *Proceed to "Shoulder Seams."*

SHOULDER SEAMS

You will now be using the Three Needle Bind Off method (page 207) to join the shoulder seams.

1. Turn your work inside out and place the RS of your front and back panels together.

2. Your front right (left, left, right, right) (left, left, right, right) shoulder stitches should still be on your needle. Place the corresponding 4 (4, 6, 8, 9) (10, 10, 12, 14) sts left on hold for the back right (left, left, right, right) (left, left, right, right) shoulder back onto the other needle. Make sure both needles are facing the same direction.

3. Insert a third needle (US 19 [15 mm] or smaller) knitwise into the first st of the panel that is facing you, then insert that same needle knitwise into the corresponding st of the other panel.

4. Continue, following the instructions for the Three Needle Bind Off method (page 207).

5. Repeat all steps for the other shoulder, using the corresponding front and back shoulder stitches left on hold.

NECK TRIM

Flip your work so that the RS are facing out and your shoulder seams are invisible.

Using US 17 (12 mm) 32-inch (80-cm) circular needles and Color B, pick up stitches in the following fashion:.

1. Pick up and knit all the live sts from the stitch holder at the back neck.

2. Pick up all sts along the left (as worn) side of the front neck.

3. Pick up 1 st to mark the center of the V-neck. For sizes - (S, M, -, -) (XXL, 3XL, -, -), pick up this st in the bound off st, for sizes XS (-, -, L, XL) (-, -, 4XL, 5XL), just pick up a st between the two sides. Mark this st with an interlocking stitch marker.

4. Continue picking up all sts along the right (as worn) side of the front neck. PM to mark the BOR.

Make sure you have an even number of stitches. You will need to use the Magic Loop method (page 207) to work the neck trim.

You are going to be working in 1x1 ribbing. Your center/marked stitch **must** be a knit stitch, so you will need to count backwards from that knit stitch in order to determine if you will start with a knit or purl stitch.

Round 1: Work in 1x1 ribbing.

Round 2: Work in 1x1 ribbing until 1 st before marked st, S2KP, **PM** on the resulting st, work in 1x1 ribbing as sts appear until end of the round.

Rounds 3–4: Repeat round 2.

BO all sts in 1x1 rib pattern until you reach 1 st before the marked st, S2KP, BO the resulting st and all sts left in the round. RM.

SLEEVE TRIMS

Left Trim

Starting at the underarm point, using US 17 (12 mm) 32-inch (80-cm) circular needles and Color D, pick up the stitches around the armhole in the following fashion: *Pick up 4 sts, skip 1 st.* Make sure you have an even number of stitches. PM to mark the BOR.

Next 2 rounds: *K1, p1*, rep ** until end of the row.

Switch to Color A.

BO in 1x1 rib pattern.

Right Trim

Starting at the underarm point, using US 17 (12 mm) 32-inch (80-cm) circular needles and Color E, pick up the stitches around the armhole in the following fashion: *Pick up 4 sts, skip 1 st.* Make sure you have an even number of stitches. PM to mark the BOR.

Next 2 rounds: *K1, p1*, rep ** until end of the row.

Switch to Color C.

BO in 1x1 rib pattern.

FINISHING

Weave in all your loose ends.

Blocking super bulky yarn is not necessary. However, if you do wish to block your vest, it is suggested that you use the spray blocking method (do *not* wet or steam block).

Zesty Vest

Add a burst of citrusy flavor to your wardrobe with the Zesty Vest! This joyful design features an adorable lemon motif at its center, created using the Duplicate stitch technique, which I like to think emulates the experience of drawing or painting with yarn. Despite using Aran weight yarn, which happens to be the lightest yarn weight you will find in this book, this project is surprisingly quick to knit. Before you know it, this vest will be flying off the needles and you'll have a zesty new addition to your wardrobe. As is the case with all the patterns in this chapter, one of the most enjoyable aspects of this project is the opportunity to explore your creativity through color selection. I encourage you to experiment with different combinations to truly make this vest your own. The possibilities are endless, and each color choice will undoubtedly infuse the Zesty Vest with its own unique personality.

Construction Notes

This seamless vest is worked mostly in the round in stockinette stitch from the bottom up. You will first work the bottom section of the vest in the round, before splitting at the underarm point to work the back panel flat, followed by the front panel where you will shape the V-neck. You will join the shoulder seams to create the neck hole and armholes using the Three Needle Bind Off method (page 207). The neck and sleeve trims are worked in the round by picking up stitches along the neck hole/armhole edges. The lemon is then worked onto the front of the vest in Duplicate stitch *(https://www.jaimecreates.me/book/tutorials)*.

Skill Level

Confident Beginner

Sizing

XS (S, M, L, XL) (XXL, 3XL, 4XL, 5XL)

Finished bust: 36.2 (40.2, 44, 48, 52.8) (56.6, 60.6, 64.6, 68.6)" / 92 (102, 112, 122, 134) (144, 154, 164, 174) cm, blocked

Recommended ease: This vest is designed with 6.3–8.3 inches / 16–21 cm of positive ease

Sample shown is knit in Size S.

MATERIALS

Yarn

Aran weight, Cowgirlblues, Aran Single (80% Wool, 20% Mohair), 131 yds (120 m) per 100-g skein, shown in Hot Pink (MC) and Lemon (CC) colorways (and scrap Aran weight yarn for leaf)

Any Aran weight yarn can be used for this pattern as long as it matches gauge.

Yardage/Meterage

Yarn estimates are approximate and refer specifically to the recommended yarn.

2 (3, 3, 3, 4) (4, 5, 5, 6) skeins of MC

1 (1, 1, 1, 2) (2, 2, 2, 2) skein(s) of CC

Needles

For body: US 10 (6 mm) 32- to 40-inch (80- to 100-cm) circular needle

For bottom ribbing: US 7 (4.5 mm) 32- to 40-inch (80- to 100-cm) circular needle

For neck and sleeve trims: US 7 (4.5 mm) 24- to 32-inch (60- to 80-cm) circular needle

Notions

Stitch markers

Tapestry needle

Scissors

Stitch holders

GAUGE

14 sts x 20 rows = 4 inches (10 cm) in stockinette stitch using larger needle (blocked)

ABBREVIATIONS

1x1 rib(bing) - *Knit 1, purl 1*

BO - Bind off

BOR - Beginning of round

CC - Contrast color

CO - Cast on

K - Knit

K2tog - Knit 2 stitches together

MC - Main color

P - Purl

P2tog - Purl 2 stitches together

PM - Place marker

Rep - Repeat

RM - Remove marker

RS - Right side

S2KP - Slip 2 stitches together knitwise, knit 1, pass slipped stitches over

Ssk - Slip, slip, knit 2 stitches together through the back loops

Ssp - Slip, slip, purl 2 stitches together through the back loops

St(s) - Stitch(es)

WS - Wrong side

SIZING CHART

Size	XS	S	M	L	XL	XXL	3XL	4XL	5XL
To fit bust	28–30"/ 71–76 cm	32–34"/ 81–86 cm	36–38"/ 91.5–96.5 cm	40–42"/ 101.5–106.5 cm	44–46"/ 111.5–117 cm	48–50"/ 122–127 cm	52–54"/ 132–137 cm	56–58"/ 142–147 cm	60–62"/ 152–158 cm
(A) Width	18.1"/ 46 cm	20.1"/ 51 cm	22"/ 56 cm	24"/ 61 cm	26.4"/ 67 cm	28.3"/ 72 cm	30.3"/ 77 cm	32.3"/ 82 cm	34.3"/ 87 cm
(B) Length	16.1"/ 41 cm	16.9" 43 cm	17.7"/ 45 cm	18.5"/ 47 cm	19.3"/ 49 cm	20.1"/ 51 cm	20.9"/ 53 cm	21.7"/ 55 cm	22.4"/ 57 cm
(C) Armhole Depth	8.7"/ 22 cm	8.7"/ 22 cm	8.7"/ 22 cm	9.8"/ 25 cm	9.8"/ 25 cm	10.6"/ 27 cm	10.6"/ 27 cm	11.8"/ 30 cm	11.8"/ 30 cm

SPECIAL TECHNIQUES

Alternating Cable Cast On (page 208)

Three Needle Bind Off (page 207)

Duplicate stitch (https://www.jaimecreates. me/book/tutorials)

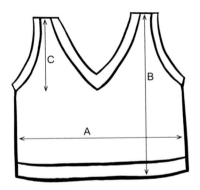

ZESTY VEST PATTERN

BOTTOM

Using US 7 (4.5 mm) 32- to 40-inch (80- to 100-cm) circular needles and the Alternating Cable Cast On (page 208), CO 128 (144, 156, 170, 188) (202, 216, 230, 244) sts in CC. Join in the round and PM to mark the BOR.

Rounds 1–2: *K1, p1*, rep ** until end of the round.

Switch to MC.

Round 3: *K1, p1*, rep ** until end of the round.

Switch to CC.

Rounds 4–9: *K1, p1*, rep ** until end of the round.

Switch to US 10 (6 mm) 32- to 40-inch (80- to 100-cm) circular needles and MC. Restart your row count here.

Work 30 (34, 38, 36, 40) (40, 44, 42, 46) rounds in stockinette stitch.

Note: If you would like to add or subtract length to/from the bottom of your vest, do so before moving on to the back panel.

BACK PANEL

You will now be working flat across **only the last 64 (72, 78, 85, 94) (101, 108, 115, 122) sts** that you just worked. Leave the remaining stitches on the cord or place them on a stitch holder. *You will come back to them later for the Front Panel.*

Restart your row count here. You will now begin making decreases for the armholes. Turn your work so you begin on a WS row. The decrease sequence is as follows:

Row 1 (WS): P across.

Row 2 (RS): K1, ssk, k to last 3 sts, k2tog, k1.

Repeat rows 1–2 until you have worked them 10 (10, 10, 11, 11) (12, 12, 13, 13) times **total** (meaning 20 (20, 20, 22, 22) (24, 24, 26, 26) total rows). You should end after a RS row and have 44 (52, 58, 63, 72) (77, 84, 89, 96) sts.

Starting on a WS row, work 21 (21, 21, 25, 25) (27, 27, 31, 31) straight rows in stockinette stitch with no decreases. *You should end after a WS row.*

BACK SHOULDERS

You will now make decreases to shape the back neckline.

Row 1 (RS): K across 10 (13, 16, 18, 22) (24, 27, 29, 32) sts, turn.

Row 2 (WS): P1, p2tog, p to end of the row.

Row 3: K across.

Cut yarn and place these 9 (12, 15, 17, 21) (23, 26, 28, 32) right shoulder sts on a stitch holder. *You will come back to them later for the Shoulder Seams.*

Place the middle 24 (26, 26, 27, 28) (29, 30, 31, 30) sts on another stitch holder. *You will come back to them later for the Neck Trim.*

Reattach yarn on the RS to the remaining 10 (13, 16, 18, 22) (24, 27, 29, 33) left shoulder sts.

Row 1 (RS): K across.

Row 2 (WS): P to last 3 sts, ssp, p1.

Row 3: K across.

Cut yarn and place these 9 (12, 15, 17, 21) (23, 26, 28, 32) sts on a stitch holder. *You will come back to them later for the Shoulder Seams.*

FRONT PANEL

You will now be working flat across the 64 (72, 78, 85, 94) (101, 108, 115, 122) sts you left on hold after the bottom section.

Reattach yarn on the WS.

You will now begin making decreases for the armholes. The decrease sequence is as follows:

Row 1 (WS): P across.

Row 2 (RS): K1, ssk, k to last 3 sts, k2tog, k1.

Repeat rows 1–2. You should have 60 (68, 74, 81, 90) (97, 104, 111, 118) sts.

You will now begin making decreases for the V-neck at the same time. You will now be working across **only the first 30 (34, 37, 40, 45) (48, 52, 55, 59) sts** to shape the front right (as worn) shoulder. Leave the remaining stitches on the cord or place them on a stitch holder. *You will come back to them later for the front left shoulder.*

Row 1 (WS): P across 30 (34, 37, 40, 45) (48, 52, 55, 59) sts, turn.

Row 2 (RS): K1, ssk, k to last 3 sts, k2tog, k1.

Repeat rows 1–2 until you have worked them 8 (8, 8, 9, 9) (10, 10, 11, 11) times **total** (meaning 16 (16, 16, 18, 18) (20, 20, 22, 22) total rows). You should end after a RS row and have 14 (18, 21, 22, 27) (28, 32, 33, 37) sts.

You will now continue making decreases for the V-neck only.

Row 1 (WS): P across.

Row 2 (RS): K1, ssk, k to end of the row.

Repeat rows 1–2 until you have worked them 5 (6, 6, 5, 6) (5, 6, 5, 5) times **total** (meaning 10 (12, 12, 10, 12) (10, 12, 10, 10) total rows). You should end after a RS row and have 9 (12, 15, 17, 21) (23, 26, 28, 32) sts.

Starting on a WS row, work 14 (12, 12, 18, 16) (20, 18, 24, 24) straight rows in stockinette stitch with no decreases. You should end after a RS row.

Cut yarn and place these 9 (12, 15, 17, 21) (23, 26, 28, 32) sts on a stitch holder. *You will come back to them later for the Shoulder Seams.*

Reattach yarn on the WS to the remaining **30 (34, 37, 41, 45) (49, 52, 56, 59) sts.** You will now shape the front left (as worn) shoulder.

Sizes XS (S, M, -, XL) (-, 3XL, -, 5XL) only

Row 1 (WS): P across.

Row 1 (WS): BO 1, P across. You should now have - (-, -, 40, -) (48, -, 55, -) sts.

All sizes continue

Row 2 (RS): K1, ssk, k to last 3 sts, k2tog, k1.

Row 3 (WS): P across.

Repeat rows 2–3 until you have worked them 8 (8, 8, 9, 9) (10, 10, 11, 11) times **total** (meaning 16 (16, 16, 18, 18) (20, 20, 22, 22) total rows). You should end after a WS row and have 14 (18, 21, 22, 27) (28, 32, 33, 37) sts.

You will now continue making decreases for the V-neck only.

Row 1 (RS): K to last 3 sts, k2tog, k1.

Row 2 (WS): P across.

Repeat rows 1–2 until you have worked them 5 (6, 6, 5, 6) (5, 6, 5, 5) times **total** (meaning 10 (12, 12, 10, 12) (10, 12, 10, 10) total rows). You should end after a WS row and have 9 (12, 15, 17, 21) (23, 26, 28, 32) sts.

Starting on a RS row, work 13 (11, 11, 17, 15) (19, 17, 23, 23) straight rows in stockinette stitch with no decreases. *You should end after a RS row.*

Leave these 9 (12, 15, 17, 21) (23, 26, 28, 32) sts on your needle and do not cut the yarn. *Proceed to "Shoulder Seams."*

SHOULDER SEAMS

You will now be using the Three Needle Bind Off method (page 207) to join the shoulder seams.

1. Turn your work inside out and place the RS of your front and back panels together.

2. Your front left (as worn) shoulder stitches should still be on your needle. Place the corresponding 9 (12, 15, 17, 21) (23, 26, 28, 32) sts left on hold for the back left shoulder onto the other needle. Make sure both needles are facing the same direction.

3. Insert a third needle (US 10 [6 mm] or smaller) knitwise into the first st of the panel that is facing you, then insert that same needle knitwise into the corresponding st of the other panel.

4. Continue, following the instructions for the Three Needle Bind Off method (page 207).

5. Repeat all steps for the right shoulder, using the corresponding front and back right shoulder stitches left on hold.

NECK TRIM

Flip your work so that the RS are facing out and your shoulder seams are invisible.

Using US 7 (4.5 mm) 24- to 32-inch (60- to 80-cm) circular needle and CC, pick up stitches in the following fashion:

1. Pick up 4 sts along the side of the back right shoulder.

2. Pick up and knit the 24 (26, 26, 27, 28) (29, 30, 31, 30) live sts from the stitch holder at the back neck.

3. Pick up 4 sts along the side of the back left shoulder.

4. Pick up sts along the left (as worn) side of the V-neck in the following fashion: *Pick up 5 sts, skip 1 st.*

5. Pick up 1 st to mark the center of the V-neck. For sizes - (-, -, L, -) (XXL, -, 4XL, -), pick up this st in the bound off st, for sizes XS (S, M, -, XL) (-, 3XL, -, 5XL), just pick up a st between the two sides. Mark this st with an interlocking stitch marker.

6. Pick up sts along the right (as worn) side of the V-neck in the following fashion: *Pick up 5 sts, skip 1 st.*

PM to mark the BOR. *Make sure you have an even number of sts.*

You are going to be working in 1x1 ribbing. Your center/marked stitch **must** be a knit stitch, so you will need to count backwards from that knit stitch to determine if you will start with a knit or purl stitch.

Round 1: Work in 1x1 ribbing.

Round 2: Work in 1x1 ribbing until 1 st before marked st, S2KP, **PM** on the resulting st, work in 1x1 ribbing as sts appear until end of the round.

Rounds 3–4: Repeat round 2.

Switch to MC.

Round 5: Repeat round 2.

Switch to CC.

Rounds 6–7: Repeat round 2.

BO all sts in 1x1 rib pattern until you reach 1 st before the marked st, S2KP, BO the resulting st and all sts left in the round. **RM.**

SLEEVE TRIMS

Starting at the underarm point, using US 7 (4.5 mm) 24- to 32-inch (60- to 80-cm) circular needle and CC, pick up and knit the stitches around the armhole in the following fashion: *Pick up 5 sts, skip 1 st.* Make sure you have an even number of stitches. PM to mark the BOR.

Rounds 1–2: *K1, p1*, rep ** until the end of the round.

Switch to MC.

Round 3: *K1, p1*, rep ** until the end of the round.

Switch to CC.

Round 4: *K1, p1*, rep ** until the end of the round.

BO all sts in 1x1 rib pattern.

ADDING SOME ZEST TO YOUR VEST

You will use the Duplicate stitch to add the lemon colorwork detailing to the front of the vest. *For a video tutorial on the Duplicate stitch, visit the following page on my site: https://www.jaimecreates.me/book/tutorials.*

Step 1: With the front of your work facing you, count 5 (5, 5, 5, 5) (7, 7, 7, 7) rows down from where you split your front piece in half to start the V-neck shaping.

Step 2: Count 6 (6, 6, 6, 6) (9, 9, 9, 9) sts to the right, and place an interlocking stitch marker on the stitch you land on.

Step 3: Count 19 (19, 19, 19, 19) (24, 24, 24, 24) rows down from this stitch, and place another interlocking stitch marker on the stitch you land on.

Follow colorwork chart A (A, A, A, A) (B, B, B, B) using Duplicate stitch *(https://www.jaimecreates.me/book/tutorials)*. The stitch/row marked as 1 on the chart can be located using the stitch marker placed in step 3. The marker placed in step 2 marks the top right corner of the chart.

FINISHING

Weave in all your loose ends.

Wash and block (see Blocking 101 [page 216] or use your preferred blocking method).

COLORWORK CHART A (SIZES XS–XL)

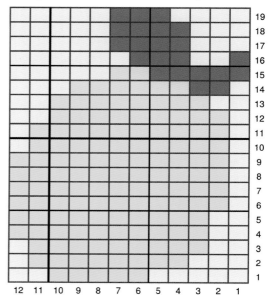

Legend		
		CC
		Scrap Yarn
		No Stitch

COLORWORK CHART B (SIZES XXL–5XL)

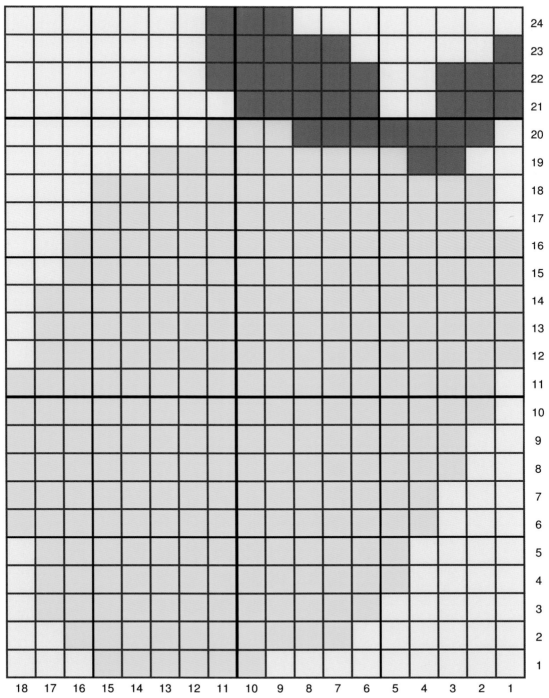

Color Me Striped Jumper

The Color Me Striped Jumper highlights the Intarsia technique, which is utilized in this pattern to create bold and vivid vertical stripes that effortlessly flow along the body. If you've never tried Intarsia before, this pattern is a great place to start, as it has been specially crafted to serve as a gentle initiation into the art of this nifty colorwork technique. Designed to be both fitted and cropped, this jumper is the perfect layering piece and will sit nicely under a coat or jacket. The bottom ribbing, cleverly seamed to the body, adds an intriguing patchwork effect that elevates the overall design and adds an extra touch of uniqueness to your finished garment.

Construction Notes

This jumper is worked mostly flat in stockinette stitch from the bottom up. You will first work the back panel flat, followed by the front panel. The vertical stripes are worked using the Intarsia technique. You will join the shoulder seams to create the neck hole using the Three Needle Bind Off method (page 207). To create the armholes, you will use a variation of the Horizontal Mattress stitch (https://www.jaimecreates.me/book/tutorials) to seam the left side together. The bottom ribbing is worked separately and is then seamed to the body. You will then use the variation of the Horizontal Mattress stitch to seam the right side of the body. The neck trim and sleeves are worked in the round by picking up stitches along the neck hole/armhole edges. To avoid weaving in so many ends, follow the instructions for the Weavin' Stephen technique (page 212) to learn how to weave in ends as you go. Follow the instructions for Jogless Stripes (page 211) to avoid jogs when knitting your stripes in the round while making the sleeves.

Skill Level

Intermediate

Sizing

XS (S, M, L, XL) (XXL, 3XL, 4XL, 5XL)

Finished bust: 30.8 (34.6, 38.6, 42.6, 46.4) (50.4, 54.4, 58.2, 63)" / 78 (88, 98, 108, 118) (128, 138, 148, 160) cm, blocked

Recommended ease: This jumper is designed with approximately 0.8–2.8 inches / 2–7 cm of positive ease

Sample shown is knit in Size S.

MATERIALS

Yarn

Bulky weight, Wool and Works, Merino Chunky (100% Superwash Merino), 110 yds (100 m) per 100-g skein, shown in Rose (Color A), Burst (Color B), Apricot (Color C) and Glacier (Color D) colorways

Any bulky weight yarn can be used for this pattern as long as it matches gauge. A good substitute would be Wool and the Gang, Alpachino Merino or Drops, Andes.

Yardage/Meterage

Yarn estimates are approximate and refer specifically to the recommended yarn.

2 (2, 2, 2, 2) (3, 4, 4, 4) skein(s) of Color A

2 (2, 2, 2, 2) (3, 4, 4, 4) skein(s) of Color B

2 (2, 2, 2, 2) (3, 3, 4, 4) skein(s) of Color C

1 (1, 2, 2, 2) (2, 2, 2, 2) skein(s) of Color D

Needles

For body: US 10.5* (7 mm) straight needles or 24- to 32-inch (60- to 80-cm) circular needle

For sleeves: US 10.5* (7 mm) 24- to 32-inch (60- to 80-cm) circular needle

For bottom ribbing: US 8 (5 mm) straight needles or 24- to 32-inch (60- to 80-cm) circular needle

For neckline and sleeve cuffs: US 8 (5 mm) 24-inch (60-cm) circular needle

There is no direct US equivalent to 7 mm needles; US 10.5 (6.5 mm) is the closest size

Notions

Stitch markers

Tapestry needle

Scissors

Stitch holders

Measuring tape

GAUGE

12 sts x 16 rows = 4 inches (10 cm) in stockinette stitch using larger needle (blocked)

ABBREVIATIONS

BO - Bind off

BOR - Beginning of round

CO - Cast on

K - Knit

K2tog - Knit 2 stitches together

P - Purl

PM - Place marker

Rep - Repeat

RS - Right side

Ssk - Slip, slip, knit 2 stitches together through the back loops

St(s) - Stitch(es)

WS - Wrong side

SIZING CHART

Size	XS	S	M	L	XL	XXL	3XL	4XL	5XL
To fit bust	28–30"/ 71–76 cm	32–34"/ 81–86 cm	36–38"/ 91.5–96.5 cm	40–42"/ 101.5–106.5 cm	44–46"/ 111.5–117 cm	48–50"/ 122–127 cm	52–54"/ 132–137 cm	56–58"/ 142–147 cm	60–62"/ 152–158 cm
(A) Width	15.4"/ 39 cm	17.3"/ 44 cm	19.3"/ 49 cm	21.3"/ 54 cm	23.2"/ 59 cm	25.2"/ 64 cm	27.2"/ 69 cm	29.1"/ 74 cm	31.5"/ 80 cm
(B) Length	16.1"/ 41 cm	16.1"/ 41 cm	17.7"/ 45 cm	17.7"/ 45 cm	19.3"/ 49 cm	19.3"/ 49 cm	20.9"/ 53 cm	20.9"/ 53 cm	22.4"/ 57 cm
(C) Upper Arm Width	7.1"/ 18 cm	7.1"/ 18 cm	7.1"/ 18 cm	8.7"/ 22 cm	8.7"/ 22 cm	8.7"/ 22 cm	10.2"/ 26 cm	10.2"/ 26 cm	10.2"/ 26 cm
(D) Sleeve Length	17.7"/ 45 cm	19.7"/ 50 cm	19.7"/ 50 cm	19.7"/ 50 cm	20.9"/ 53 cm	20.9"/ 53 cm	20.9"/ 53 cm	22"/ 56 cm	22"/ 56 cm

SPECIAL TECHNIQUES

Intarsia (https://www.jaimecreates.me/book/tutorials)

Three Needle Bind Off (page 207)

Alternating Cable Cast On (page 208)

Stretchy Bind Off (page 211)

Tubular Bind Off (page 209)

Magic Loop method (page 207)

Jogless Stripes (page 211)

Weavin' Stephen (page 212)

Horizontal Mattress stitch variation (https://www.jaimecreates.me/book/tutorials)

Mattress stitch (page 209)

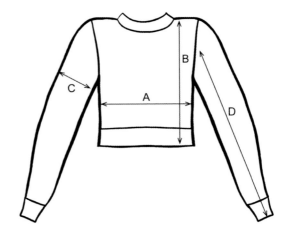

BACK PANEL

Using US 10.5* (7 mm) straight needles or 24- to 32-inch (60- to 80-cm) circular needles and the Long Tail Cast On, CO sts with Colors A, B and C according to the table below. Read from right to left, matching the direction that the stitches are added to your needle as you cast on. *Be sure to attach a new working yarn for each color switch.*

For example (Size XS): CO 9 sts in Color A, CO 8 sts in Color B, CO 8 sts in Color C, CO 8 sts in Color A, CO 8 sts in Color B, CO 9 sts in Color C.

You should have a total of 50 (56, 62, 68, 74) (80, 86, 92, 99) sts.

Using the Intarsia technique, work 53 (53, 61, 61, 66) (66, 73, 73, 80) rows in stockinette stitch, starting with a knit (RS) row, changing colors as they appear. *You should end after a RS (RS, RS, RS, WS) (WS, RS, RS, WS) row. For a video tutorial on the Intarsia technique, visit the following page on my site: https://www.jaimecreates.me/book/tutorials.*

> **Note:** If you would like to add or subtract length to/from your jumper, do so here, but make note of how many total rows you work so that you can work your Front Panel to match. Make sure you still end after a RS (RS, RS, RS, WS) (WS, RS, RS, WS) row. Keep in mind that the bottom ribbing will add approximately 2.8 inches (7 cm).

B	A	C	B	A	C	B	A	C	B	A	
					9	8	8	8	8	9	XS
				8	8	8	8	8	8	8	S
			7	8	8	8	8	8	8	7	M
			10	8	8	8	8	8	8	10	L
		9	8	8	8	8	8	8	8	9	XL
	8	8	8	8	8	8	8	8	8	8	XXL
7	8	8	8	8	8	8	8	8	8	7	3XL
	10	9	9	9	9	9	9	9	9	10	4XL
9	9	9	9	9	9	9	9	9	9	9	5XL

BACK SHOULDERS

You will now bind off stitches to shape the back neckline whilst working in pattern. *If/when you need to bind off the last remaining stitch of a color section, work that bind off using the next color.*

Sizes XS (S, M, L, -) (-, 3XL, 4XL, -) only

Row 1 (WS): Work in pattern across the first 14 (16, 19, 22, -) (-, 30, 33, -) sts, turn.

Row 2 (RS): BO 1, work in pattern to end of the row.

Row 3: Work in pattern to end of the row.

Cut yarn and place these 13 (15, 18, 21, -) (-, 29, 32, -) left shoulder sts on a stitch holder. *You will come back to them later for the Shoulder Seams.*

Place the middle 22 (24, 24, 24, -) (-, 26, 26, -) sts on another stitch holder. *You will come back to them later for the Neck Trim.*

Reattach yarn on the WS to the remaining 14 (16, 19, 22, -) (-, 30, 33, -) right shoulder sts.

Row 1 (WS): BO 1, work in pattern to end of the row.

Rows 2–3: Work in pattern to end of the row.

Cut yarn and place these 13 (15, 18, 21, -) (-, 29, 32, -) right shoulder sts on a stitch holder. *You will come back to them later for the Shoulder Seams.*

Sizes - (-, -, -, XL) (XXL, -, -, 5XL) only

Row 1 (RS): Work in pattern across the first - (-, -, -, 25) (27, -, -, 36) sts, turn.

Row 2 (WS): BO 1, work in pattern to end of the row.

Row 3: Work in pattern to end of the row.

Cut yarn and place these - (-, -, -, 24) (26, -, -, 35) right shoulder sts on a stitch holder. *You will come back to them later for the Shoulder Seams.*

Place the middle - (-, -, -, 24) (26, -, -, 27) sts on another stitch holder. *You will come back to them later for the Neck Trim.*

Reattach yarn on the RS to the remaining - (-, -, -, 25) (27, -, -, 36) left shoulder sts.

Row 1 (WS): BO 1, work in pattern to end of the row.

Rows 2–3: Work in pattern to end of the row.

Cut yarn and place these - (-, -, -, 24) (26, -, -, 35) left shoulder sts on a stitch holder. *You will come back to them later for the Shoulder Seams.*

FRONT PANEL

Follow Back Panel instructions until you have worked 46 (46, 54, 54, 59) (59, 66, 66, 73) rows total. *You should end after a WS (WS, WS, WS, RS) (RS, WS, WS, RS) row.*

> **Note:** If you are adding or subtracting length to/from your jumper, work 7 less rows than you did for the Back Panel.

FRONT SHOULDERS

You will now bind off stitches to shape the front neckline whilst working in pattern. *If/when you need to bind off the last remaining stitch of a color section, work that bind off using the next color.*

Sizes XS (S, M, L, -) (-, 3XL, 4XL, -) only

Row 1 (RS): Work in pattern across the first 17 (19, 22, 25, -) (-, 33, 36, -) sts, turn.

Row 2 (WS): BO 1, work in pattern to end of the row.

Row 3: Work in pattern to end of the row.

Rows 4–9: Repeat rows 2–3.

Row 10: Work in pattern to end of the row.

Cut yarn and place these 13 (15, 18, 21, -) (-, 29, 32, -) left (as worn) shoulder sts on a stitch holder. *You will come back to them later for the Shoulder Seams.*

Place the middle 16 (18, 18, 18, -) (-, 20, 20, -) sts on another stitch holder. *You will come back to them later for the Neck Trim.*

Reattach yarn on the RS to the remaining 17 (19, 22, 25, -) (-, 33, 36, -) right (as worn) shoulder sts.

Row 1 (RS): BO 1, work in pattern to end of the row.

Row 2 (WS): Work in pattern to end of the row.

Rows 3–8: Repeat rows 1–2.

Rows 9–10: Work in pattern to end of the row.

Leave these 13 (15, 18, 21, -) (-, 29, 32, -) sts on the needle and do not cut the yarn. *Proceed to "Shoulder Seams."*

Sizes - (-, -, -, XL) (XXL, -, -, 5XL) only

Row 1 (WS): Work in pattern across the first - (-, -, -, 28) (30, -, -, 39) sts, turn.

Row 2 (RS): BO 1, work in pattern to end of the row.

Row 3: Work in pattern to end of the row.

Rows 4–9: Repeat rows 2–3.

Row 10: Work in pattern to end of the row.

Cut yarn and place these - (-, -, -, 24) (26, -, -, 35) right (as worn) shoulder sts on a stitch holder. *You will come back to them later for the Shoulder Seams.*

Place the middle - (-, -, -, 18) (20, -, -, 21) sts on another stitch holder. *You will come back to them later for the Neck Trim.*

Reattach yarn on the WS to the remaining - (-, -, -, 28) (30, -, -, 39) left (as worn) shoulder sts.

Row 1 (WS): BO 1, work in pattern to end of the row.

Row 2 (RS): Work in pattern to end of the row.

Rows 3–8: Repeat rows 1–2.

Rows 9–10: Work in pattern to end of the row.

Leave these - (-, -, -, 24) (26, -, -, 35) sts on the needle and do not cut the yarn. *Proceed to "Shoulder Seams."*

SHOULDER SEAMS

You will now be using the Three Needle Bind Off method (page 207) to join the shoulder seams.

1. Turn your work inside out and place the RS of your front and back panels together.

2. Your front left (left, left, left, right) (right, left, left, right) (as worn) shoulder stitches should still be on your needle. Place the corresponding 13 (15, 18, 21, 24) (26, 29, 32, 35) sts left on hold for the back right left (left, left, left, right) (right, left, left, right) shoulder onto the other needle. Make sure both needles are facing the same direction.

3. Insert a third needle (US 10.5* [7 mm] or smaller) knitwise into the first st of the panel that is facing you, then insert that same needle knitwise into the corresponding st of the other panel.

4. Continue, following the instructions for the Three Needle Bind Off method (page 207).

5. Repeat all steps for the other shoulder, using the corresponding front and back right shoulder stitches left on hold.

BOTTOM RIBBING

Using US 8 (5 mm) straight needles or 24- to 32-inch (60- to 80-cm) circular needles and the Alternating Cable Cast On (page 208), CO 98 (110, 122, 134, 146) (158, 170, 182, 196) sts in Color D.

Rows 1–12: *K1, p1*, rep ** until end of the row.

BO all sts using the Stretchy Bind Off (page 211).

SEAMS

1. Flip your work so that the RS are now facing out (your shoulder seams should be invisible).

2. With the front panel facing you, take a measuring tape and measure from the shoulder seam down. Place an interlocking stitch marker on the outside edge of your work at the 7.1 (7.1, 7.1, 8.7, 8.7) (8.7, 10.2, 10.2, 10.2) inch / 18 (18, 18, 22, 22) (22, 26, 26, 26) cm mark. Repeat on the other side.

3. Use the Mattress stitch (page 209) to seam the front and back panels together on the left side, starting from the bottom, until you reach the marker. *Leave the right side unseamed for now—you will come back to it later.*

4. You will now seam the ribbing to the body. You will be using a variation of the Horizontal Mattress stitch to work this seam. *For a video tutorial on this technique, visit the following page on my site: https://www.jaimecreates.me/book/tutorials.*

5. With the front panel facing you, use the Mattress stitch (page 209) to seam the front and back panels together on the right side, starting from the bottom of the ribbing, until you reach the marker. *You may now remove both markers.*

You should now have 66 (70, 70, 70, 70) (74, 74, 74, 76) sts. PM to mark the BOR.

Rounds 1–9: *K1, p1*, rep ** until end of the round.

BO all sts using the Tubular Bind Off (page 209).

SLEEVES

Using US 10.5* (7 mm) 24- to 32-inch (60- to 80-cm) circular needles and Color B (B, C, C, B) (B, C, B, C), starting at the underarm point, pick up 49 (49, 49, 57, 57) (57, 65, 65, 65) sts, evenly spaced around the armhole. PM to mark the BOR.

Rounds 1–11: K across.

Switch to Color C (C, A, A, C) (C, A, C, A).

> **A note on changing colors:** When introducing a new color, the first row you work will show up as a row of the previous color. To prevent confusion and ensure accuracy when counting how many rows you have worked with the current color before switching to the next color, count the live stitches that are on your needles as a row.

Rounds 12–13: K across.

You will now begin making decreases.

Round 14: K1, k2tog, k to last 3 sts, ssk, k1.

Rounds 15–19: K across.

Round 20: Repeat round 14.

Rounds 21–23: K across.

Switch to Color A (A, B, B, A) (A, B, A, B).

Rounds 24–25: K across.

Round 26: Repeat round 14.

Rounds 27–31: K across.

NECK TRIM

Using US 8 (5 mm) 24-inch (60-cm) circular needles and Color D, pick up stitches in the following fashion:

1. Pick up 4 sts along the side of the back right shoulder.
2. Pick up and knit the 22 (24, 24, 24, 24) (26, 26, 26, 27) live sts from the stitch holder at the back neck.
3. Pick up 4 sts along the side of the back left shoulder.
4. Pick up 10 sts along the side of the front left shoulder.
5. Pick up and knit the 16 (18, 18, 18, 18) (20, 20, 20, 21) live sts from the stitch holder at the front neck.
6. Pick up 10 sts along the side of the front right shoulder.

Round 32: Repeat round 14.

Rounds 33–35: K across.

Switch to Color B (B, C, C, B) (B, C, B, C).

Rounds 36–47: Repeat rounds 24–35.

Switch to Color C (C, A, A, C) (C, A, C, A).

Rounds 48–59: Repeat rounds 24–35.

You should now have 33 (33, 33, 41, 41) (41, 49, 49, 49) sts.

Switch to Color A (A, B, B, A) (A, B, A, B).

Next 5 (12, 12, 12, 12) (12, 12, 12, 12) rounds: K across.

Sizes XS (S, M, L, -) (-, -, -, -) proceed to "All sizes continue."

Sizes XS (S, M, L, -) (-, -, -, -) proceed to "All sizes continue."

Sizes - (-, -, -, XL) (XXL, 3XL, 4XL, 5XL) only

Switch to Color - (-, -, -, B) (B, C, B, C).

Next - (-, -, -, 6) (6, 6, 11, 11) rounds: K across.

Proceed to "All sizes continue."

All sizes continue

Switch to Color D.

You will now make decreases before working the sleeve cuffs.

Sizes XS (S, M, -, -) (-, -, -, -) only

Next round: *K2tog, k1*, rep ** until end of the round.

Sizes - (-, -, L, XL) (XXL, -, -, -) only

Next round: *K2tog, k2*, rep ** until last st, k1.

Next round: *K2tog, k4*, rep ** until last st, k1.

Sizes - (-, -, -, -) (-, 3XL, 4XL 5XL) only

Next round: *K2tog, k1*, rep ** until last st, k1.

Next round: *K2tog, k9*, rep ** until end of the round.

All sizes continue

You should now have 22 (22, 22, 26, 26) (26, 30, 30, 30) sts.

Switch to US 8 (5 mm) 24-inch (60-cm) circular needles. *You will need to use the Magic Loop method (page 207).*

Next 9 rounds: *K1, p1*, rep ** until end of the round.

BO all sts using the Tubular Bind Off (page 209).

FINISHING

Weave in any remaining loose ends.

Wash and block (see Blocking 101 [page 216] or use your preferred blocking method).

Lace Is More

If you're familiar with lace knitting, you'd know that lacework patterns that call for bulkier yarn are few and far between, which is why I felt it was important to include a chapter dedicated to lacework in this book. Although traditional lace knitting is usually done with finer yarns, there is no real reason why it cannot be done using bulkier yarn. In fact, I find the process far more rewarding and much less tedious when using thicker yarn, and the result is just as beautiful!

The four pieces in this chapter were thoughtfully designed to demonstrate the versatility of lacework, with each pattern providing the knitter with a unique lace knitting experience. The ethereal Lily Cardigan (page 183) is a stunning staple piece featuring understated yet elegant lace detailing. The Twist and Shout Vest (page 175) is an exciting fusion of lace and cable work, whereas the Bambi Jumper (page 195) exhibits how simple lace stitches can create a cable-like texture. If you're after a project that will exercise your mind and produce a finished piece that is simply to die for, the Ivy Jumper (page 167) has you covered.

Ivy Jumper

Meet the Ivy Jumper, a personal favorite of mine that combines the elegance of lacework with the comfort of bulky weight yarn, providing an exciting challenge for seasoned knitters that won't take months to complete. The Ivy Jumper showcases the beauty of the Traveling Vine stitch, an intricate design that weaves a captivating story throughout the fabric and is quite addictive to knit up. The lacework pattern evokes the image of lush vines gracefully entwining, creating a mesmerizing visual effect. This pattern is not for the faint of heart and demands your full attention, so perhaps save your binge-watching for another time, and allow yourself to fully immerse in this rewarding knitting experience.

Construction Notes

This jumper is worked mostly flat in charted lace from the bottom up. You will first work the back panel flat, followed by the front panel. You will join the shoulder seams to create the neck hole using the Three Needle Bind Off method (page 207). To create the armholes, you will use the Mattress stitch (page 209) to seam the sides together. The neck trim and sleeves are worked in the round by picking up stitches along the neck hole/armhole edges.

Skill Level

Intermediate

Sizing

XS (S, M, L, XL) (XXL, 3XL, 4XL, 5XL)

Finished bust: 39.4 (44.8, 49.6, 51.2, 56.6) (61.4, 63, 69.4, 73.2)" / 100 (114, 126, 130, 144) (156, 160, 176, 186) cm, blocked

Recommended ease: This jumper is designed with approximately 11–13 inches / 28–33 cm of positive ease

Sample shown is knit in Size S.

MATERIALS

Yarn

Bulky weight, Wool and the Gang, Alpachino Merino (60% Merino Wool, 40% Baby Alpaca), 110 yds (100 m) per 100-g skein, shown in Lime Sorbet colorway

Any bulky weight yarn can be used for this pattern as long as it matches gauge. A good substitute would be Drops, Andes or Wool and Works, Chunky Merino.

Yardage/Meterage

473 (554, 632, 677, 744) (776, 868, 976, 1020) yds / 433 (507, 578, 619, 680) (710, 794, 892, 933) m

Needles

For body: US 11 (8 mm) straight needles or 24- to 32-inch (60- to 80-cm) circular needle

For sleeves: US 11 (8 mm) 24- to 32-inch (60- to 80-cm) circular needle

For bottom ribbing: US 10 (6 mm) straight needles or 24- to 32-inch (60- to 80-cm) circular needle

For neckline: US 10 (6 mm) 24-inch (60-cm) circular needle

Notions

Stitch markers

Tapestry needle

Scissors

Stitch holders

Measuring tape

GAUGE

10.5 sts x 14 rows = 4 inches (10 cm) in Traveling Vine stitch (explained below) using larger needle (blocked)

To Knit Gauge Swatch

CO 20 sts.

RS rows: K2, rep corresponding row of the chart (page 174) 2 times, K2.

WS rows: P2, rep corresponding row of the chart 2 times, P2.

Work at least 14 rows.

> Note: When worked flat, odd (RS) rows of the chart are read from right to left, and even (WS) rows are read from left to right.

> Note: The "no stitch" symbols on the WS rows are there to account for the extra stitch you will have created on the RS rows. As you only decrease once per repeat on the RS rows but increase twice with the two yarn overs, you will make the second decrease on the WS rows. Do not skip a stitch or bind off when you reach a "no stitch" symbol; simply ignore it and move on to the next stitch of that row.

Don't forget to block your swatch before casting on to ensure you have the correct gauge!

ABBREVIATIONS

1x1 rib(bing) - *Knit 1, purl 1*

BO - Bind off

BOR - Beginning of round

CO - Cast on

K - Knit

K2tog - Knit 2 stitches together

P - Purl

P2tog - Purl 2 stitches together

PM - Place marker

Rep - Repeat

RS - Right side

Ssk - Slip, slip, knit 2 stitches together through the back loops

Ssp - Slip, slip, purl 2 stitches together through the back loops

St(s) - Stitch(es)

Tbl - Through the back loop

WS - Wrong side

YO - Yarn over

SPECIAL TECHNIQUES

Alternating Cable Cast On (page 208)

Three Needle Bind Off (page 207)

Mattress stitch (page 209)

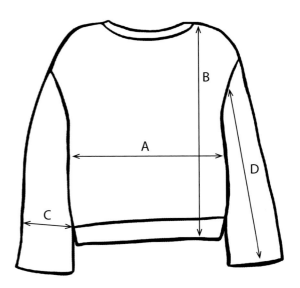

SIZING CHART

Size	XS	S	M	L	XL	XXL	3XL	4XL	5XL
To fit bust	28–30"/ 71–76 cm	32–34"/ 81–86 cm	36–38"/ 91.5–96.5 cm	40–42"/ 101.5–106.5 cm	44–46"/ 111.5–117 cm	48–50"/ 122–127 cm	52–54"/ 132–137 cm	56–58"/ 142–147 cm	60–62"/ 152–158 cm
(A) Width	19.7"/ 50 cm	22.4"/ 57 cm	24.8"/ 63 cm	25.6"/ 65 cm	28.3"/ 72 cm	30.7"/ 78 cm	31.5"/ 80 cm	34.7"/ 88 cm	36.6"/ 93 cm
(B) Length	18.1"/ 46 cm	19.3"/ 49 cm	19.3"/ 49 cm	20.5"/ 52 cm	20.5"/ 52 cm	21.7"/ 55 cm	21.7"/ 55 cm	22.8"/ 58 cm	22.8"/ 58 cm
(C) Sleeve Width	7.9"/ 20 cm	7.9"/ 20 cm	7.9"/ 20 cm	9.4"/ 24 cm	9.4"/ 24 cm	9.4"/ 24 cm	11"/ 28 cm	11"/ 28 cm	11.8"/ 30 cm
(D) Sleeve Length	15.7"/ 40 cm	16.5"/ 42 cm	16.5"/ 42 cm	17.3"/ 44 cm	17.3"/ 44 cm	17.3"/ 44 cm	18.1"/ 46 cm	18.1"/ 46 cm	18.1"/ 46 cm

IVY JUMPER PATTERN

BACK PANEL

Using US 10 (6 mm) straight needles or 24- to 32-inch (60- to 80-cm) circular needles and the Alternating Cable Cast On (page 208), CO 52 (60, 66, 68, 76) (82, 84, 92, 98) sts.

Rows 1–10: *K1, p1*, rep ** until end of the row.

Switch to US 11 (8 mm) straight needles or 24- to 32-inch (60- to 80-cm) circular needles.

Restart your row count here. You will now begin working in Traveling Vine stitch.

Repeat the following 12 rows until you have worked 50 (56, 56, 62, 62) (68, 68, 74, 74) rows total. *You should end after row 2 (8, 8, 2, 2) (8, 8, 2, 2) of the chart (page 174).*

Note: If you would like to add or subtract length to/from your jumper, do so here, but ensure you still end after row 2 (8, 8, 2, 2) (8, 8, 2, 2) of the chart, or knit to your desired length, making note of what row of the chart you end after, as this will change which row you start with for the Back Shoulders. Make note of how many total rows you work so that you can work your Front Panel to match.

Rows 1, 3, 5, 7, 9, 11 (RS): K2 (2, 1, 2, 2) (1, 2, 2, 1), rep corresponding row of the chart (page 174) 6 (7, 8, 8, 9) (10, 10, 11, 12) times, K2 (2, 1, 2, 2) (1, 2, 2, 1).

Rows 2, 4, 6, 8, 10, 12 (WS): P2 (2, 1, 2, 2) (1, 2, 2, 1), rep corresponding row of the chart 6 (7, 8, 8, 9) (10, 10, 11, 12) times, P2 (2, 1, 2, 2) (1, 2, 2, 1).

BACK SHOULDERS

You will now make decreases to shape the back neckline, whilst continuing to work in Traveling Vine stitch.

You should be on row 3 (9, 9, 3, 3) (9, 9, 3, 3) of the chart.

Setup row (RS): K2 (2, 1, 2, 2) (1, 2, 2, 1), rep corresponding row of the chart (page 174) 1 (1, 2, 2, 2) (3, 3, 3, 4) time(s), k7 (10, 6, 5, 9) (5, 4, 8, 4), BO 18 (20, 20, 22, 22) (22, 24, 24, 24) sts, k7 (10, 6, 5, 9) (5, 4, 8, 4), rep corresponding row of the chart 1 (1, 2, 2, 2) (3, 3, 3, 4) time(s), k2 (2, 1, 2, 2) (1, 2, 2, 1).

You will start with the back left shoulder, followed by the back right shoulder. *You may leave the back right shoulder stitches on the cord or place them on a stitch holder.*

You should be on row 4 (10, 10, 4, 4) (10, 10, 4, 4) of the chart.

Next row (WS): P2 (2, 1, 2, 2) (1, 2, 2, 1), rep corresponding row of the chart 1 (1, 2, 2, 2) (3, 3, 3, 4) time(s), p to last 3 sts, ssp, p1.

Next row (RS): K across.

Cut yarn and place these 16 (19, 22, 22, 26) (29, 29, 33, 36) left shoulder sts on a stitch holder. *You will come back to them later for the Shoulder Seams.*

Reattach yarn on the WS to the remaining right shoulder stitches. *You should be on row 4 (10, 10, 4, 4) (10, 10, 4, 4) of the chart.*

Next row (WS): P1, p2tog, p4 (7, 3, 2, 6) (2, 1, 5, 1), rep corresponding row of the chart 1 (1, 2, 2, 2) (3, 3, 3, 4) time(s), p2 (2, 1, 2, 2) (1, 2, 2, 1).

Next row (RS): K across.

Cut yarn and place these 16 (19, 22, 22, 26) (29, 29, 33, 36) right shoulder sts on a stitch holder. *You will come back to them later for the Shoulder Seams.*

FRONT PANEL

Follow Back Panel instructions until you have worked 48 (54, 54, 60, 60) (66, 66, 72, 72) rows **total** of Traveling Vine stitch (not including ribbing). *You should end after row 12 (6, 6, 12, 12) (6, 6, 12, 12) of the chart.*

> **Note:** If you are adding or subtracting length to/from your jumper, work 2 rows less than you did for the Back Panel. Make note of what row of the chart you end after, as this will change which row you start with for the Front Shoulders.

FRONT SHOULDERS

You will now make decreases to shape the front neckline whilst continuing to work in Traveling Vine stitch.

You should now be on row 1 (7, 7, 1, 1) (7, 7, 1, 1) of the chart.

Setup row (RS): K2 (2, 1, 2, 2) (1, 2, 2, 1), rep corresponding row of the chart (page 174) 1 (1, 2, 2, 2) (3, 3, 3, 4) time(s), k8 (11, 7, 6, 10) (6, 5, 9, 5), BO 16 (18, 18, 20, 20) (20, 22, 22, 22) sts, k8 (11, 7, 6, 10) (6, 5, 9, 5), rep corresponding row of the chart 1 (1, 2, 2, 2) (3, 3, 3, 4) time(s), k2 (2, 1, 2, 2) (1, 2, 2, 1).

You will start with the front right (as worn) shoulder, followed by the front left (as worn) shoulder. *You may leave the front left shoulder stitches on the cord or place them on a stitch holder.*

You should now be on row 2 (8, 8, 2, 2) (8, 8, 2, 2) of the chart.

Next row (WS): P2 (2, 1, 2, 2) (1, 2, 2, 1), rep corresponding row of the chart 1 (1, 2, 2, 2) (3, 3, 3, 4) time(s), p to last 3 sts, ssp, p1.

Next row (RS): K7 (10, 6, 5, 9) (5, 4, 8, 4), rep corresponding row of the chart 1 (1, 2, 2, 2) (3, 3, 3, 4) time(s), k2 (2, 1, 2, 2) (1, 2, 2, 1).

Next row: P2 (2, 1, 2, 2) (1, 2, 2, 1), rep corresponding row of the chart 1 (1, 2, 2, 2) (3, 3, 3, 4) time(s), p to last 3 sts, ssp, p1.

Next row: K across.

Cut yarn and place these 16 (19, 22, 22, 26) (29, 29, 33, 36) right shoulder sts on a stitch holder. *You will come back to them later for the Shoulder Seams.*

Reattach yarn on the WS to the remaining left shoulder stitches. *You should be on row 2 (8, 8, 2, 2) (8, 8, 2, 2) of the chart.*

Next row (WS): P1, p2tog, p5 (8, 4, 3, 7) (3, 2, 6, 2), rep corresponding row of the chart 1 (1, 2, 2, 2) (3, 3, 3, 4) time(s), p2 (2, 1, 2, 2) (1, 2, 2, 1).

Next row (RS): K2 (2, 1, 2, 2) (1, 2, 2, 1), rep corresponding row of the chart 1 (1, 2, 2, 2) (3, 3, 3, 4) time(s), k7 (10, 6, 5, 9) (5, 4, 8, 4).

Next row: P1, p2tog, p4 (7, 3, 2, 6) (2, 1, 5, 1), rep corresponding row of the chart 1 (1, 2, 2, 2) (3, 3, 3, 4) time(s), p2 (2, 1, 2, 2) (1, 2, 2, 1).

Next row: K across.

Leave these 16 (19, 22, 22, 26) (29, 29, 33, 36) left shoulder sts on your needle and do not cut the yarn. *Proceed to "Shoulder Seams."*

SHOULDER SEAMS

You will now be using the Three Needle Bind Off method (page 207) to join the shoulder seams.

1. Place the RS of your front and back panels together.

2. Your front left (as worn) shoulder stitches should still be on your needle. Place the corresponding 16 (19, 22, 22, 26) (29, 29, 33, 36) sts left on hold for the back left shoulder onto the other needle. Make sure both needles are facing the same direction.

3. Insert a third needle (US 11 [8 mm] or smaller) knitwise into the first st of the panel that is facing you, then insert that same needle knitwise into the corresponding st of the other panel.

4. Continue, following the instructions for the Three Needle Bind Off method (page 207).

5. Repeat all steps for the other shoulder, using the corresponding front right and back right shoulder stitches left on hold.

SIDE SEAMS

1. Flip your work so that the RS are now facing out (your shoulder seams should be invisible).

2. Take a measuring tape and measure from the shoulder seam down. Place an interlocking stitch marker on the outside edge of your work at the 7.9 (7.9, 7.9, 9.4, 9.4) (9.4, 11, 11, 11) inch / 20 (20, 20, 24, 24) (24, 28, 28, 28) cm mark. Repeat this on both sides.

3. Use the Mattress stitch (page 209) to seam the sides, starting at the bottom.

4. Seam until you reach the stitch markers (you may now remove the markers).

NECK TRIM

Using US 10 (6 mm) 24-inch (60-cm) circular needles, pick up stitches in the following fashion:

1. Pick up 2 sts along the side of the back right shoulder.

2. Pick up 18 (20, 20, 22, 22) (22, 24, 24, 24) sts along the back neck.

3. Pick up 2 sts along the side of the back left shoulder.

4. Pick up 6 sts along the side of the front left shoulder.

5. Pick up 16 (18, 18, 20, 20) (20, 22, 22, 22) sts along the front neck.

6. Pick up 6 sts along the side of the front right shoulder.

You should now have 50 (54, 54, 58, 58) (58, 62, 62, 62) sts. PM to mark the BOR.

Rounds 1–4: *K1, p1*, rep ** until end of the round. *You may need to use the Magic Loop method (page 207).*

BO loosely in 1x1 rib pattern.

SLEEVES

Using US 11 (8 mm) 24- to 32-inch (60- to 80-cm) circular needles, starting at the underarm point, pick up 48 (48, 48, 56, 56) (56, 64, 64, 64) sts, evenly spaced, around the armhole. PM to mark the BOR.

You will now begin working in Traveling Vine stitch in the round.

Repeat the following 12 rounds until you have worked 46 (48, 48, 50, 50) (50, 52, 52, 52) rounds **total**. *You should end after round 10 (12, 12, 2, 2) (2, 4, 4, 4) of the chart.*

> **Note:** If you would like to add or subtract length to/from your sleeve, do so here, but ensure you still end after an even-numbered round. Make note of how many total rows you work so that you can work your second sleeve to match.

Rounds 1–12: Rep corresponding round of the chart (written instructions below) until end of the round. *You should repeat the chart 6 (6, 6, 7, 7) (7, 8, 8, 8) times per round. You may need to use the Magic Loop method (page 207).*

> **Note:** When worked in the round, the chart is read from right to left on every row.

Round 1: YO, k1 tbl, YO, ssk, k5.

Round 2: K3, ssk, k4.

Round 3: YO, k1 tbl, YO, k2, ssk, k3.

Round 4: K5, ssk, k2.

Round 5: K1 tbl, YO, k4, ssk, k1, YO.

Round 6: K6, ssk, k1.

Round 7: K5, k2tog, YO, k1 tbl, YO.

Round 8: K4, k2tog, k3.

Round 9: K3, k2tog, k2, YO, k1 tbl, YO.

CHART

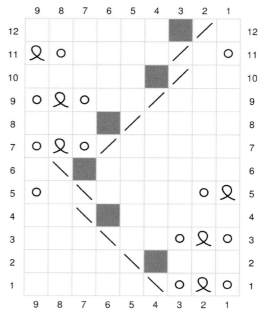

Round 10: K2, k2tog, k5.

Round 11: YO, k1, k2tog, k4, YO, k1 tbl.

Round 12: K1, k2tog, k6.

BO all sts.

FINISHING

Weave in any remaining loose ends.

Wash and block (see Blocking 101 [page 216] or use your preferred blocking method).

Legend		
☐		RS: Knit WS: Purl
▉		No Stitch
╲		Ssk
╱		K2tog
○		YO
☿		K1 tbl

CHART PATTERN WORKED FLAT

Row 1 (RS): YO, k1 tbl, YO, ssk, k5.

Row 2 (WS): P4, ssp, p3.

Row 3: YO, k1 tbl, YO, k2, ssk, k3.

Row 4: P2, ssp, p5.

Row 5: K1 tbl, YO, k4, ssk, k1, YO.

Row 6: P1, ssp, p6.

Row 7: K5, k2tog, YO, k1 tbl, YO.

Row 8: P3, p2tog, p4.

Row 9: K3, k2tog, k2, YO, k1 tbl, YO.

Row 10: P5, p2tog, p2.

Row 11: YO, k1, k2tog, k4, YO, k1 tbl.

Row 12: P6, p2tog, p1.

Twist and Shout Vest

The Twist and Shout Vest is an ultra-quick knit featuring a striking lace cable detailing that is sure to impress any knitting enthusiast. The Lace Cable stitch is a perfect example of why I will never get bored of knitting, as there are so many ways one can combine different techniques to create a stunning, unique texture. Knitted with super bulky yarn, this vest is a quick and easy project that is perfect for both experienced knitters and beginners looking to challenge themselves with some fun, new techniques. With its distinctive design and trendy, cropped fit, this vest is sure to become a beloved addition to your handmade wardrobe.

Construction Notes

This vest is worked mostly flat in reverse stockinette and charted lace/cables from the bottom up. You will first work the back panel flat, followed by the front panel. You will join the shoulder seams to create the neck hole using the Grafting method (page 214). To create the armholes, you will use the Mattress stitch (page 209) to seam the sides together. The neck and sleeve trims are worked in the round by picking up stitches along the neck hole/armhole edges. Instructions on how to adjust the body length of your vest are included.

Skill Level

Advanced Beginner

Sizing

XS (S, M, L, XL) (XXL, 3XL, 4XL, 5XL)

Finished bust: 32.3 (36.2, 40.2, 44, 48) (52, 56, 59.8, 64.6)" / 82 (92, 102, 112, 122) (132, 142, 152, 164) cm

Recommended ease: This vest is designed with 2.4–4.3 inches / 6–11 cm of positive ease

Sample shown is knit in Size S.

MATERIALS

Yarn

Super bulky weight, Cardigang, Chunky Merino Wool (100% merino wool), 87 yds (80 m) per 200-g skein, shown in Tangerine Dream colorway

Any super bulky weight yarn can be used for this pattern as long as it matches gauge. A good substitute would be Wool and the Gang, Crazy Sexy Wool or Malabrigo, Rasta.

Yardage/Meterage

167 (179, 213, 252, 304) (322, 374, 422, 480) yds / 153 (164, 195, 230, 278) (294, 342, 386, 439) m

Needles

For body: US 17 (12 mm) straight needles or 32-inch (80-cm) circular needle

For bottom ribbing, sleeve and neck trims: US 15 (10 mm) 24- to 32-inch (60- to 80-cm) circular needle

Notions

Stitch markers

Tapestry needles

Scissors

Stitch holders

GAUGE

8 sts x 11 rows = 4 inches (10 cm) in stockinette stitch using larger needle

ABBREVIATIONS

1x1 rib(bing) - *Knit 1, purl 1*

C4F - Cable 4 front (place 2 sts on cable needle and hold to front of work. K2, k2 from cable needle)

CO - Cast on

BO - Bind off

BOR - Beginning of round

K - Knit

K2tog - Knit 2 stitches together

P - Purl

P2tog - Purl 2 stitches together

PM - Place marker

Rep - Repeat

RS - Right side

SM - Slip marker

Ssk - Slip, slip, knit 2 stitches together through the back loops

Ssp - Slip, slip, purl 2 stitches together through the back loops

St(s) - Stitch(es)

WS - Wrong side

YO - Yarn over

SIZING CHART

Size	XS	S	M	L	XL	XXL	3XL	4XL	5XL
To fit bust	28–30"/ 71–76 cm	32–34"/ 81–86 cm	36–38"/ 91.5–96.5 cm	40–42"/ 101.5–106.5 cm	44–46"/ 111.5–117 cm	48–50"/ 122–127 cm	52–54"/ 132–137 cm	56–58"/ 142–147 cm	60–62"/ 152–158 cm
(A) Width	16.1"/ 41 cm	18.1"/ 46 cm	20.1"/ 51 cm	22"/ 56 cm	24"/ 61 cm	26"/ 66 cm	28"/ 71 cm	29.9"/ 76 cm	32.3"/ 82 cm
(B) Length	15.7"/ 40 cm	15.7"/ 40 cm	16.9"/ 43 cm	18.1"/ 46 cm	18.9"/ 48 cm	19.7"/ 50 cm	21.3"/ 54 cm	22.4"/ 57 cm	23.6"/ 60 cm
(C) Armhole Depth	8.3"/ 21 cm	8.3"/ 21 cm	8.3"/ 21 cm	9.8"/ 25 cm	9.8"/ 25 cm	10.6"/ 27 cm	10.6"/ 27 cm	11.8"/ 30 cm	11.8"/ 30 cm

SPECIAL TECHNIQUES

Alternating Cable Cast On (page 208)

Magic Loop method (page 207)

Grafting (page 214)

Mattress stitch (page 209)

TWIST AND SHOUT VEST PATTERN

BACK PANEL

Using US 15 (10 mm) 24- to 32-inch (60- to 80-cm) circular needles and the Alternating Cable Cast On (page 208), CO 34 (38, 42, 46, 50) (54, 58, 62, 68) sts.

Rows 1–6: *K1, p1*, rep ** until end of the row.

Switch to US 17 (12 mm) straight needles or 32-inch (80-cm) circular needles. Restart your row count here.

Row 1 (RS): P across.

Row 2 (WS): K across.

Next 13 (13, 17, 17, 19) (19, 23, 23, 25) rows: Repeat rows 1–2, ending after a RS row.

Place an interlocking stitch marker on the stitch on both edges of row 15 (15, 19, 19, 21) (21, 25, 25, 27).

Note: If you would like to add or subtract length to/from your vest, do so here. Make note of how many rows you add or subtract so you can work your Front Panel to match.

Restart your row count here. You will now begin making decreases for the armholes. The decrease sequence is as follows:

Row 1 (WS): K1, ssk, k until last 3 sts, k2tog, k1.

Row 2 (RS): P across.

Repeat rows 1–2 until you have worked them 6 (6, 6, 7, 7) (8, 8, 9, 9) times **total** (meaning 12 (12, 12, 14, 14) (16, 16, 18, 18) total rows). You should end after a RS row and have 22 (26, 30, 32, 36) (38, 42, 44, 50) sts.

Work 8 (8, 8, 10, 10) (10, 10, 12, 12) straight rows in reverse stockinette stitch with no decreases.

BACK SHOULDERS

Setup row (WS): K4 (6, 8, 8, 10) (11, 12, 13, 15), BO 14 (14, 14, 16, 16) (16, 18, 18, 20), k to end of the row.

You will now be working across only the first 4 (6, 8, 8, 10) (11, 12, 13, 15) sts. Leave the remaining stitches on the cord or place them on a stitch holder. *You will come back to them later for the left shoulder.*

Row 1 (RS): P1 (3, 5, 5, 7) (8, 9, 10, 12), ssp, p1.

Row 2 (WS): K across.

Cut yarn and place these 3 (5, 7, 7, 9) (10, 11, 12, 14) right shoulder sts on a stitch holder. *You will come back to them later for the Shoulder Seams.*

Reattach yarn on the RS to work the remaining 4 (6, 8, 8, 10) (11, 12, 13, 15) sts for the left shoulder.

Row 1 (RS): P1, p2tog, p1 (3, 5, 5, 7) (8, 9, 10, 12).

Row 2 (WS): K across.

Cut yarn and place these 3 (5, 7, 7, 9) (10, 11, 12, 14) left shoulder sts on a stitch holder. *You will come back to them later for the Shoulder Seams.*

FRONT PANEL

Using US 15 (10 mm) 24- to 32-inch (60- to 80-cm) circular needles and the Alternating Cable Cast On (page 208), CO 34 (38, 42, 46, 50) (54, 58, 62, 68) sts.

Rows 1–6: *K1, p1*, rep ** until end of the row.

Switch to US 17 (12 mm) straight needles or 32-inch (80-cm) circular needles. Restart your row count here.

You will now begin to follow the chart (page 182).

Restart your row count here. You will now begin making decreases for the armholes. **Continue following the chart** between markers.

The decrease sequence is as follows:

Row 1 (WS): K1, ssk, work in pattern until last 3 sts, k2tog, k1.

Row 2 (RS): Work in pattern.

Repeat rows 1–2 until you have worked them 6 (6, 6, 7, 7) (8, 8, 9, 9) times **total** (meaning 12 (12, 12, 14, 14) (16, 16, 18, 18) total rows). You should end after row 3 (3, 7, 1, 3) (5, 1, 3, 5) of the chart and have 22 (26, 30, 32, 36) (38, 42, 44, 50) sts.

Work 3 (3, 3, 5, 5) (5, 5, 7, 7) straight rows with no decreases, continuing to follow the chart between the markers.

You should end after row 6 (6, 2, 6, 8) (2, 6, 2, 4) of the chart.

FRONT SHOULDERS

Setup row (RS): P6 (8, 10, 10, 12) (13, 14, 15, 17), BO 10 (10, 10, 12, 12) (12, 14, 14, 16), p to end of the row.

You will now be working across **only the first 6 (8, 10, 10, 12) (13, 14, 15, 17) sts.** Leave the remaining sts on the cord or place them on a stitch holder. *You will come back to them later for the left shoulder.*

Row 1 (WS): K until last 3 sts, k2tog, k1.

Row 2 (RS): P across.

Rows 3–6: Repeat rows 1–2. You should now have 3 (5, 7, 7, 9) (10, 11, 12, 14) sts.

Row 7: K across.

Row 8: P across.

Cut yarn and place these 3 (5, 7, 7, 9) (10, 11, 12, 14) right (as worn) shoulder sts on hold. *You will come back to them later for the Shoulder Seams.*

Setup row (RS): P9 (11, 13, 15, 17) (19, 21, 23, 26), PM, work row 1 of the chart, PM, p to the end of the row.

Row 1 (WS): K to marker, SM, work next row of the chart, SM, k to the end of the row.

Row 2: P to marker, SM, work next row of the chart, SM, p to the end of the row.

Repeat rows 1–2 until you have worked 15 (15, 19, 19, 21) (21, 25, 25, 27) rows (including the setup row). *You should end after row 7 (7, 3, 3, 5) (5, 1, 1, 3) of the chart.*

> **Note:** If you would like to add or subtract length to/from your vest, do so here, but be sure to add or subtract the same number of rows as you did for the back panel. Note—this will impact which row of the chart you end on. This is fine, just continue to work from whichever row you are up to.

Reattach yarn on the WS to work the remaining 6 (8, 10, 10, 12) (13, 14, 15, 17) left (as worn) shoulder sts.

Row 1 (WS): K1, ssk, k to end of the row.

Row 2 (RS): P across.

Rows 3–6: Repeat rows 1–2. You should now have 3 (5, 7, 7, 9) (10, 11, 12, 14) sts.

Row 7: K across.

Row 8: P across.

Leave your 3 (5, 7, 7, 9) (10, 11, 12, 14) sts on your needles and do not cut the yarn.

SHOULDER SEAMS

You will now be using the Grafting method (page 214) to join the shoulder seams.

1. Place the WS of your front panel and back panel together.

2. Your front left (as worn) shoulder stitches should still be on your needle. Place the corresponding 3 (5, 7, 7, 9) (10, 11, 12, 14) sts left on hold for the back left shoulder onto the other needle. Make sure both needles are facing the same direction.

3. Cut working yarn leaving a tail that is 2–3 times longer than the width of the shoulder.

4. Continue, following the instructions for Grafting (page 214).

5. Repeat all steps for the other shoulder, using the corresponding front right (as worn) and back right shoulder stitches left on hold.

SIDE SEAMS

1. Use the Mattress stitch (page 209) for reverse stockinette stitch to seam the sides, starting at the bottom.

2. Seam until you reach the stitch markers (you may now remove the markers).

NECK TRIM

Using US 15 (10 mm) 24- to 32-inch (60- to 80-cm) circular needles, pick up stitches in the following fashion:

1. Pick up 16 (16, 16, 18, 18) (18, 20, 20, 22) sts along the back neck.

2. Pick up 8 sts along the side of the front left (as worn) shoulder.

3. Pick up 10 (10, 10, 12, 12) (12, 14, 14, 16) sts along the front neck.

4. Pick up 8 sts along the side of the front right (as worn) shoulder.

You should now have 42 (42, 42, 46, 46) (46, 50, 50, 54) sts. PM to mark the BOR.

Rounds 1–3: *K1, p1*, rep ** until end of the round. *You will need to use the Magic Loop method (page 207).*

BO all sts loosely in 1x1 rib pattern.

SLEEVE TRIMS

Using US 15 (10 mm) 24- to 32-inch (60- to 80-cm) circular needles, pick up stitches in the following fashion: *Pick up 5 sts, skip 1 st.* Make sure you have an even number of stitches. PM to mark the BOR.

Round 1: *K1, p1*, rep ** until end of the round. *You will need to use the Magic Loop method (page 207).*

BO all sts loosely in 1x1 rib pattern.

CHART

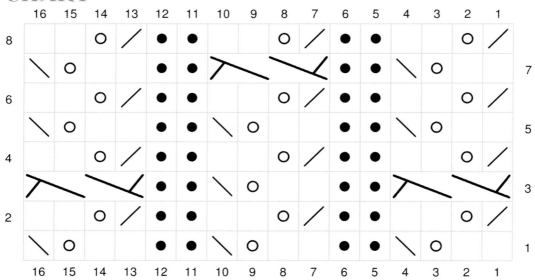

FINISHING

Weave in all your loose ends.

Blocking super bulky yarn is not necessary. However, if you do wish to block your vest, which will help open up the eyelets, it is suggested that you use the spray blocking method (do *not* wet or steam block).

Legend		
☐		RS: Knit WS: Purl
●		RS: Purl WS: Knit
╲		Ssk
╱		P2tog
○		YO
⟋⟍		C4F

CHART PATTERN

Row 1 (RS): *K2, YO, ssk, p2*, rep ** 1 more time, k2, YO, ssk.

Row 2 (WS): *P2, YO, p2tog, k2* rep ** 1 more time, p2, YO, p2tog.

Row 3: C4F, p2, k2, YO, ssk, p2, C4F.

Row 4: Repeat row 2.

Row 5: Repeat row 1.

Row 6: Repeat row 2.

Row 7: K2, YO, ssk, p2, C4F, p2, k2, YO, ssk.

Row 8: Repeat row 2.

Lily Cardigan

Whilst I love incorporating intricate textures and bold colorwork into my designs, I also believe in the beauty of simplicity, where less becomes more. The Lily Cardigan embodies this sentiment, boasting an understated elegance that captures the essence of timeless fashion. The ethereal lacework pattern is a breeze to memorize, consisting of just three rows. For those eager to embark on their lacework journey, the Lily Cardigan serves as an excellent introduction. Furthermore, the cardigan provides a canvas for personalization, allowing you to infuse your own unique personality and flair by choosing the perfect buttons to complement your style.

Construction Notes

This seamless cardigan is worked in stockinette stitch and charted lace from the bottom up. You will first work the bottom section of the cardigan flat, before splitting at the underarm point to work the front left panel, then the back panel, followed by the front right panel. You will join the shoulder seams to create the armholes using the Three Needle Bind Off method (page 207). The sleeves are worked in the round by picking up stitches along the armhole edges. You will then work the button bands flat by picking up stitches along the inside edges. You will finish by working the neck trim flat by picking up stitches along the neckline edge. Instructions on how to adjust the body and sleeve length of your cardigan are included.

Skill Level

Intermediate

Sizing

XS (S, M, L, XL) (XXL, 3XL, 4XL, 5XL)

Finished bust: 41 (44.8, 48.8, 52.8, 56.6) (60.6, 64.6, 68.6, 73.2)" / 104 (114, 124, 134, 144) (154, 164, 174, 186) cm, blocked

Recommended ease: This cardigan is designed with approximately 11–13 inches / 28–33 cm of positive ease

Sample shown is knit in Size S.

MATERIALS

Yarn

Aran weight, Wool and the Gang, Take Care Mohair (78% Mohair, 13% Wool, 9% Polyamide), 109 yds (100 m) per 50-g skein, shown in Lovely Lilac colorway

Any Aran weight fluffy yarn can be used for this pattern as long as it matches gauge. A good substitute would be Hip Knit Shop, Fluff or Cardigang, Chunky Mohair.

Yardage/Meterage

437 (470, 546, 630, 699) (782, 889, 972, 1068) yds / 400 (430, 500, 576, 639) (715, 813, 889, 977) m

Needles

For body: US 10 (6.5 mm) 32- to 40-inch (80- to 100-cm) circular needle

For sleeves: US 10 (6.5 mm) 24- to 32-inch (60- to 80-cm) circular needle

For sleeve cuffs: US 8 (5 mm) 16- to 24-inch (40- to 60-cm) circular needle or DPNs

For button bands and neck trim: US 8 (5 mm) 24- to 32-inch (60- to 80-cm) circular needle

For bottom ribbing: US 8 (5 mm) 32- to 40-inch (80- to 100-cm) circular needle

Notions

Buttons (can be 1" / 25 mm or larger) x 4 (4, 4, 5, 5) (5, 6, 6, 6)

Stitch markers

Tapestry needle

Scissors

Stitch holders

GAUGE

10.5 sts x 16 rows = 4 inches (10 cm) in stockinette stitch using larger needle (blocked)

ABBREVIATIONS

1x1 rib(bing) - *Knit 1, purl 1*

BO - Bind off

BOR - Beginning of round

CO - Cast on

DPNs - Double pointed needles

K - Knit

K2tog - Knit 2 stitches together

P - Purl

P2tog - Purl 2 stitches together

PM - Place marker

PSSO - Pass slipped stitch over

Rep - Repeat

RM - Remove marker

RS - Right side

Sl wyib - Slip stitch purlwise with yarn held in back

SM - Slip marker

Ssk - Slip, slip, knit 2 stitches together through the back loops

Ssp - Slip, slip, purl 2 stitches together through the back loops

St(s) - Stitch(es)

Tbl – Through the back loop

WS - Wrong side

Wyif – With yarn held in front

YO - Yarn over

SIZING CHART

Size	XS	S	M	L	XL	XXL	3XL	4XL	5XL
To fit bust	28–30"/ 71–76 cm	32–34"/ 81–86 cm	36–38"/ 91.5–96.5 cm	40–42"/ 101.5–106.5 cm	44–46"/ 111.5–117 cm	48–50"/ 122–127 cm	52–54"/ 132–137 cm	56–58"/ 142–147 cm	60–62"/ 152–158 cm
(A) Width	20.5"/ 52 cm	22.4"/ 57 cm	24.4"/ 62 cm	26.4"/ 67 cm	28.3"/ 72 cm	30.3"/ 77 cm	32.3"/ 82 cm	34.3"/ 87 cm	36.6"/ 93 cm
(B) Length	16.1"/ 41 cm	16.1"/ 41 cm	17.3"/ 44 cm	18.5"/ 47 cm	19.7"/ 50 cm	20.9"/ 53 cm	22"/ 56 cm	23.2"/ 59 cm	24.4"/ 62 cm
(C) Sleeve Width	7.1"/ 18 cm	7.1"/ 18 cm	7.1"/ 18 cm	8.7"/ 22 cm	8.7"/ 22 cm	8.7"/ 22 cm	10.2"/ 26 cm	10.2"/ 26 cm	10.2"/ 26 cm
(D) Sleeve Length	15"/ 38 cm	16.1"/ 41 cm	16.1"/ 41 cm	17.3"/ 44 cm	17.3"/ 44 cm	18.5"/ 47 cm	18.5"/ 47 cm	18.5"/ 47 cm	18.5"/ 47 cm

SPECIAL TECHNIQUES

Three Needle Bind Off (page 207)

Magic Loop method (page 207)

Horizontal One Row Buttonhole (page 215)

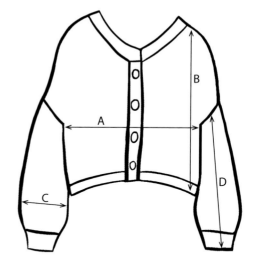

BOTTOM

Using US 8 (5 mm) 32- to 40-inch (80- to 100-cm) circular needles and the Long Tail Cast On, CO 103 (112, 123, 132, 144) (153, 164, 173, 188) sts.

Sizes XS (-, M, -, -) (XXL, -, 4XL, -) only

Row 1: *K1, p1*, rep ** until last st, k1.

Row 2: *P1, k1*, rep ** until last st, p1.

Rows 3–6: Repeat rows 1–2.

Sizes XS (-, M, -, -) (XXL, -, 4XL, -) proceed to "All sizes continue."

Sizes - (S, -, L, XL) (-, 3XL, -, 5XL) only

Row 1: *K1, p1*, rep ** until end of the row.

Rows 2–6: Repeat row 1.

Proceed to "All sizes continue."

All sizes continue

Switch to US 10 (6.5 mm) 32- to 40-inch (80- to 100-cm) circular needles. Restart your row count here.

You will now begin to follow the chart (page 193).

> **Note:** When worked flat, odd (RS) rows of the chart are read from right to left, and even (WS) rows are read from left to right.

Setup row (RS): K7 (8, 9, 10, 12) (13, 14, 15, 17), **PM**, work row 1 of the chart, **PM**, k12 (14, 18, 20, 22) (24, 28, 30, 34), **PM**, work row 1 of the chart, **PM**, k21 (24, 25, 28, 32) (35, 36, 39, 42), **PM**, work row 1 of the chart, **PM**, k12 (14, 18, 20, 22) (24, 28, 30, 34), **PM**, work row 1 of the chart, **PM**, k to end of the row.

Row 1 (WS): *P to marker, SM, work next row of the chart, SM*, rep ** 3 more times, p to end of the row.

Row 2: *K to marker, SM, work next row of the chart, SM*, rep ** 3 more times, k to end of the row.

Repeat rows 1–2 until you have worked 33 (33, 37, 37, 41) (45, 45, 49, 53) rows total (including the setup row). *You should end after row 1 of the chart.*

> **Note:** If you would like to add or subtract length to/from your cardigan, do so here, but make sure to keep track of which row of the chart you end on.

FRONT LEFT PANEL

You will now be working across **only the first 24 (26, 29, 31, 34) (36, 39, 41, 45) sts.** Leave the remaining stitches on the cord or place them on a stitch holder. *You will come back to them later for the Back and Front Right Panels.*

You should be on row 2 of the chart.

Row 1 (WS): P to marker, SM, work next row of the chart, SM, p to end of the row.

Row 2 (RS): K to marker, SM, work next row of the chart, SM, k to end of the row.

Repeat rows 1–2 until you have worked a **total** of 11 (11, 11, 15, 15) (17, 19, 19, 21) rows **from the underarm separation.** *You should end after row 4 (4, 4, 4, 4) (2, 4, 4, 2) of the chart.*

Place an interlocking stitch marker on the st on the edge of the last row you work. This will mark where you start the Button Band.

You will now make decreases to shape the front left (as worn) neckline, whilst continuing to work in pattern (including the non-charted edge stitches that have been established during the previous section).

A note on working in pattern: As you decrease during this section, you may no longer always be able to complete a full repeat of the Chart pattern at the inner edges of the neckline. This means you will not necessarily begin with stitch 1 (RS) or stitch 11 (WS) of the chart when it says "work in pattern"; instead you would start with the stitch that vertically matches the stitch column below it. If/when you start decreasing into the chart section, you may remove the marker.

You should be on row 1 (1, 1, 1, 1) (3, 1, 1, 3) of the chart.

Row 1 (RS): Work in pattern to last 3 sts, k2tog, k1.

Row 2 (WS): P2, work in pattern until end of the row.

Repeat rows 1–2 until you have worked them 7 (7, 7, 8, 8) (8, 9, 9, 9) times **total** (meaning 14 (14, 14, 16, 16) (16, 18, 18, 18) total rows). You should end after a WS row and have 17 (19, 22, 23, 26) (28, 30, 32, 36) sts.

You will now be working straight with no decreases. *You should be on row 3 (3, 3, 1, 1) (3, 3, 3, 1) of the chart.*

Sizes XS (S, -, L, -) (XXL, 3XL, -, 5XL) only

Row 1 (RS): Work in pattern to last 2 sts, k2.

Row 2 (WS): P2, work in pattern until end of the row.

Cut yarn and place these 17 (19, -, 23, -) (28, 30, -, 36) sts on a stitch holder. *You will come back to them later for the Shoulder Seams.*

Row 1 (RS): Work in pattern to last 2 sts, k2.

Row 2 (WS): P2, work in pattern until end of the row.

Row 3: Repeat row 1.

Cut yarn and place these - (-, 22, -, 26) (-, -, 32, -) sts on a stitch holder. *You will come back to them later for the Shoulder Seams.*

BACK PANEL

You will now be working across **only the next 55 (60, 65, 70, 76) (81, 86, 91, 98) sts.** Leave the remaining stitches on the cord or place them on a stitch holder. *You will come back to them later for the Front Right Panel.* Reattach yarn on the WS.

You should be on row 2 of the chart.

Row 1 (WS): *P to marker, SM, work next row of the chart, SM*, rep ** 1 more time, p to end of the row.

Row 2 (RS): *K to marker, SM, work next row of the chart, SM*, rep ** 1 more time, k to end of the row.

Repeat rows 1–2 until you have worked a total of 24 (24, 25, 30, 31) (32, 36, 37, 38) rows from the underarm separation. *You should end after a RS (RS, WS, RS, WS) (RS, RS, WS, RS) row.*

BACK SHOULDERS

You will now make decreases to shape the back neckline, whilst continuing to work in pattern (including the non-charted stitches that have been established during the previous section).

You should be on row 2 (2, 3, 4, 1) (2, 2, 3, 4) of the chart.

Row 1 (WS): Work in pattern across 18 (20, -, 24, -) (29, 31, -, 37) sts, turn.

Row 2 (RS): K1, ssk, work in pattern until end of the row.

Row 3: Work in pattern until last 2 sts, p2.

Cut yarn and place these 17 (19, -, 23, -) (28, 30, -, 36) sts on a stitch holder. *You will come back to them later for the Shoulder Seams.*

Place the middle 19 (20, -, 22, -) (23, 24, -, 24) sts on another stitch holder. *You will come back to them later for the Neck Trim.*

Reattach yarn on the WS to the remaining 18 (20, -, 24, -) (29, 31, -, 37) right shoulder sts.

Row 1 (WS): Work in pattern until end of the row.

Row 2 (RS): Work in pattern until last 3 sts, k2tog, k1.

Row 3: P2, work in pattern until end of the row.

Cut yarn and place these 17 (19, -, 23, -) (28, 30, -, 36) sts on a stitch holder. *You will come back to them later for the Shoulder Seams.*

Sizes - (-, M, -, XL) (-, -, 4XL, -) only

Row 1 (RS): Work in pattern across - (-, 23, -, 27) (-, -, 33, -) sts, turn.

Row 2 (WS): P1, p2tog, work in pattern until end of the row.

Row 3: Work in pattern until last 2 sts, k2.

Cut yarn and place these - (-, 22, -, 26) (-, -, 32, -) sts on a stitch holder. *You will come back to them later for the Shoulder Seams.*

Place the middle - (-, 19, -, 22) (-, -, 25, -) sts on another stitch holder. *You will come back to them later for the Neck Trim.*

Reattach yarn on the RS to the remaining - (-, 23, -, 27) (-, -, 33, -) left shoulder sts.

Row 1 (RS): Work in pattern until end of the row.

Row 2 (WS): Work in pattern until last 3 sts, ssp, p1.

Row 3: K2, work in pattern until end of the row.

Cut yarn and place these - (-, 22, -, 26) (-, -, 32, -) sts on a stitch holder. *You will come back to them later for the Shoulder Seams.*

FRONT RIGHT PANEL

Reattach yarn on the WS to the remaining 24 (26, 29, 31, 34) (36, 39, 41, 45) sts.

You should be on row 2 of the chart.

Row 1 (WS): P to marker, SM, work next row of the chart, SM, p to end of the row.

Row 2 (RS): K to marker, SM, work next row of the chart, SM, k to end of the row.

Repeat rows 1–2 until you have worked a **total** of 11 (11, 11, 15, 15) (17, 19, 19, 21) rows from the underarm separation. *You should end after a WS row.*

Place an interlocking stitch marker on the st on the edge of the last row you work. This will mark where you end the Button Band.

You will now make decreases to shape the front right (as worn) neckline, whilst continuing to work in pattern (including the non-charted edge stitches that have been established during the previous section).

You should be on row 1 (1, 1, 1, 1) (3, 1, 1, 3) of the chart.

Row 1 (RS): K1, ssk, work in pattern until end of the row.

Row 2 (WS): Work in pattern until last 2 sts, p2.

Repeat rows 1–2 until you have worked them 7 (7, 7, 8, 8) (8, 9, 9, 9) times **total** (meaning 14 (14, 14, 16, 16) (16, 18, 18, 18) total rows). You should end after a WS row and have 17 (19, 22, 23, 26) (28, 30, 32, 36) sts.

You will now be working straight with no decreases. *You should be on row 3 (3, 3, 1, 1) (3, 3, 3, 1) of the chart.*

Sizes XS (S, -, L, -) (XXL, 3XL, -, 5XL) only

Row 1 (RS): K2, work in pattern until end of the row.

Row 2 (WS): Work in pattern until last 2 sts, p2.

Leave these 17 (19, -, 23, -) (28, 30, -, 36) sts on the needle and do not cut the yarn. *Proceed to "Shoulder Seams."*

Sizes - (-, M, -, XL) (-, -, 4XL, -) only

Row 1 (RS): K2, work in pattern until end of the row.

Row 2 (WS): Work in pattern until last 2 sts, p2.

Row 3: Repeat row 1.

Leave these - (-, 22, -, 26) (-, -, 32, -) sts on the needle and do not cut the yarn. *Proceed to "Shoulder Seams."*

SHOULDER SEAMS

You will now be using the Three Needle Bind Off method (page 207) to join the shoulder seams.

1. Place the RS of your front and back panels together.

2. Your front right (as worn) shoulder stitches should still be on your needle. Place the corresponding 17 (19, 22, 23, 26) (28, 30, 32, 36) sts left on hold for the back right shoulder onto the other needle. Make sure both needles are facing the same direction.

3. Insert a third needle (US 10 [6.5 mm] or smaller) knitwise into the first st of the panel that is facing you, then insert that same needle knitwise into the corresponding st of the other panel.

4. Continue, following the instructions for the Three Needle Bind Off method (page 207).

5. Repeat all steps for the other shoulder, using the corresponding front left and back left shoulder stitches left on hold.

SLEEVES

Flip your work so that the RS are now facing out (your shoulder seams should be invisible).

Using US 10 (6.5 mm) 24- to 32-inch (60- to 80-cm) circular needles, starting at the underarm point, pick up 47 (47, 47, 55, 55) (55, 63, 63, 63) sts, evenly spaced, around the armhole. *You may need to use the Magic Loop method (page 207).* Ensure that the 24th (24th, 24th, 28th, 28th) (28th, 32nd, 32nd, 32nd) stitch you pick up aligns with your shoulder seam—this will ensure that your lacework section will be centered.

PM to mark the BOR. *Ensure this marker can be differentiated from the two stitch markers you'll place in the setup round.*

You will now begin to follow the chart (written instructions on page 193) in the round.

> **Note:** When worked in the round, the chart is read from right to left on every row.

Setup round: K18 (18, 18, 22, 22) (22, 26, 26, 26), **PM**, work round 1 of chart, **PM**, k to end of the round.

Round 1: K to marker, SM, work next round of chart, SM, k to end of the round.

Repeat round 1 until you have worked 52 (56, 56, 62, 62) (66, 66, 66, 66) rounds **total**, or to desired length. *Keep in mind the sleeve cuff will add approximately 2.4 inches (6 cm). Ensure you end after round 2 or 4 of the chart. Make note of how many total rows you work so that you can work your second sleeve to match.*

You will now make decreases before working the sleeve cuffs.

Next round: K1, *k2tog*, rep ** until end of the round.

You should now have 24 (24, 24, 28, 28) (28, 32, 32, 32) sts.

Switch to US 8 (5 mm) 16- to 24-inch (40- to 60-cm) circular needles or DPNs. *If using circular needles, you will need to use the Magic Loop method (page 207).*

Next 10 rounds: *K1, p1*, rep ** until end of the round.

BO all sts loosely in 1x1 ribbing.

LEFT BUTTON BAND

You will now work the left (as worn) button band.

Using US 8 (5 mm) straight needles or 24- to 32-inch (60- to 80-cm) circular needles, starting from where you placed the stitch marker underneath the neckline shaping on the Front Left (as worn) Panel, with the RS facing you, pick up stitches along the inside edge in the following pattern: *pick up 4 sts, skip 1 st*, ensuring you end up with an even number of stitches.

Rows 1–5: *K1, p1*, rep ** until end of the row.

BO all sts loosely in 1x1 ribbing.

RIGHT BUTTON BAND

You will now work the right (as worn) button band.

Using US 8 (5 mm) straight needles or 24- to 32-inch (60- to 80-cm) circular needles, starting from the bottom of the Front Right (as worn) Panel, with the RS facing you, pick up stitches along the inside edge in the following pattern: *pick up 4 sts, skip 1 st*, until you reach the stitch marker, ensuring you end up with an even number of stitches.

Rows 1–2: *K1, p1*, rep ** until end of the row.

You will now place stitch markers to mark where you will create the buttonholes.

Mark 4 (4, 4, 5, 5) (5, 6, 6, 6) spots where you will start each buttonhole. Your buttonholes should be evenly spaced. Each buttonhole will comprise 4 sts, and there should be approximately 4–5 sts between each buttonhole. The markers will mark the top of the buttonhole.

Follow instructions for the Horizontal One Row Buttonhole (page 215) where it says "work buttonhole."

Row 3 (WS): *Work in 1x1 ribbing until marker, RM, work buttonhole*, rep ** until you have worked all buttonholes, work in 1x1 ribbing until end of the row.

Rows 4–5: *K1, p1*, rep ** until end of the row.

BO all sts loosely in 1x1 ribbing.

Neck Trim

Using US 8 (5 mm) 24- to 32-inch (60- to 80-cm) circular needles, pick up stitches in the following fashion:

1. Starting from the top of the Right (as worn) Button Band, pick up stitches in the following fashion: *pick up 4 sts, skip 1 st*. Stop when you reach the live stitches you left on hold for the back neck.

2. Pick up and knit the 19 (20, 19, 22, 22) (23, 24, 25, 24) live sts from the stitch holder at the back neck.

3. Continue to pick up stitches in the same fashion as Step 1 until you reach the edge of the Left (as worn) Button Band. *Make sure you have an even number of stitches.*

Rows 1–5: *K1, p1*, rep ** until end of the row.

BO all sts loosely in 1x1 ribbing.

FINISHING

Attach buttons along the left (as worn) side of the button band in line with buttonholes.

Weave in any remaining loose ends.

Wash and block (see Blocking 101 [page 216] or use your preferred blocking method).

CHART

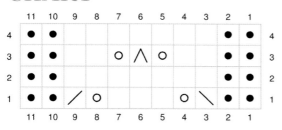

CHART PATTERN WORKED FLAT

Row 1 (RS): P2, ssk, YO, k3, YO, k2tog, p2.

Row 2 (WS): K2, p7, k2.

Row 3: P2, k2, YO, sl1 wyib, k2tog, PSSO, YO, k2, p2.

Row 4: K2, p7, k2.

CHART PATTERN WORKED IN THE ROUND

Round 1: P2, ssk, YO, k3, YO, k2tog, p2.

Round 2: P2, k7, p2.

Round 3: P2, k2, YO, sl1 wyib, k2tog, PSSO, YO, k2, p2.

Round 4: P2, k7, p2.

Legend	
□	RS: Knit WS: Purl
●	RS: Purl WS: Knit
\	Ssk
/	P2tog
o	YO
/\	Sl1, k1, PSSO

Bambi Jumper

There is more to the Bambi Jumper than meets the eye, thanks to the remarkable Faux Cable stitch, which creates a mesmerizing optical illusion. At first glance, it appears to be an intricate cable pattern, but upon closer inspection, you'll discover the clever placement of simple lacework stitches that ingeniously mimic cable-like textures. The result is a beautiful fabric that exemplifies how lace stitches can be manipulated to create stunning visual effects. My goal when designing this piece was to showcase the versatility of lacework beyond its conventional usage. Crafted with super bulky yarn, the Bambi Jumper pushes the boundaries of traditional lacework patterns and recontextualizes this classic knitting style in a way that is both fresh and functional.

Construction Notes

This seamless jumper is worked entirely in the round in stockinette stitch and charted cables from the top down. You will first work the neck trim before working the yoke. You will then divide the body from the sleeves at the underarm point, and continue to work the body in the round, before knitting the sleeves in the round.

Skill Level

Intermediate

Sizing

XS (S, M, L, XL) (XXL, 3XL, 4XL, 5XL)

Finished bust: 41.8 (45.6, 49.6, 53.6, 57.4) (61.4, 65.4, 69.2, 74)" / 106 (116, 126, 136, 146) (156, 166, 176, 188) cm

Recommended ease: This jumper is designed with approximately 11.8–13.8 inches / 30–35 cm of positive ease

Sample shown is knit in Size S.

MATERIALS

Yarn

Super bulky weight, Malabrigo, Rasta (100% Merino Wool), 90 yds (82 m) per 150-g skein, shown in Melon colorway

Any super bulky weight yarn can be used for this pattern as long as it matches gauge. A good substitute would be Wool and the Gang, Crazy Sexy Wool or Cardigang, Chunky Merino.

Yardage/Meterage

465 (548, 591, 665, 703) (784, 851, 939, 991) yds / 426 (501, 540, 608, 643) (717, 778, 859, 906) m

Needles

For body and sleeves: US 17 (12 mm) 32- to 40-inch (80- to 100-cm) circular needle

For bottom ribbing, sleeve and neck trims: US 15 (10 mm) 24- to 32-inch (60- to 80-cm) circular needle

Notions

Stitch markers

Tapestry needle

Scissors

Stitch holders

Scrap yarn

GAUGE

8 sts x 12 rows = 4 inches (10 cm) in stockinette stitch using larger needle

SPECIAL TECHNIQUES

Magic Loop method (page 207)

ABBREVIATIONS

1x1 rib(bing) - *Knit 1, purl 1*

BO - Bind off

BOR - Beginning of round

CO - Cast on

K - Knit

K2tog - Knit 2 stitches together

K3tog - Knit 3 stitches together

M1L - Make 1 left

M1R - Make 1 right

P - Purl

PM - Place marker

Rep - Repeat

RM - Remove marker

S2KP - Slip 2 stitches together knitwise, knit 1, pass slipped stitches over

SM - Slip marker

Ssk - Slip, slip, knit 2 stitches together through the back loops

St(s) - Stitch(es)

YO - Yarn over

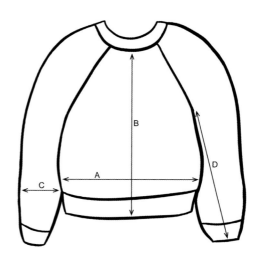

SIZING CHART

Size	XS	S	M	L	XL	XXL	3XL	4XL	5XL
To fit bust	28–30"/ 71–76 cm	32–34"/ 81–86 cm	36–38"/ 91.5–96.5 cm	40–42"/ 101.5–106.5 cm	44–46"/ 111.5–117 cm	48–50"/ 122–127 cm	52–54"/ 132–137 cm	56–58"/ 142–147 cm	60–62"/ 152–158 cm
(A) Width	20.9"/ 53 cm	22.8"/ 58 cm	24.8"/ 63 cm	26.8"/ 68 cm	28.7"/ 73 cm	30.7"/ 78 cm	32.7"/ 83 cm	34.6"/ 88 cm	37"/ 94 cm
(B) Length	17.3"/ 44 cm	18.5"/ 47 cm	18.5"/ 47 cm	19.7"/ 50 cm	19.7"/ 50 cm	20.9"/ 53 cm	20.9"/ 53 cm	22"/ 56 cm	22"/ 56 cm
(C) Sleeve Width	9.1"/ 23 cm	10.2"/ 26 cm	10.6"/ 27 cm	10.6"/ 27 cm	11"/ 28 cm	11"/ 28 cm	11"/ 28 cm	11.4"/ 29 cm	11.4"/ 29 cm
(D) Sleeve Length	14.2"/ 36 cm	14.2"/ 36 cm	15"/ 38 cm	15.7"/ 40 cm	15.7"/ 40 cm	16.5"/ 42 cm	16.5"/ 42 cm	17.3"/ 44 cm	17.3"/ 44 cm

BAMBI JUMPER PATTERN

NECK TRIM

Using US 15 (10 mm) 24- to 32-inch (60- to 80-cm) circular needles and the Long Tail Cast On, CO 48 (50, 52, 52, 54) (58, 58, 62, 62) sts. Join in the round and PM to mark the BOR. *You will need to use the Magic Loop method (page 207).*

Rounds 1–6: *K1, p1*, rep ** until end of the round.

YOKE

Switch to US 17 (12 mm) 32- to 40-inch (80- to 100-cm) circular needles. Restart your row count here.

You will now place 3 additional markers to divide your stitches into 4 sections (front, sleeve 1, back, sleeve 2). Ensure your BOR marker can be easily distinguished from the other markers.

Setup round 1: K17 (17, 19, 19, 19) (21, 21, 23, 23), PM, k7 (8, 7, 7, 8) (8, 8, 8, 8), PM, k17 (17, 19, 19, 19) (21, 21, 23, 23), PM, k7 (8, 7, 7, 8) (8, 8, 8, 8).

You will now place additional markers to mark where you will work in Faux Braid stitch on the front and back sections.

Setup round 2: *K2 (2, 3, 3, 3) (4, 4, 5, 5), p1, PM, k6, k2tog, k2, YO, PM, p1, k to marker, SM, k to marker, SM*, rep ** until end of the round.

Restart your row count here. You will now begin to follow the chart for the Faux Braid stitch (page 205). *Begin with round 12 of the chart during Round 1 below where it says "work next round of the chart."*

Round 1: *K1, M1L, k to 1 st before marker, p1, SM, work next round of the chart, SM, p1, k to 1 st before marker, M1R, k1, SM, k1, M1L, k to 1 st before marker, M1R, k1, SM*, rep ** until end of the round.

Round 2: *K to 1 st before marker, p1, SM, work next round of the chart, SM, p1, k to marker, SM, k to marker, SM*, rep ** until end of the round.

Repeat rounds 1–2 until you have worked them 3 (2, 3, 3, 2) (2, 2, 2, 2) times total (meaning 6 (4, 6, 6, 4) (4, 4, 4, 4) total rounds). You should now have a total of 72 (66, 76, 76, 70) (74, 74, 78, 78) sts, with 23 (21, 25, 25, 23) (25, 25, 27, 27) sts for the front and back sections, and 13 (12, 13, 13, 12) (12, 12, 12, 12) sts for each sleeve. *You should end after round 5 (3, 5, 5, 3) (3, 3, 3, 3) of the chart.*

Next round: Repeat round 1.

You will now place additional markers to mark where you will work in Faux Braid stitch on the sleeves. *Begin working the chart for the sleeves with the same current round of the chart as the front/back sections. You should be on round 7 (5, 7, 7, 5) (5, 5, 5, 5) of the chart.*

Next round: *K to 1 st before marker, p1, SM, work next round of the chart, SM, p1, k to marker, SM, k2 (1, 2, 2, 1) (1, 1, 1, 1), p1, PM, work next round of the chart, PM, p1, k to marker, SM*, rep ** until end of the round.

Restart your row count here. *You should be on round 8 (6, 8, 8, 6) (6, 6, 6, 6) of the chart.*

Round 1: *K1, M1L, k to 1 st before marker, p1, SM, work next row of the chart, SM, p1, k to 1 st before marker, M1R, k1, SM*, rep ** until end of the round.

Round 2: *K to 1 st before marker, p1, SM, work next round of the chart, SM, p1, k to marker, SM*, rep ** until end of the round.

Repeat rounds 1–2 until you have worked them 5 (6, 5, 5, 6) (4, 4, 4, 4) times total (meaning 10 (12, 10, 10, 12) (8, 8, 8, 8) total rounds). You should now have a total of 120 (122, 124, 124, 126) (114, 114, 118, 118) sts, with 35 (35, 37, 37, 37) (35, 35, 37, 37) sts for the front and back sections, and 25 (26, 25, 25, 26) (22, 22, 22, 22) sts for each sleeve. *You should end after round 5 (5, 5, 5, 5) (1, 1, 1, 1) of the chart.*

Next round: *K1, M1L, k to 1 st before marker, p1, RM, work next round of the chart, RM, p1, k to 1 st before marker, M1R, k1, SM, K1, M1L, k to 1 st before marker, p1, SM, work next round of the chart, SM, p1, k to 1 st before marker, M1R, k1, SM, *, rep ** until end of the round.

You will now place additional markers to mark where you will work additional repeats of Faux Braid stitch on the front and back sections. *Begin working the additional repeats with the same current round of the chart as the front/back/sleeves. You should be on round 7 (7, 7, 7, 7) (3, 3, 3, 3) of the chart.*

Next round: *K1 (1, 2, 2, 2) (1, 1, 2, 2), p1, PM, (work next round of the chart, p1) 2 times, work next round of the chart, PM, p1, k to marker, SM, k to 1 st before marker, p1, SM, work next round of the chart, SM, p1, k to marker, SM*, rep ** until end of the round.

Restart your row count here. *You should be on round 8 (8, 8, 8, 8) (4, 4, 4, 4) of the chart.*

Round 1: *K1, M1L, k to 1 st before marker, p1, SM, (work next round of the chart, p1) 2 times, work next round of the chart, SM, p1, k to 1 st before marker, M1R, k1, SM, k1, M1L, k to 1 st before marker, p1, SM, work next round of the chart, SM, p1, k to 1 st before marker, M1R, k1, SM*, rep ** until end of the round.

Round 2: *K to 1 st before marker, p1, SM, (work next round of the chart, p1) 2 times, work next round of the chart, SM, p1, k to marker, SM, k to 1 st before marker, p1, SM, work next round of the chart, SM, p1, k to marker, SM*, rep ** until end of the round.

Repeat rounds 1–2 until you have worked them 4 (3, 4, 4, 3) (5, 5, 5, 5) times **total** (meaning 8 (6, 8, 8, 6) (10, 10, 10, 10) total rounds). You should now have a **total** of 160 (154, 164, 164, 158) (162, 162, 166, 166) sts, with 45 (43, 47, 47, 45) (47, 47, 49, 49) sts for the front and back sections, and 35 (34, 35, 35, 34) (34, 34, 34, 34) sts for each sleeve. *You should end after round 3 (1, 3, 3, 1) (1, 1, 1, 1) of the chart.*

Size XS proceed to "Body."

Sizes - (S, M, L, XL) (XXL, 3XL, 4XL, 5XL) only

Next round: *K1, M1L, k to 1 st before marker, p1, SM, (work next round of the chart, p1) 2 times, work next round of the chart, SM, p1, k to 1 st before marker, M1R, k1, SM, k1, M1L, k to 1 st before marker, p1, RM, work next round of the chart, RM, p1, k to 1 st before marker, M1R, k1, SM*, rep ** until end of the round.

You will now place additional markers to mark where you will work additional repeats of Faux Braid stitch on the sleeve sections. *Begin working the additional repeats with the same current round of the chart as the front/back/sleeves. You should be on round - (3, 5, 5, 3) (3, 3, 3, 3) of the chart.*

Next round: *K to 1 st before marker, p1, SM, (work next round of the chart, p1) 2 times, work next round of the chart, SM, p1, k to marker, SM, k- (1, 2, 2, 1) (1, 1, 1, 1), p1, PM, (work next round of the chart, p1) 2 times, work next round of the chart, PM, p1, k to marker, SM*, rep ** until end of the round.

Restart your row count here. *You should be on round - (4, 6, 6, 4) (4, 4, 4, 4) of the chart.*

Round 1: *K1, M1L, k to 1 st before marker, p1, SM, (work next round of the chart, p1) 2 times, work next round of the chart, SM, p1, k to 1 st before marker, M1R, k1, SM*, rep ** until end of the round.

Round 2: *K to 1 st before marker, p1, SM, (work next round of the chart, p1) 2 times, work next round of the chart, SM, p1, k to marker, SM*, rep ** until end of the round.

Next round: *K1, M1L, k to 1 st before marker, p1, **RM**, (work next round of the chart, p1) 2 times, work next round of the chart, **RM**, p1, k to 1 st before marker, M1R, k1, SM, k1, M1L, k to 1 st before marker, p1, SM, (work next round of the chart, p1) 2 times, work next round of the chart, SM, p1, k to 1 st before marker, M1R, k1, SM, rep ** until end of the round.

You will now place additional markers to mark where you will work additional repeats of Faux Braid stitch on the front and back sections. *Begin working the additional repeats with the same current round of the chart as the front/back/sleeves. You should be on round - (-, -, -, -) (-, -, 11, 11) of the chart.*

Next round: *K1, p1, **PM**, (work next round of the chart, p1) 4 times, work next round of the chart, **PM**, p1, k to marker, SM, k to 1 st before marker, p1, SM, (work next round of the chart, p1) 2 times, work next round of the chart, SM, p1, k to marker, SM*, rep ** until end of the round.

Proceed to "Body."

Repeat rounds 1–2 until you have worked them - (2, 2, 2, 3) (3, 3, 3, 3) times **total** (meaning - (4, 4, 4, 6) (6, 6, 6, 6) total rounds). You should now have a **total** of - (178, 188, 188, 190) (194, 194, 198, 198) sts, with - (49, 53, 53, 53) (55, 55, 57, 57) sts for the front and back sections, and - (40, 41, 41, 42) (42, 42, 42, 42) sts for each sleeve. *You should end after round - (7, 9, 9, 9) (9, 9, 9, 9) of the chart.*

Sizes - (S, M, L, XL) (XXL, 3XL, -, -) proceed to "Body."

BODY

You will now divide the sleeves from the body. *When placing sleeve stitches on scrap yarn, do not remove the stitch markers that marked where you will work the Faux Braid stitch, as you will need them when you come back to the sleeve stitches later.*

You should be on round 4 (8, 10, 10, 10) (10, 10, 12, 12) of the chart.

Sizes XS (S, M, -, -) (-, -, -, -) only

Next round: *K to 1 st before marker, p1, SM, (work next round of the chart, p1) 2 times, work next round of the chart, SM, p1, k to next marker, **RM**, place the next 35 (40, 41, -, -) (-, -, -, -) sts on scrap yarn, SM*, rep ** until end of the round.

Sizes - (-, -, L, XL) (XXL, 3XL, 4XL, 5XL) only

Next round: *K1, M1L, k to 1 st before marker, p1, SM, (work next round of the chart, p1) - (-, -, 2, 2) (2, 2, 4, 4) times, work next round of the chart, SM, p1, k to 1 st before next marker, M1R, k1, **RM**, place the next - (-, -, 41, 42) (42, 42, 44, 44) sts on scrap yarn, SM*, rep ** until end of the round.

All sizes continue

You should now have a **total** of 90 (98, 106, 110, 110) (114, 114, 122, 122) sts on your needles, with 45 (49, 53, 55, 55) (57, 57, 61, 61) sts each for the front and back sections, and two sections of 35 (40, 41, 41, 42) (42, 42, 44, 44) sts on scrap yarn.

Sizes XS (S, M, -, -) (-, -, -, -) proceed to "All sizes continue."

Restart your row count here. *You should be on round - (-, -, 11, 11) (11, 11, 1, 1) of the chart.*

Size L only

Round 1: *K to 1 st before marker, p1, SM, (work next round of the chart, p1) 2 times, work next round of the chart, SM, p1, k to marker, SM*, rep ** until end of the round.

Round 2: *K1, M1L, k to 1 st before marker, p1, SM, (work next round of the chart, p1) 2 times, work next round of the chart, SM, p1, k to 1 st before next marker, M1R, k1, SM*, rep ** until end of the round.

You should now have a **total** of 114 sts, with 57 sts for the front and back sections. *You should end after round 12 of the chart.*

Size L proceed to "All sizes continue."

Size XL only

Round 1: *K to 1 st before marker, p1, SM, (work next round of the chart, p1) 2 times, work next round of the chart, SM, p1, k to marker, SM*, rep ** until end of the round.

Round 2: *K1, M1L, k to 1 st before marker, p1, SM, (work next round of the chart, p1) 2 times, work next round of the chart, SM, p1, k to 1 st before next marker, M1R, k1, SM*, rep ** until end of the round.

Round 3: Repeat round 1.

Round 4: *K1, M1L, k to 1 st before marker, p1, **RM**, (work next round of the chart, p1) 2 times, work next round of the chart, **RM**, p1, k to 1 st before marker, M1R, k1, SM*, rep ** until end of the round.

You will now place additional markers to mark where you will work additional repeats of Faux Braid stitch on the front and back sections. *Begin working the additional repeats with the same current round of the chart as the front/back sections. You should be on round 3 of the chart.*

Round 5: *K1, p1, **PM**, (work next round of the chart, p1) 4 times, work next round of the chart, **PM**, p1, k to marker, SM*, rep ** until end of the round.

Round 6: *K1, M1L, k to 1 st before marker, p1, SM, (work next round of the chart, p1) 4 times, work next round of the chart, SM, p1, k to 1 st before next marker, M1R, k1, SM*, rep ** until end of the round.

You should now have a **total** of 122 sts, with 61 sts for the front and back sections. *You should end after round 4 of the chart.*

Size XL proceed to "All sizes continue."

Sizes - (-, -, -, -) (XXL, 3XL, -, -) only

Round 1: *K to 1 st before marker, p1, SM, (work next round of the chart, p1) 2 times, work next round of the chart, SM, p1, k to marker, SM*, rep ** until end of the round.

Round 2: *K1, M1L, k to 1 st before marker, p1, **RM**, (work next round of the chart, p1) 2 times, work next round of the chart, **RM**, p1, k to 1 st before marker, M1R, k1, SM*, rep ** until end of the round.

You will now place additional markers to mark where you will work additional repeats of Faux Braid stitch on the front and back sections. *Begin working the additional repeats with the same current round of the chart as the front/back sections. You should be on round - (-, -, -, -) (1, 1, -, -) of the chart.*

Round 3: *K1, p1, **PM**, (work next round of the chart, p1) 4 times, work next round of the chart, **PM**, p1, k to marker, SM*, rep ** until end of the round.

Round 4: *K1, M1L, k to 1 st before marker, p1, SM, (work next round of the chart, p1) 4 times, work next round of the chart, SM, p1, k to 1 st before next marker, M1R, k1, SM*, rep ** until end of the round.

Round 5: *K to 1 st before marker, p1, SM, (work next round of the chart, p1) 4 times, work next round of the chart, SM, p1, k to marker, SM*, rep ** until end of the round.

Round 6: Repeat round 4.

Repeat rounds 5–6 until you have worked them - (-, -, -, -) (2, 4, -, -) times **total** (meaning - (-, -, -, -) (4, 8, -, -) total rounds). You should now have a **total** of - (-, -, -, -) (130, 138, -, -) sts, with - (-, -, -, -) (65, 69, -, -) sts each for the front and back sections. *You should end after round - (-, -, -, -) (6, 10, -, -) of the chart.*

Sizes - (-, -, -, -) (XXL, 3XL, -, -) proceed to "All sizes continue."

Round 1: *K to 1 st before marker, p1, SM, (work next round of the chart, p1) 4 times, work next round of the chart, SM, p1, k to marker, SM*, rep ** until end of the round.

Round 2: *K1, M1L, k to 1 st before marker, p1, SM, (work next round of the chart, p1) 4 times, work next round of the chart, SM, p1, k to 1 st before next marker, M1R, k1, SM*, rep ** until end of the round.

Repeat rounds 1–2 until you have worked them - (-, -, -, -) (-, -, 6, 8) times **total** (meaning - (-, -, -, -) (-, -, 12, 16) total rounds). You should now have a **total** of - (-, -, -, -) (-, -, 146, 154) sts, with - (-, -, -, -) (-, -, 73, 77) sts each for the front and back sections. *You should end after round - (-, -, -, -) (-, -, 12, 4) of the chart.*

Proceed to "All sizes continue."

All sizes continue

Restart your row count here. *You should be on round 5 (9, 11, 1, 5) (7, 11, 1, 5) of the chart.*

Round 1: *K to 1 st before marker, p1, SM, (work next round of the chart, p1) 2 (2, 2, 2, 4) (4, 4, 4, 4) times, work next round of the chart, SM, p1, k to marker, SM*, rep ** until end of the round.

Repeat round 1 until you have worked 12 (16, 16, 14, 12) (10, 10, 8, 6) rounds **total**. *You should end after round 4 (12, 2, 2, 4) (4, 8, 8, 10) of the chart.*

> **Note:** If you would like to add or subtract length to/from your jumper, do so here, keeping in mind the ribbing will add approximately 2.4 inches (6 cm).

Switch to US 15 (10 mm) 24- to 32-inch (60- to 80-cm) circular needles. Remove all markers as they appear **except** for the BOR marker whilst working the next round.

Next 6 rounds: *K1, p1*, rep ** until end of the round.

BO all sts in 1x1 ribbing.

SLEEVES

Place one of the sections of 35 (40, 41, 41, 42) (42, 42, 44, 44) sts you left on scrap yarn, as well as the stitch markers, onto your US 17 (12 mm) 32- to 40-inch (80- to 100-cm) circular needles.

Setup round: Starting at the underarm point, pick up 1 st, k the next 35 (40, 41, 41, 42) (42, 42, 44, 44) live sts (slipping markers as they appear), pick up 1 st, **PM to mark the BOR.**

You should now have 37 (42, 43, 43, 44) (44, 44, 46, 46) sts. *You should be on round 4 (8, 10, 10, 10) (10, 10, 12, 12) of the chart.*

Size XS only

Round 1: K to 1 st before marker, p1, **RM**, work next round of the chart, p1, **RM**, p1, k to end of the round.

You will now place additional markers to mark where you will work additional repeats of Faux Braid stitch. *Begin working the additional repeats with the same current round of the chart as the sleeve section. You should be on round 5 of the chart.*

Round 2: K2, p1, **PM**, (work next round of the chart, p1) 2 times, work next round of the chart, **PM**, p1, k to end of the round.

All sizes continue

Next round: K to 1 st before marker, p1, SM, (work respective round of the chart, p1) 2 times, work respective round of the chart, SM, p1, k to end of the round.

Repeat the last round until you have worked 34 (34, 36, 38, 38) (40, 40, 42, 42) rounds **total.** *You should end after round 3 (5, 9, 11, 11) (1, 1, 5, 5) of the chart.*

> **Note:** If you would like to add or subtract length to/from your sleeve, do so here, keeping in mind the sleeve cuff will add approximately 2.8 inches (7 cm). Make note of how many total rows you work so that you can work your second sleeve to match.

Next round: K to 1 st before marker, p1, **RM**, (work next round of the chart, p1) 2 times, work next round of the chart, **RM**, p1, k to end of the round.

You will now make decreases for the sleeve cuffs.

Size XS only

Next round: K1, *k2tog*, rep ** until end of the round.

Size S only

Next round: *K2tog*, rep ** until end of the round.

Next round: *K5, k2tog*, rep ** until end of the round.

Sizes - (-, M, L, -) (-, -, -, -) only

Next round: *K2tog*, rep ** until last st, k1.

Next round: *K3, k2tog*, rep ** until last 2 sts, k2.

Sizes - (-, -, -, XL) (XXL, 3XL, -, -) only

Next round: *K2tog*, rep ** until end of the round.

Next round: *K6, k2tog*, rep ** until last 6 sts, k6.

Sizes - (-, -, -, -) (-, -, 4XL, 5XL) only

Next round: *K2tog*, rep ** until end of the round.

All sizes continue

You should now have 19 (18, 18, 18, 20) (20, 20, 23, 23) sts.

Switch to US 15 (10 mm) 24- to 32-inch (60- to 80-cm) circular needles. *You will need to use the Magic Loop method (page 207) to work the sleeve cuffs.* Restart your row count here.

Sizes XS (-, -, -, -) (-, -, 4XL, 5XL) only

Round 1: K2tog, p1, *k1, p1*, rep ** until end of the round.

You should now have 18 (-, -, -, -) (-, -, 22, 22) sts.

All sizes continue

Next 5 (6, 6, 6, 6) (6, 6, 5, 5) rounds: *K1, p1*, rep ** until end of the round.

BO all sts loosely in 1x1 rib pattern.

FINISHING

Weave in all your loose ends.

Blocking super bulky yarn is not necessary. However, if you do wish to block your jumper, which will help open up the eyelets, it is suggested that you use the spray blocking method (do *not* wet or steam block).

CHART

10	9	8	7	6	5	4	3	2	1	
										12
O			K3tog			O				11
										10
			Ssk			O				9
										8
				Ssk				O		7
										6
		O				S2KP			O	5
										4
	O			K2tog						3
										2
	O			K2tog						1

| 10 | 9 | 8 | 7 | 6 | 5 | 4 | 3 | 2 | 1 |

Legend

☐	Knit
\	Ssk
/	K2tog
O	YO
⋏	K3tog
⋀	S2KP

CHART PATTERN

Round 1: K5, k2tog, k2, YO, k1.

Round 2, 4, 6, 8, 10, 12: K across.

Round 3: K4, k2tog, k2, YO, k2.

Round 5: YO, k2, S2KP, k2, YO, k3.

Round 7: K1, YO, k2, ssk, k5.

Round 9: K2, YO, k2, ssk, k4.

Round 11: K3, YO, k2, k3tog, k2, YO.

TECHNIQUES

Here you will find step-by-step instructions for all the special techniques used more than once throughout the book. Instructions for any special techniques that are only used in one pattern in this book can be found within the pattern in which they appear. The techniques in this section are listed in order of most to least frequently used throughout the book.

Magic Loop Method

This technique is most useful when you are knitting in the round and do not have enough stitches to fit comfortably around your cord (i.e., your cord is too long), as the Magic Loop method allows you to knit small circumference sections, such as a sleeve, using any size cord length.

1. Divide your stitches so that half are on one needle and half are on the other.

2. Pull the cord through the gap between the two sets of stitches.

3. Pull the right needle so the stitches on this needle sit on the cord. *Make sure there is still a loop between the two sets of stitches.*

4. Grab the working yarn and begin knitting the stitches on the left needle like normal.

5. Once you have knit all the stitches on the left needle, rotate your work and repeat steps 1–4.

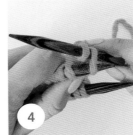

Three Needle Bind Off

1. Insert a third needle knitwise into the first stitch of the panel that is facing you, then insert that same needle knitwise into the corresponding stitch of the other panel.

2. Wrap the yarn around the needle and pull through both loops and drop both stitches off the needle. *You should now have 1 stitch on your right needle, as you have knitted the first stitch from each panel together.*

3. Repeat steps 1–2. *You should now have 2 stitches on your right needle.*

4. Bind off one stitch on your right needle by passing the stitch on the right over the stitch on the left.

5. Repeat steps 3–4 until you have bound off all stitches.

6. Cut the yarn and pull through the last stitch on your needle to secure the bind off.

1a
2a

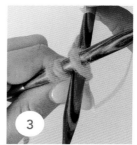

2b
3

Alternating Cable Cast On

This is a great cast on to use before working in 1x1 ribbing that leaves a nice, clean, invisible edge to your work.

To set up, make a slip knot and place it on the left needle. Insert the right needle into the slip knot knitwise, wrap the yarn around the needle and draw a loop. Place this loop onto the left needle by inserting the left needle through the loop from front to back.

1. Insert the right needle in between the first two stitches from front to back.

2. Wrap the yarn around the needle and draw a loop. Place this loop onto the left needle by inserting the left needle through the loop from front to back.

3. Insert the right needle in between the first two stitches from back to front.

4. Repeat Step 2.

5. Repeat steps 1–4.

MATTRESS STITCH

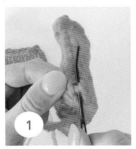

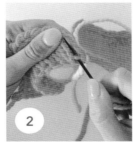

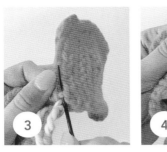

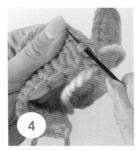

TUBULAR BIND OFF SET UP

Mattress Stitch

To set up, place the two panels you want to join side by side with the RS (knit side for stockinette stitch and purl side for reverse stockinette stitch) facing you. Attach yarn at the bottom corner of the left panel. Cut a tail that is longer than the length of your desired seam. Thread your tail onto a tapestry needle.

1. Insert the needle under the first horizontal ladder in between the first and second stitch of the right panel. Pull the yarn through.

2. Insert the needle under the corresponding ladder in between the first and second stitch of the left panel. Pull the yarn through.

3. Insert the needle under the next horizontal ladder in between the first and second stitch of the right panel. Pull the yarn through.

4. Insert the needle under the next horizontal ladder in between the first and second stitch of the left panel. Pull the yarn through.

5. Repeat steps 3-4.

Tubular Bind Off

This is a sewn bind off that can be used to create a nice, stretchy, invisible edge after working in 1x1 ribbing.

Cut a long tail approximately 3–4 times the circumference of your bind off. Thread your tail on a tapestry needle.

To set up, insert the needle into the first stitch (this should be a knit stitch) purlwise. Pull the yarn through. Then, insert the needle in between the first two stitches from the back to the front. Then, insert the needle into the second stitch (this should be a purl stitch) knitwise. Pull the yarn through.

TUBULAR BIND OFF

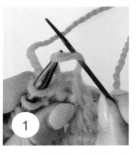

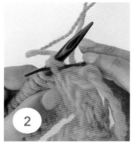

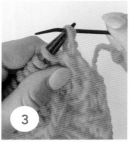

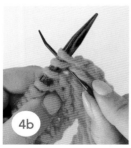

1. Insert the needle into the first stitch knitwise and slip this stitch off the needle.

2. Insert the needle into the second stitch (this should be a knit stitch) purlwise. Pull the yarn through.

3. Insert the needle into the first stitch purlwise and slip this stitch off the needle.

4. Insert the needle in between the first two stitches from the back to the front. Then, insert the needle into the second stitch (this should be a purl stitch) knitwise. Pull the yarn through.

5. Repeat steps 1–4 until you have 2 stitches remaining.

6. Insert the needle into the first stitch knitwise and slip this stitch off the needle.

7. Insert the needle into the right leg of the first stitch you bound off purlwise. Pull the yarn through.

8. Insert the needle into the first stitch purlwise and slip this stitch off the needle.

9. Insert the needle into the left leg of the first stitch you bound off knitwise. Pull the yarn through to secure.

Jogless Stripes

When knitting stripes in the round, you can use this simple technique to prevent the jog that would typically appear when changing colors due to the spiral nature of knitting in the round. This method will create the illusion of seamless stripes, resulting in a neater finish.

1. Join new color and knit first round normally.
2. Slip first stitch of the next round purlwise with yarn held in back. Then continue knitting the remaining stitches of this round normally.
3. Repeat steps 1–2 when you start each new color.

Stretchy Bind Off

This is a knitted bind off that can be used to create a nice, stretchy, invisible edge after working in 1x1 ribbing. It is particularly useful for binding off neck trims or tight sleeve cuffs.

To set up: K1, p1.

1. Insert the left needle into the last 2 stitches on the right needle through the back loops.
2. Purl these 2 stitches together.
3. K1.
4. Insert the left needle into the last 2 stitches on the right needle through the front loops.
5. Knit these 2 stitches together.
6. P1.
7. Repeat steps 1–6.

STRETCHY BIND OFF

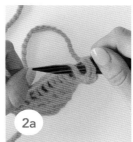

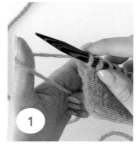

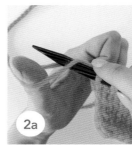

Weavin' Stephen

When changing colors frequently in a project, you are bound to be left with a plethora of ends to weave in once you finish. This clever technique enables you to save some precious time by "weaving" in these ends as you go.

1. Knit the first stitch with new color.

2. Cross tail from previous color over working yarn from right to left.

3. Repeat steps 1–2 for approximately 8–10 stitches.

4. Cut the remaining tail (I like to do this at the end of the project).

Backwards Loop Cast On

This is a simple cast on to use when you need to cast on new stitches in the middle of your work.

1. Place the working yarn over your left thumb so that the tail end is towards you.

2. Insert your right needle underneath the front strand that is wrapped around your thumb. Drop the loop off your thumb and pull working yarn to tighten.

Adding Elastic

Turn your project inside out. Cut a piece of thin elastic string that is 2–3 times the circumference of your neckline. Thread the elastic on a tapestry needle.

To set up, starting from any *knit* stitch, 2–3 rows below the top edge of the neckline, insert the needle into the right leg of the stitch. Pull the elastic through, leaving a tail long enough to weave in. Then, insert the needle into the right leg of the same stitch again and pull through to secure the elastic thread.

1. Insert the needle into the right leg of the next knit stitch (skipping the purl stitch). Pull the elastic through.

2. Repeat step 1 all the way around the neckline.

You will now be working into the stitches that are 2–3 rows above the bottom of the neckline.

3. Insert the needle into the right leg of the next knit stitch (this stitch will be in line with the first stitch you worked into during the set up). Pull the elastic through.

4. Insert the needle into the right leg of the next knit stitch. Pull the elastic through.

5. Repeat step 4 all the way around the neckline.

6. Pull the elastic thread to tighten to your desired fit. It will be helpful to try on your project to help determine how tight to pull the elastic.

7. Secure the two ends of the elastic using a double slip knot and then weave them in as you would with a normal yarn tail.

ADDING ELASTIC SET UP

ADDING ELASTIC

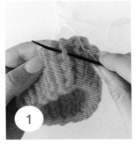

GRAFTING SET UP

GRAFTING

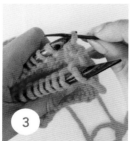
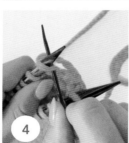

Grafting

The following instructions are written for stockinette stitch. For working the Grafting method for reverse stockinette stitch (Twist and Shout Vest [page 175] and Heartstrings Vest [page 27]): When instructed to insert the needle into a stitch knitwise, insert purlwise instead, and vice versa.

Thread your yarn tail on a tapestry needle.

To set up, insert the tapestry needle into the first stitch of the front tapestry needle purlwise. Pull the yarn through. Insert the needle into the first stitch of the back needle knitwise. Pull the yarn through.

1. Insert the tapestry needle into the first stitch of the front needle knitwise and slip this stitch off the needle. Pull the yarn through.

2. Insert the tapestry needle into the next stitch of the front needle purlwise. Pull the yarn through.

3. Insert the tapestry needle into the first stitch of the back needle purlwise and slip this stitch off the needle. Pull the yarn through.

4. Insert the tapestry needle into the next stitch of the back needle knitwise. Pull the yarn through.

5. Repeat steps 1–4 until you have 1 stitch remaining on each needle.

6. Insert the tapestry needle into the first stitch of the front needle knitwise and slip this stitch off the needle. Pull the yarn through.

7. Insert the tapestry needle into the first stitch of the back needle purlwise and slip this stitch off the needle. Pull the yarn through.

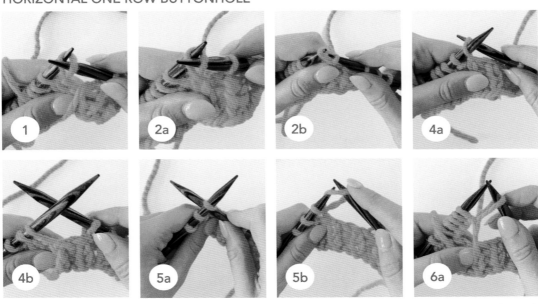

Horizontal One Row Buttonhole

1. Sl1 purlwise tbl wyif.

2. Sl1 purlwise tbl wyib, BO 1 st.

3. Repeat step 2 until you have bound off as many sts as indicated in your pattern (e.g., if your pattern states that your buttonhole will comprise 4 sts, you will need to bind off 4 sts).

4. Place resulting st onto the left needle. Turn your work.

5. CO the number of sts you bound off using the Cable Cast On (e.g., if you bound off 4 sts, you will cast on 4 sts).

6. CO 1 more stitch using the Cable Cast On, but before you place the stitch on the needle, bring your yarn to the front between the previous stitch you casted on and the stitch you are currently casting on. Turn your work.

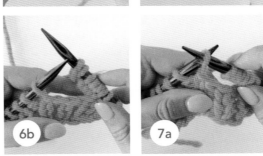

7. Sl1 purlwise wyib (this is the resulting bind off stitch from step 3), BO 1 st by passing the last cast on stitch over this stitch.

BLOCKING 101

The term blocking refers to the process of setting the finished size and shape of a knitting project, as well as evening out the stitches and allowing the fibers to relax. There are several methods of blocking one can use, e.g., wet, steam or spray blocking. As a beginner, I never quite understood the importance of blocking and I will be the first to admit that it took me a while before I started blocking my projects consistently. I find it quite strange that beginners often aren't taught how to block, as I've now come to understand how much of a difference it can make to your finished project.

For all patterns in the book except for those that call for super bulky yarn*, the sizing and gauge information listed are based on blocked measurements. This means that your project will only achieve the intended fit and drape after it has been blocked. On that note, it is therefore very important that you block your swatch, for what I hope are now obvious reasons.

> Note: *Super bulky yarn refers specifically to super bulky roving style yarn (single ply).

It is important to consider that different fibers will behave differently both before and after blocking. Some fibers grow more than others when blocked, so if you are using an alternative to the recommended yarn in a particular pattern, take this into account when making your selection. It's best to choose a yarn that not only has a similar weight/yardage but also has similar fiber content to the suggested yarn.

Wet Blocking

My preferred blocking method is wet blocking, as this allows you to wash and block your project simultaneously. This method is relatively easy and will become second nature once you've done it a few times.

1. Immerse your garment in cold or lukewarm water with a small amount of gentle wool wash. Let it soak for 10 to 15 minutes.

2. Rinse out excess detergent, then gently squeeze out (do *not* wring) as much water from the garment as possible.

3. Lay a towel on the floor and place the garment flat on the towel.

4. Roll up the towel, then step on the towel to help squeeze out any remaining excess water. Remove the towel.

5. Place the garment on some blocking mats (alternatives include foam puzzle play mats or a towel), ideally somewhere warm that won't be exposed to any direct sunlight.

6. Stretch out your garment to the desired shape and measurements as per the sizing chart. This may take some maneuvering and manipulation of the fibers, but it's worth taking some time to ensure your stitches look nice and neat.

7. If you are using some form of blocking mat (i.e., not a towel), pin the garment along the edges and in any other places that may need it (e.g., lace stitches). This will ensure the garment holds its shape while it dries. *I like to use knit blockers, but any pin will do.*

8. Wait for the garment to dry fully. This may take a while depending on the fiber and the climate, but it is very important that you have patience and do not prematurely remove the garment from the mat. If you're unsure if it is fully dry, it probably isn't.

YARN SUPPLIERS

Below is a list of yarn companies whose yarn is featured in this book. A special thanks to Wool and Works, Cardigang and Malabrigo for providing yarn support.

Cardigang

www.cardigang.com.au

Heartstrings Vest (page 27)

Magnolia Jumper (page 37)

Miss Ziggy Vest (page 67)

Twist and Shout Vest (page 175)

Cowgirlblues

www.cowgirlblues.co.za

Zesty Vest (page 145)

Malabrigo

www.malabrigoyarn.com

Kaleidoscope Cardigan (page 127)

Bambi Jumper (page 195)

Wool and the Gang

www.woolandthegang.com

Orla Cardigan (page 47)

Attention Deficit Jumper (page 101)

Bright Like a Diamond Cardigan (page 75)

Cassie Cardigan (page 95)

Somewhere Over the Raglan Jumper (page 121)

V-Stripy Vest (page 135)

Lily Cardigan (page 183)

Ivy Jumper (page 167)

Wool and Works

www.woolandworks.com.au

Sweet as Pie Jumper (page 19)

Stairway to Heaven Vest (page 85)

Color Me Striped Jumper (page 155)

ACKNOWLEDGMENTS

Without the support of the incredible people behind the scenes, the creation of this book simply would not have been possible, and I truly could not be more grateful.

Thank you to Emily and the team at Page Street for believing in me and providing the opportunity for me to write this book—something I never ever thought I would be able to do. Thank you for making this process so enjoyable, for answering all my questions as a first-time author and for giving me the creative freedom to make this book my own.

To my amazing tech editor Sara, thank you so much for your invaluable feedback and insights that took these patterns from drab to fab, for patiently correcting my (many) mathematical errors and for trying to make sense of my long-winded voice notes that never really made any sense to begin with. I have learned so much from working with you and hope to continue working together in the future.

A huge thank you to my unbelievable, dedicated and talented team of over 300 test knitters from all over the world for volunteering your time and skills to help me perfect these patterns and ensure they would fit as intended within a tight deadline. A special mention to those of you who were willing to test more than one pattern—you are genuine superstars! The knitting community is truly extraordinary when it comes to sheer kindness and generosity, and I am so grateful and lucky to have connected with each and every one of you.

Words cannot express my gratitude to my beautiful internet-turned-real-life friend Chloe. Your unwavering support throughout the process of writing this book was truly unmatched and I am so thankful that our shared love of knitting brought you into my life. Thank you for always hyping me up, for being my sounding board for virtually every idea I had for this book, for putting up with my rants, for our late-night knitting sessions and of course for being so generous to provide yarn for three of these designs. I am so excited and honored to feature Wool and Works in this book and put your incredible talent on display.

To my phenomenal photographer Alex, you are such a visionary and an absolute dream to work with. I couldn't be prouder of what we created together, and I will be eternally grateful that you agreed to come on board to photograph my book. A tremendous thank you for everything.

I owe endless thank-yous to my loving parents, supportive siblings, amazing partner and incredible friends for encouraging me to pursue my passions, and for always being my biggest cheerleaders. You all kept me sane throughout the process of writing this book and showed me unconditional love and support, for which I feel very lucky and couldn't be more grateful.

Finally, to anyone who has followed my journey on social media, bought my patterns or shared my work with others, your support means the world to me, and *you* are the reason I was able to write this book, so thank you from the bottom of my heart for everything you have given me. The knitting community is truly a special one that I'm so lucky to be a part of, and I am constantly in awe of the incredible creativity and craftsmanship I see on my Instagram feed every single day. Thank you for inspiring me, and I hope this book brings you joy, satisfaction and a few new handmade masterpieces to add to your collection.

ABOUT THE AUTHOR

Jaime Dorfman is an independent and free-lance knitwear designer from Melbourne, Australia.

She first learned to crochet in 2018 after finishing high school, but in 2019 she fell in love with knitting and hasn't looked back since then. She started actively sharing her work online in 2020 and began writing and releasing her own knitting patterns in 2021. Jaime has become known for creating modern, youthful, trendy designs which embrace and experiment with fun, bold colors and textures. She strongly believes that knitting is for everyone, regardless of age, gender, race, body size, ability or class, and she hopes to inspire a new generation of knitters to pick up the needles and reap the many benefits of this incredible craft.

Jaime's patterns are available to purchase online from www.jaimecreates.me, as well as on Ravelry, Etsy and Ribblr. You can follow her on Instagram, TikTok and YouTube @jaime_creates, where you can keep up to date with her latest designs and catch plenty of behind-the-scenes knitting content.

Fast and Fabulous Knits is her first book.

INDEX

Note: the notations **(CB), (AB)** and **(I)** following a pattern name indicate the level of knitting skills needed as explained on page 11.